Hudson Tuttle

Arcana of Spiritualism

A Manual of Spiritual Science and Philosophy

Hudson Tuttle

Arcana of Spiritualism
A Manual of Spiritual Science and Philosophy

ISBN/EAN: 9783337337117

Printed in Europe, USA, Canada, Australia, Japan

Cover: Foto ©Lupo / pixelio.de

More available books at **www.hansebooks.com**

ARCANA

OF

SPIRITUALISM:

A MANUAL OF

SPIRITUAL SCIENCE AND PHILOSOPHY.

BY HUDSON TUTTLE,

AUTHOR OF "LIFE IN THE SPHERES," "ARCANA OF NATURE," "ORIGIN AND ANTIQUITY OF MAN," "CAREER OF THE GOD-IDEA IN HISTORY," "CAREER OF THE CHRIST-IDEA IN HISTORY," ETC.

When Alps dissolve, and worlds shall fade away,
When suns go out, and stars no longer blaze,
I scarcely shall have reached my primal day.
I, only I, can claim to be the real:
I am the type of Nature, — her Ideal.
                                SPIRIT.

The Soul is immortal. — PYTHAGORAS.

BOSTON:
ADAMS & CO., 25 BROMFIELD STREET.
1871.

PREFACE.

MINE is the task of an amanuensis, writing that which is revealed to me. Doubtless I have often failed in my endeavor to comprehend the meaning of the impressions I have received, or in clothing them with appropriate words. I presume many questions remain unanswered. The field of inquiry is vast as space and time; and often there are not words to describe the spiritual realities and relations which hitherto have not been unfolded to mortal understanding.

I have faithfully, carefully, and conscientiously presented my impressions as they have been given me by my masters, the invisible spirits, claiming neither the honor nor dishonor pertaining thereto. I have written in hours of pleasure and of pain; when life was a joy, and when, overtasked, it became a weariness: but ever have I been cheered by the presence of spirit-friends, and, bathed in their magnetism, been supremely blessed.

Preface.

I cannot resist expressing my thanks to the many friends who have aided me in publishing and disseminating my previous works, and my appreciation of the kind words they have spoken and written. Many of them I may never meet on earth; but they will be ever cherished in most sacred remembrance, until we clasp each other's hands on the "Ever Green Mountains of Life."

H. T.

BOSTON, 1870.

CONTENTS.

GENERAL STATEMENT OF PRINCIPLES . . . 13

I.

INTRODUCTION 19

II.

EVIDENCES OF SPIRITUALISM: A DISCUSSION OF THE VARIOUS THEORIES ADVANCED FOR ITS EXPOSITION.

The necessities of immortal being. Proofs of immortality drawn from the constitution of the mind. Science not necessarily conflicting. Are we self-deceived? Unreliability of the senses in the border-land. Hallucinations. The circle, — are its members hallucinated? Theories examined. Evil spirits. The Devil. Electricity. Magnetism. Od force. Failure of any one theory to explain all phenomena. Interposition of spirits must be accepted. Identification of spirits 35

III.

EVIDENCES OF SPIRITUALISM.

Materialism. The impossible. The positive. The senses. Belief educational. Why have not these phenomena occurred before? Spirit is individualized force. One fact of more value than a thousand theories. How is it possible for spirits to return? Not new. First manifestations. They assume a new character. They extend to other localities. Spiritualism in France. Unexpected report. The evidence of psychometry. Spirit-identification by psychometry. What good? Personal experience   58

IV.

MATTER AND FORCE: THEIR RELATIONS TO SPIRIT.

The present tendency of thought. Force. Motion,— resolution of into heat, light, electricity, magnetism. Atomic attraction. Chemical affinity. Theories. Speculations. Grand cycle of correlation. Cause of motion in living beings. Cause of heat, light, electricity. Relation of this doctrine to life. Intelligence. Spirit . . 91

V.

PHYSICAL MATTER AND SPIRIT.

Divisibility of matter. Its eternity. What is matter? What an atom? An attribute? A principle? Properties? Resolution of all phenomena. The chemical atom. The basis of positive science. The theory of atoms and of forces. Shape of the atom. Space, is it an entity? The old notion of the impenetrability and inertia of matter discarded. Cause of change in properties by chemical union. The atom nothing: force everything. The highest philosophical ground. The spiritual sense . . 116

VI.

SPIRITUAL ATMOSPHERE OF THE UNIVERSE.

Instrument employed in investigation. The impressibility of the brain. Impressibility of animals. Sympathy a form of impressibility. Influence of the external world on the nervous system. Reichenbach's experiments. Influence of magnets. Influence of crystals. Crystallic flame. Impartation of influence. Polarity of the body. Abnormal sensitiveness of the diseased. Disease and sleep. Influence of the moon. Of the sun. Of locality. Of churchyard ghosts. The image sometimes remains. Individual spheres. Conclusions 133

VII.

RELATION OF THE SPIRITUAL TO THE ANIMAL IN MAN.

The lower faculties of the mind traced in the animal world. Their necessity. The spirit cannot lose any of its propensities at death. Instinct never misdirects. Perfectly selfish. Man never satisfied. Sin, cause of. The animal faculties united with the intellect, insatiable. Their true relations. Illustrations 164

VIII.

ANIMAL MAGNETISM, — ITS BOUNDARIES, LAWS, AND RELATION TO SPIRIT.

Necessity of investigating the laws of magnetism. Magnetism among the ancients. Man possesses this influence over animals. Animals can influence man. Each other. Why do we think of those who are thinking of us? Influence of man over man. Generalization. Atmospheric ether. Impressibility of the brain. Psychometry applied. Application to fortune-telling. Animal magnetism as a curative agent. Application to spirit-communion . . 174

IX.

SPIRIT — ITS PHENOMENA AND LAWS.

Immortality the base of all religion. Tendency of savage mind. Definitions of spirit. Pre-existence. Evolution of the spiritual body from the physical. Degrees of the magnetic state. Natural and induced. Illustrations 198

X.

SPIRIT — ITS PHENOMENA AND LAWS.

Magnetism intensifies the spiritual perceptions. Not imagination. Clairvoyance: applied to the realm of spirit. Testimony of the seeress of Prevorst. Of Swedenborg. Spirits retain and appear in their earthly form. Do the senses of spirits recognize physical objects? Does the spirit of the clairvoyant leave the body? Double presence. Impressions made on the mind never effaced. Prophecy 222

XI.

SPIRIT — ITS PHENOMENA AND LAWS.

Cause of failure. Value of Clairvoyance. Condition of the freed spirit. Can the spirit possess senses independent of the physical body? The spiritual organism. The most subtle form of matter. An erroneous hypothesis. Electricity not employed. Progress of the elements. Spiritual elements realities. Spirits of animals. Spiritual attraction and repulsion. In the spiritual world the same law holds supreme. Why, if material, spirits cannot be seen. Why seek immortal existence outside of physical matter? Origin of the spiritual body. How far the body affects the spirit 249

XII.

PHILOSOPHY OF DEATH: A REVIEW OF SOME OLD THEORIES.

What is life? What is death? Christian idea of death terrible, but that of the ancient Greeks beautiful. Terrors of death. Myths of the resurrection of the body. Christianity takes a deep draught from Paganism. Mohammed receives the dogma of the resurrection. Teachings of the Bible. Resurrection of Christ . . . 269

XIII.

THE CHANGE CALLED DEATH.

Ultimate of nature's plan. Death is not change of being: it is change of spheres. The spirit and the body. Man should mature like the fruit of autumn before death. Death no occasion for rejoicing. The spirit after death. How received 282

XIV.

MEDIUMSHIP.

Mediumship and spirit-influence among savages. The Australians. The Maori. The African and New Zealander. Connection between the person and his name. The hermits of the Ganges. The Red Indian. The Pythonic oracles. Position of the medium. Why disreputable media are used. Sensitiveness does not exonerate media for their waywardness. Mediumship constitutional. Impressibility, how induced. Mediumship. Mental excitement. Sickness. Fasting. Death. Organic impressibility preferable to induced. Desire for mediumship. How to become a medium. Influence of individuals on the communications. A physical state negative to mediumship. Why communications are contradictory. Contradictions referred to the circle. How circles should be formed. Responsibility of mediumship 289

XV.

MEDIUMSHIP DURING SLEEP.

Sleep. Dreams. Somnambulism. Spiritual communications given in dreams. Presentiments. Prophetic dreams, origin of. Facts from Martineau. Abercrombie. Macnish. Addison. Coleridge. Dreams of animals. The dreaming dog. Presentiments. Mr. Calderhood.

Prof. Bohm. Of accidents. Future events. Death. Prophetic dreams. Susceptibility during sleep. . . . 315

XVI.

Heaven and Hell, the Supposed Abodes of the Departed.

Where located by the ancients. Beneath the earth. Above the clouds: between the earth and moon. Comets the location of hell. The childhood of the race outgrown. Heaven the actual of desires. Why another state is asked for. The "New Jerusalem." The popular idea. Election, how known. From whence come these dogmas. The terrors of hell. The joys of the redeemed . . 351

XVII.

The Spirit's Home.

Law rules supreme. The same holds good in the spirit-world. No miracle. An unknown universe. What and where is the spirit-world? The testimony of spirits reliable. What they say. Nature works in cycles. Where do the refined atoms go? Form of the zones. Distance of the spheres from the earth's surface. Their thickness. Matter when it aggregates takes the form in which it existed on earth. Relation of the spirit. Spirit-locomotion. Can they pass to other globes? Relation of light to the spheres 375

XVIII.

Religious Aspect of Spiritualism.

Spiritualism considered wanting in a vital system of ethics. Reasons offered by the church for doing right. Not an easy affair to become a Spiritualist. Spiritualism the essence of philosophy. Doctrine of salvation. We are responsible for the thoughts and actions of all others. The teachings of spirits on the moral capabilities of man. Equality in the future. The *ideal* of Spiritualism. How may it be obtained? The object of being. The creed of Spiritualism 394

XIX.

THE OLD AND THE NEW.

The Radical and Radicalism. Protestantism brings from Catholicism everything but the Pope. A religion of abnegation. Religionists not necessarily insincere. Is the present form of religion demanded? Christian and infidel. Can Christianity live? Churchianity bedridden. Churchianity dying. Spiritualism. Comprehends the universe. An American religion. Perfectly democratic. Leaderless. Persistency and extension. The Spiritualist. Pleasures of a belief in Spiritualism. The coming contest. The totality of Spiritualism 412

LIST OF AUTHORITIES 448

INDEX 451

SPIRITUALISM.

GENERAL STATEMENT OF PRINCIPLES.

What is Spiritualism?

SPIRITUALISM is the knowledge of everything pertaining to the spiritual nature of man; and, as spirit is the moving force of the universe in its widest scope, it grasps the domain of nature. It embraces all that is known, and all that ever can be known. It is cosmopolitan eclecticism, receiving all that is good, and rejecting all that is bad. (324, 9.) *

Who are Spiritualists?

Those who believe that departed spirits communicate with man, however else they disagree, are Spiritualists; but only as they cultivate the noble faculties, and harmonize their lives, are they entitled to the name in its highest meaning. (330, 332.)

Principles on which All Agree.

There are certain fundamental principles on which all agree as forming the basis of the Spiritual philosophy.

* The references indicate chapters and sections in the body of the work.

Man a Dual Being.

Man is a duality,—a physical structure and a spirit. The spirit is an organized form, evolved by and out of the physical body, having corresponding organs and development. (155, 6, 8.)

Immortality.

This spiritual being is immortal. (ii., iii.)

Death.

Death is the separation of this duality, and effects no change in the spirit, morally nor intellectually. (xii., xiii., 183, 219.)

Relations of the Spirit to the Spirit-World.

The spirit holds the same relations to the spirit-world that man holds to physical nature. (xvii., 189, 190, 197.)

A Future State of Awards.

The spirit there, as here, works out its own salvation, receiving the reward of well-doing, and suffering for wrongful action.

Salvation — how Attained.

Salvation is only attainable through growth. (305, 312.)

No Arbitrary Decree.

There is no arbitrary decree, final judgment, or

atonement for wrong, except through the suffering of the guilty. (xvi., xvii.)

Relation of the Earth-Life to Spirit-Being.

The knowledge, attainment, and experience of the earth-life form the basis of the spirit-life. (159.)

Destiny of Spirit.

Progressive evolution of intellectual and moral power is the endless destiny of individual spirits. (152.)

The Spirit–World.

In the spirit-world, as on earth, we receive all we are capable of receiving; all seeking congenial employment, and gratifying their tastes. (xvii.)

Hell and Heaven.

Hell and heaven are not places, but conditions of mind. Inharmony is hell; harmony, heaven. (xvi., 271.)

Origin of Spiritual Beings.

All spiritual beings were eliminated from physical bodies. (157.)

Grades.

There are all grades, from the sage of ten thousand years to the idiot and infant. (xvii.)

They are Frequent Visitors.

They are often near those they love, and strive to warn, protect, and influence them.

MEDIUMSHIP.

The departed, whatever may have been their moral or intellectual condition, can return, and communicate through properly endowed mediums. (ii., xiv.)

CHARACTER OF THEIR INFLUENCE.

This influence may be for evil as well as for good. (247.)

COMMUNICATIONS FALLIBLE.

Communications from spirits must thus be fallible, partaking of the nature of their source. (245, 247.)

ALL COMMUNICATIONS FROM ONE SOURCE.

The spiritual communications of all ages emanate from this one source, and must be alike tried by the test of reason.

THERE CAN BE NO MIRACLE.

As law rules supreme in the spiritual as well as physical realm, there can be no miracle nor supernatural event. (198.)

BROTHERHOOD AND DIVINITY OF MAN.

Spirit is the reality, and individualized spirit the highest type, of creation. In this sense, mankind become brethren, commencing and continuing their progress on the same plane of development. In this sense all men are divine, and are endowed with infinite capabilities.

INCENTIVES OF SPIRITUALISM.

Spiritualism encourages the loftiest spiritual aspirations, energizes the soul by presenting only exalted motives, prompts to highest endeavors, and inculcates noble self-reliance. It frees man from the bondage of authority of book and creed. Its only authority is truth; its interpreter, reason. (324.)

ITS OBJECT.

It seeks for a whole and complete cultivation of man,—physically, morally, and intellectually. (324.)

INFLUENCE OF THE DEPARTED.

As the departed take deep interest in the affairs of earth, they mingle in all the reforms of the day. The temperance movement, women's rights, the high duties and responsibilities of parentage, abolition of all slavery, the thorough education of all, the establishment of universal peace, the promulgation of correct religious views in contradiction to prevailing errors, and all movements for the elevation and improvement of mankind, claim their attention. (ii.)

IT CAN HAVE NO CREED.

Every individual must be a law unto himself, and draft his own creed, but not seek to force such on others.

ORGANIZATION.

If Spiritualists organize, it is because organization is the best method to reach desirable results, and the means by which each receives the combined strength of all.

Such organization must be based on absolute personal freedom, and unquestioned right to individual opinion and action, so far as the rights of others remain inviolate. There must be agreement to differ.

I.

INTRODUCTION.

THE Reformation was the proclamation of salvation by grace, once preached by Paul and his companions. — D'AUBIGNÉ.

Reform is evolved by the progressive growth of the human intellect.

HOW often do we hear it said, in derision, this or that man is a theorist, a visionary, an idealist, and has no practical powers! Is this prevalent impression, that the ideal is valueless, correct? Is the world of the senses the only world? and are the men of the yardstick and scale the only valuable portion of mankind?

If we look deeper into this question, we shall find that the ideal world is the real, of which the vaunted real world is but the shadow.

What are these realities? They are incarnations of ideas. Look at the ponderous engine! Its bones are wrought of iron; its sinews are of steel; its vital energy is fire. How perfectly it performs its work! How wonderfully its parts are adjusted to each other! It is the very embodiment of the real and the practical. Yet what would it be without the thought that gave it birth? A mass of inert metal slumbering in the earth. Ideas have found expression in the length of that piston, in the form of those valves, in the polish of that cylinder, in the condensation of that steam, in the draft of that fire; and, from those ideas, the engine has been actualized. Whether it be placed in the hull of a ship to propel it against adverse waves and winds, or mounted on wheels to drag freighted cars with the speed of the wind, it once formed a part of the mind of its architect.

Before the iron of which it is formed is mined, the machine exists in the mental world. The inventor plans and projects; and when he enters the shop, and by his hands builds after these plans, he but clothes, with iron and steel and brass, his ideal.

What this machine does, results from the amount of mind he imparts to it. So far as it represents his idea, it is perfect; and, so far as it does not, it is imperfect. The idea is its soul, which we discern when we examine its motions, clearly visible through the garb of metal. The boiler is tested at forty pounds' pressure. We see the index move at forty-two; and the steam escapes to restore the necessary equilibrium. The inert metal has life, it is intelligent, it relieves itself when endangered. Mind has fashioned it: it retains the skill of the molding hand.

The picture exists in the mind of the painter before he places it on canvas, and often with a force and beauty, an exquisiteness of outline, a brilliancy of coloring, which shames his every attempt at reproduction. The statue exists in the mind of the sculptor before it is chiseled in marble; and how often does he revile the unyielding stone!

This is all plain enough; but, in the higher walks of morality, what there? Vastly more. Not to the actualizing man belongs the honor of the grand achievements of history. It is to the idealists, the fanatics, we owe everything.

The spread of Islamism was the actualization of an idea. Mohammed, in his tent in the desert, with only his wife, surrounded by the awful and terrible sublimities of nature, felt the promptings of a spiritual presence, and that "*there is but one God:*" all the idol worship of his people was vain, all their mythology childish. "There is but one God." He, the first to receive the sublime knowledge of the grand unity of all things, — he was the "prophet of God." Chadisjah, his beloved wife, said, in the simple, trustful, all-receiving faith of a wife, "I believe;" and, thus strengthened, he went forth.

What was there, against the bigotry, intolerance, superstition, and ignorance of those who surrounded this plain, simple man, that bore him up, and in the end subjugated all adverse elements? It was an IDEA. "*There is one God, and Mohammed is his prophet.*" That is a plain thought; but, to that people and time, it was a clean Damascus blade. It destroyed the old; and, like a whirlwind gathering force, it spread from people to people, and still rolls onward along the African continent, displacing the tenets of all other sects, not excepting those of Christianity. Beginning with the humble man in his tent in the desert, it is now received by 300,000,000 souls, or more than one-fourth of the human family.

The ideas of universal brotherhood floating in the atmosphere of the world gather around a child born to a poor carpenter in Nazareth, and so destitute they cradle him in a manger. When the child matures, he becomes possessed with the idea of brotherly love. He scorns the inequality, injustice, and shams of the world. He believes in the universal applicability of love, and that it is better to suffer wrong than to do wrong; to do as we would be done by.

We may ask, Is there power in these? Yes: there is power enough to overturn a world, and resurrect a new and glorious race of angelic beings. Those ideas have worked through eighteen centuries, and are still at work with stronger force than ever.

There is this singular peculiarity about the men who first receive ideas,—they cannot keep them. When the rising sun gilded the face of the Egyptian Memnon, he answered the light with songs; so, when the sun of truth gilds our mental horizon, we cry out at the beautiful vision. No sooner does the man perceive that he has a new idea, than he becomes impressed that he has a mission. It is not egotism; it is not a desire for notoriety. The same power which gives him the idea fills him with an irresistible impulse to reveal it. He cannot conceal it: he rushes forth to light the lamp of his neighbors.

He cannot be diverted. Wealth, ease, comfort, home, wife, children, friends, the gentle amenities of life, may plead; and poverty, disgrace, ruin, and martyrdom with rod, fire, and dungeon, may menace, — he rushes on to promulgate the new. He has gained an insight into the everlasting, the inscrutable; and his lips glow with the words with which he sets it forth. He controlled by the soft pleasures of this life? They are ephemeral. He proselyted? Never. In him, an idea, for the first time since creation, has found a tongue of flame. It is no fault of his that he becomes fanatical, and overestimates the importance of his treasure. The world gains by the equilibrium resulting from a thousand such. Stand aloof, men of the world, who cannot understand anything unless it is set down in dollars and cents, quarts and bushels. Stand aside! you are the freight, the dead freight, which such fanatics are to carry through; and the only possible use you serve is a retarding influence, which, out of kindness, we call conservative, by which you keep them in sight.

Spiritualism, in its rapid growth, illustrates the power of an idea. That idea is the grandest as well as dearest possible to conceive. Immortality of our being, and of our ties and bonds of affection and intelligence.

It comes to prove this, and does so through the sweet voices of the loved departed. The idea of "one God" is cold and far off compared with this. Immortality demonstrated is above all else what we most desire. The voice of prayer has daily and hourly pleaded for this great revelation, now freely shed like the light of the morning sun. The world has been slowly preparing for its advent. Ideas do not burst suddenly on the minds of men, like flashing meteors, but rather like the slowly breaking twilight of the perfect day. Their dawn is determined by the advance of culture.

There is growth in the human race, from infancy to manhood. When civilization flourished on the fertile banks of the Nile, and the Hebrew warrior tended his flocks on Assyrian plains, it was in its infancy. Its birth is shrouded by impenetrable mists of mythology; and its early history is the record of its childish prattle, a description of its toys and cobble-houses. The actions of the greatest, most learned, and accomplished of the Egyptians possess a marked puerility, such as is expected of children. The early nations represent the childhood of the race, — rude, fearful, revengeful, superstitious, believers in devils, hobgoblins, and afraid of the dark.

The present is the age of dawning manhood. The baby-clothes (creeds, superstitions, traditions) are fast being laid away in the world's lumber-room, with all the useless utensils former generations considered necessary for the government of the people. The rack, the gibbet, the gallows, the guillotine, horrid engines of torture, once thought requisite to maintain government, are cast off with the ignorance which prompted their use.

The world to-day has outgrown its yesterday thoughts; and to-morrow will outgrow the best performances of to-day. Each year adds growth to the moral and intellectual world, as the circling sun adds a new layer to the tree. Each year's growth encircles all others; or, in other words, the ideas of the race are higher, its attainments more noble, and it basks in a brighter light. Each year adds to the moral and intellectual temperature of mind; makes it glow with superior truth and wisdom. This growth, slow, but visible, is a progress as uncontrollable as the movement of the heavenly bodies around their central suns.

Grown to manhood, the infant garments cannot be strained on; and, were it possible to force them on, they would cramp the free movement of his body, bind his limbs in stiff contortions, and destroy freedom and manliness. Creeds, dogmas, beliefs, are such garments to the spirit. When the expanding mind is forced to take up its abode in the habiliments of the past, its best motives are crushed; its feelings are stifled; its holiest emanations dried up; and it becomes as barren as the desert-sands of Sahara, as cold and frigid as the icebergs around the frozen poles.

Everything moves toward a crisis, attains its maximum, and then declines, performing a perpetual oscillation. The planet departs from its orbit; the world varies in its motions: but a deviation in one extreme is counterbalanced by a deviation in the other; and, through a perpetual oscillation, the world moves in a given orbit around the sun.

So with the inhabitants of the world, — like a ship crossing the ocean, driven hither and thither by storm and current in many a devious wandering, but, as a whole, making a straight course to the destined port.

Underneath the superficial dross is an omnipotent principle which none can resist nor gainsay. By the force of this principle, the race moves faster or slower in proportion to the number at the oars, and the vigor of their exertions.

Great men, leaders of the race, are thrown up from the waves of the intellectual sea, and mounted on the highest billow's crest, not so much by their own exertions as by the irresistible undulations of that sea. It is not difficult for them to lead, but the easiest thing in the world. They lead because they cannot help it. Some enter one sphere of action, doing good; some, another. All are for their place and season.

Sensual and crude as the doctrines of Mohammed are, the beliefs before him were more sensual and depraved. He had a far more ignorant and animal race to reform than had Christ; and hence it was impossible for him to institute the transcendental doctrines of the Nazarene. Had Mohammed appeared in Jerusalem, he could have worked no reform. Had Christ appeared in Mecca, his sublime visions of universal love and wisdom would have been lost; for the sensual Arabians could not appreciate such transcendental ideas. They would far exceed the perfection with which he invests his God. But Christ in his place, and Mohammed in his, were where they should be to do the most good.

Reformers may introduce and sustain a few fundamental truths; but the great mass of their teachings must necessarily be erroneous. None are born so far in advance as to see the absolute right. Their words, in consequence, are comparative. As the ages pass, the ideas of yesterday become obsolete, giving place to the new of to-day, which are destined to become old to-morrow.

There are a few principles which are established here for time and eternity; but the mass of knowledge styled truth is only true for its time, and liable at any moment to be outgrown. There is a class which desires to make this imperfect truth eternal truth, by preventing mankind from outgrowing it. These are the conservatives, — poor men who have turned their eyes backward, looking the wrong way. Against these, reformation must wage open war.

While the reformer would have mankind throw off the garments of boyhood, — cast aside the top, the doll, and toy, which pacified its babyhood, and occupy its mind with manly things, — the conservative would compel it to wear its infant dress, clinging for safety to its leading-strings, and delight itself with gewgaws and tinsel. Even its new clothes must be cut after the old infantile pattern. But, despite the stoutness of the seams, human minds will grow. They cannot arrest their own growth, though they strive ever so hard to starve themselves into mental dwarfs. Reform takes even these; and, though they may not remain afar in the rear, they are moved along.

We said there were levelers and builders, and that both were useful. The radical utters his thoughts in so rabid a form; is so cutting, harsh, and vindictive; and comes down on his hearers with such crushing force,—they become angry, and will not hear him. He misses the mark; for men, when excited by anger, lose reason, and refuse persuasion. They cannot be driven into a new belief, but a well-known call they will follow anywhere.

The builder comes along, and finds a state of confusion left by the leveler. He sets himself at work to heal the laceration, applying balm and healing ointment. His words are so sweet, that, although new, they are palatable; and men incline to accept them. He comes not with the grim battle-ax and brand, rushing to the fray with clang of arms; but gently, as a south wind reviving the drooping flower, he stoops over fainting humanity, and speaks cheeringly of a better life and more exalted aims. My heart is with such. The temple's spire of their construction glitters in the sunlight of peace and love.

Great changes can be wrought in peace, or by concentrating giant forces, in confusion, convulsion, and ruin. Niagara's stream, in its never-ceasing flow, little by little, undermines and wears the rock away; but should we concentrate the work of ages in a single effort, and compel the waters to plow out that channel at once, the mighty rush would sweep clear the country from Erie's tide to the Atlantic main. So, if we would destroy long-standing institutions, however erroneous, we must proceed by degrees, else disorder and the horrors of anarchy result.

We do not dishonor the institutions of the past, but profoundly respect them for the good they have accomplished. They have been the instruments through which mind has attained its present perfection; the steps by which it arose; and now are the landmarks set up along the shores of the wild sea of life, marking the deeds of its various ages. But they are not for the present: they cramp its vital energies, and restrain the best emotions of the soul.

We lament the error, sin, and depravity, which exist, and justly too; but we forget that there is a cause, and that cause — ignorance. Alas for human ignorance! It has immolated its myriad victims; and still its all-devouring jaws are stretched wide with insatiable rapacity. It is the prolific cause of *all* crime, *all* degradation, *all* misery. It is an accepted truth, that, if man perfectly obeyed every law of his moral, intellectual, and physical nature, he would be perfectly happy, perfectly free from all pain, unnatural desires, and sufferings. He obeys not, because he is ignorant. Give him knowledge upon these great subjects; and he would do better in proportion to the light he receives. Pour a flood of wisdom into the world, so much that every by-lane and every alley shall be filled, and evil will expire. Error, sin, and evil, are the results of subjecting ourselves to other laws than those of our normal being. If we sufficiently understood these laws, we should never suffer from them.

The child, before it learns the nature of physical matter, is delighted with the brilliant flame, reaches forth its tender hand to grasp the glittering object, and is burnt.

Henceforth it understands the relations of heat to its physical frame, — that it causes intense pain, — and avoids it, however much it glitters. Man, taken collectively, has been a child. When first an inhabitant of the globe, a rude savage, totally unacquainted with the material universe, and its controlling laws, he was surrounded by darkness, and was compelled to walk empirically. Like the child, attracted by brilliant objects, he strove to obtain, perhaps finding them useful in supplying his wants, perhaps causing him intense suffering. In either case, he discovered their nature, and the relations they sustained to him. By degrees, the light dawned. Fact after fact was learned, law after law deduced, until he knew the general bearing he sustained to the microcosm of which he is a part.

Still the unknown far exceeds the known, and the anxious student of nature, who has surpassed all his contemporaries, looks off on the limitless sea of knowledge which stretches beyond the shores of his present acquirements, and, in an agony of aspiration after the unknown truths of the mystic beyond, is abashed at his own insignificance; that he is a traveler on the shores of the intellectual sea, and has tasted but a few drops of its waters. Newton gives voice to his feelings, exclaiming, "I am but a boy gathering a few pebbles on the ocean's strand."

Being thus ignorant of the laws which govern the external and internal universes, we must expect transgressions, and their accompanying punishments in the form of misery and suffering. As soon as man learns the higher principles of right and wrong, so soon will suffering cease. This must be learned empirically, as he learned the properties of fire, air, and water. In these experiments, he will often make missteps, and suffer many a fall. Some there are, who, guided by superior intuition, safely steer their barks among shoals and rocks, where others, less gifted, would certainly perish. Such are born reformers, — men who see far down the vista of a thousand ages, and chart the unknown seas for the direction of future generations. These are the true reformers, which the world finds or evolves at long intervals, to clear away the accumulations of rubbish, and build new systems for expanding thought. Theirs it is to walk far ahead of their times, and mark the way by the recognition of before unknown laws, throwing a strong, clear light over the darkness.

It matters little whether born on a throne or in a manger: when they arise in their manhood, all conventionalisms crumble away, and king and peasant stand in the same light. When sublime intuitions fill their overflowing souls, and they reveal man's relations to the universe and to his fellow-man, all distinctions vanish in the rapturous gush of eloquence, as the frost-work of night vanishes in the rays of the rising sun. Confucius was nobly born; Zoroaster stated his ideas from a throne; Mohammed was a noble: their converts count by the hundred million. Some eighteen centuries ago, a poor carpenter's son, of so low origin he was cradled in a manger, arose, and with a breath overturned all the cherished idols of his time, and founded a transcendental system of purity, which is the ideal, even now, of the civilized world.

So it is written in all history. The origin of the man is of small account: the truths he utters avail everything. Say you there is no need of new truths; that, the older the world grows, the worse it becomes? You contradict history, the all-answering experience of the past. You repeat a myth, first dreamed by the poets, and since set up as a revelation. The golden age is the goal towards which we are going, not the one we left. It is in the future, not in the past, which only reveals fitful gleams through the thick night of its darkness. There is the turmoil and conflict of animal passions, with here and there a noble man, a great thought, a glorious deed. Such are the redeemers of history. All have perished in oblivion. The great conquerors, who, with their murderous hordes, rushed across the world, scattering the affrighted nations, have scarce a place left to write their names. A few years, or centuries,—all the same in time,—have obliterated their ravages, as they do the path of the avalanche. The disturbances they caused were no more than ripples on the surface, soon subsiding in the smooth outline of history. Great crimes, as well as great benevolence, are all lost in the sea of life. They are all forgotten. They are but the accidental ripples beneath which the vast, interminable sea ebbs and flows, controlled by undeviating laws.

Oblivion, which devours the dross of the world, leaves only the great and shining truths. A truth once revealed is never forgotten. All that mankind has conquered from nature remains conquered forever. No inquisition can suppress it; no irruption of savage hordes blot it out.

Creeds, dogmas, superstitions, shall pass away,— all the paraphernalia by which mock legislators seek to force men to be moral; governments shall fade; and the ephemeral world grow old, and perish: but the least thought of truth lives forever! It is endowed with productive power; and, as each age claims it, it gives birth to truths for that age, and thus grows continually, extending its influence broader and broader; and mankind, in remote generations, drinks at its fountain of clear waters, pronouncing the name of its author, calling him blessed.

There is need of untiring action. Each reform presupposes and calls for a greater. The desires of humanity are not left long unanswered before fresh thoughts are ushered into the world, at whose breath old institutions crumble away, and new start up as by the touch of the magician's wand.

Is not reform needed? Shall we be content? There is no content. As long as a slave sends up a petition to sympathizing Heaven; as long as the chains of despotism canker the limbs of the downtrodden masses; as long as ignorance and attendant crimes encompass us, — so long will the world, lost in darkness, cry loudly, wildly, from its bed of torture, "Light! more light!"

Tell us not of the past. I respect it for its truths; but the world's genii have elevated us far, far above the bravest thoughts of our forefathers. We have actualized their wildest idealities. Our own ideal is for the future. Men, one and all, feel, deeply feel, that great wrongs are to be righted, great errors to be overcome, and anxiously wait the blast the trump of their leader shall send down the gale. They expect a higher, purer morality. They feel that the age of thought is in store for the future, dimly seen through the long vista of events by the Hebrew seers and prophets of past ages, shadowed forth in the constitution of mind, — an age of thought whose brilliant morning lights up the mental world by its rapid coming.

The age of thought is full of promise. Ignorance shall vanish, and, with it, its viper-brood, — crime, error, evil, misery, and suffering. A thousand or a million years may intervene; but, surely as mind progresses, the future shall yield this fruit, and the whole earth shall partake of it in harmony.

II.

EVIDENCES OF SPIRITUALISM: A DISCUSSION OF THE VARIOUS THEORIES ADVANCED FOR ITS EXPOSITION.

WE ask no one to come to the investigation of Spiritualism biased in its favor. We only ask that there be no prejudice against it, and vision directed through a perfectly clear glass.

How vast is the power of spirits! An ocean of invisible intelligences surround us everywhere. If you look for them, you cannot see them. If you listen, you cannot hear them. Identified with the substance of all things, they cannot be separated from it. They cause men to sanctify and purify their hearts. . . . They are everywhere; above us, on the right, and on the left. Their coming cannot be calculated. How important we do not neglect them! — CONFUCIUS, B.C. 551.

1. IF A MAN DIE, SHALL HE LIVE AGAIN?

NO question can be asked so full of import, or appealing with greater force to the human consciousness. On its affirmation depend our hopes and aspirations: its negation converts creation into a sham, into which man seems thrust for no purpose but to have the brief hour of his existence, fraught with pain and disappointment, blotted out in eternal night.

2. ATHEISM

Is a mental state into which some of the most profound thinkers fall. The student of nature cannot avoid, if he logically follows the views science at present entertains, arriving at its goal. This tendency has been long foreseen by the theological world, which, in various ways, has sought to arrest its progress. The shafts hurled by dogmatic believers have always rebounded against themselves. Nothing is gained by denial. It is the responsibility of every new truth to vindicate itself: it must not only produce positive evidence in its favor, but reveal the errors in the theories it would supplant. Cicero gave more attention to the arguments brought against him than those he could urge in his favor. To show the old false is essential to establish the new.

3. IMMORTALITY AND SCIENCE.

Science is an interpreter of the senses. The phenomena attending the death of man and of animals are apparently the same. The processes of decay destroy their bodies, resolving them into identical elements. In vain is appeal made to the senses for knowledge of existence beyond the grave. Their voice is, "Dust to dust;" a resurrection of new organic life out of the dead atoms. Man's physical body is composed of perishable compounds, and, of necessity, must perish. Dissolution is the terrible, but unavoidable, end of living beings. Composed as they are of elements antagonistic, gross, and conflicting, the embryonic, called life, cannot be preserved. A living being represents a balance of the forces of decay and renovation. In the maturing organism, the latter predominate ; in age, the former rule with constantly increasing power until they gain the victory in death. Such is the history of all organic forms. Out of the imperfect material afforded by the physical world, immortal beings cannot be produced.

4. Conditions of Immortality.

An immortal being presupposes the perfect harmony of its constituent elements. The forces of decay and renovation must not only balance, they must so remain forever. Immortality is this harmony eternally preserved ; and, if attainable with physical elements, an immortal lion or panther, oak or pine, would be as possible as an immortal man.

5. Impossible with Physical Elements.

But such conditions cannot obtain. Organic forms live for an hour, and perish. They revolve in designated orbits, fulfill appointed missions, and pass back to elementary atoms. The grass and herbs of the fields, the trees of centuries' growth, the deer browsing the branches, the lion devouring the deer, all the multitudinous forms of animated nature, with man boasting of his superiority, grow old, and die. Identically do they all decay. Their dissolving elements are absorbed by the earth, drunk by the rains, wafted away by the winds. All are resolved, and mingle. The farthest oasis in the desert is refreshed by the gifts brought by the winds and rain : the palm is taller, the grass greener. Life rejoices in the harvest of the old. So is it always: life preys on death; and, in a perpetual cycle of change from death to life, the world is filled with beings, and a fleeting happiness secured to each.

6. Does the Mind perish?

Man's aspirations—are they also to perish? Physically, man is an animal; mentally, "Ah! what?" asks the skeptic. "What is memory but an interpreted succession of what before were automatic actions? And reason, godlike reason, which places an impassable abyss between man and animals,— what is it but comparison of perceptions? What is mind, as a whole, but the result of certain chemical changes in the grate, or electricity of changes in the battery? Does not the brain secrete thought as the liver secretes bile?"* These questions are very well, but they yield no explanation of spiritual ideas: they only give new names to well-known facts.

Man has the wants of the animal; but, after these are supplied, he feels the breath of new and vastly higher aspirations. Indefinable, awful, inexpressible desires and longings seize him. He feels that he is akin to that which is supreme. He thinks blindly that this afflatus is the breath of Deity, and shadowing forth his ideal. He describes it as God, endowed with all the attributes he admires,—justice, love, wisdom, all infinite in quantity and degree. What is this shadow, which the mortal, man the animal,

* Carl Vogt.

calls God, and worships with such devotion? Startling is the revelation. It is man's own immortal essence. As in a mirror, he sees his own divine qualities reflected back from the domain of nature. It is not true, as has been said, that men assimilate to their gods: on the contrary, their gods are concrete representatives of themselves.

How do these ideas of immortality arise, if not true? Nature, interpreted by the senses, demonstrates mortality. How, then, did man learn this wonderful truth? Savage man, standing by his dying brother, who presented the same appearance as the deer pierced by his arrow, said, "The deer is dead, but my brother still lives," and solved the problem. Did he learn this by dreams? He dreamed of meeting his departed friends, just as we now dream, and supposed they still existed. But he dreamed of seeing animals also; and why did he not bestow immortality on them?

7. IF MAN IS NOT IMMORTAL, HOW CAN HE UNDERSTAND IMMORTALITY?

You might as well talk mathematics as immortality to an ox, so far as his understanding is concerned. Why? Because he has not the elements of either in his organization. The ox never counts the blades of grass, nor estimates their form or size. Only so far as they appease his hunger, can he appreciate their qualities. He has no comprehension of anything beyond the gratification of his appetite.

In man, these relations are suggested because he has the mental qualities which represent the laws of mathematics.

So, if man were mortal, vain would it be to talk to him of immortality; for, not having the capabilities, he could not understand that existence. As well a finite being comprehend an infinite, as a mortal immortality. That man aspires for immortal life is presumptive evidence that he has the possibilities of that life.

8. Opposition of Science and Spiritualism.

The facts of science are opposed to Spiritualism: at least, such is their interpretation, as given by scientific men, who ignore the facts of Spiritualism as miraculous, and do not even recognize their existence. But spiritual phenomena are as positive, and amenable to law, as physical, and quite as far removed from the supernatural. They cannot be explained by orthodox science. Scientists have, without exception, signally failed; and the magnitude of their failure has been in direct proportion to their greatness. They start wrong, with the supposition that everything claiming to be spiritual must be miraculous; and, the further they go, the more erroneous they become.

9. This Conflict is not Necessary.

Science has become exclusively external. One does not penetrate beneath the outer garb of appearances: the other seeks the vital soul of things, and works outward. Physical science has not the whole, complete truth. Spiritualism supplies the deficiency. It adds new elements to every fact, and modifies the conclusions drawn therefrom. Shall its facts be accepted?

10. Are they Legerdemain?

When an investigator enters a circle, and witnesses manifestations, the first explanation which suggests itself is that they are produced by legerdemain. The precautions of honest skepticism against fraud are not detrimental nor offensive; and every precaution should be taken to render the facts trustworthy. A manifestation which admits of doubt is valueless, although it may be genuine. Experiments should always be instituted in such a manner as to avoid all possibility of error. Spiritualists usually are more severe in their tests than skeptics; and it is improbable that they are self-deceived. Mediums rely on their own communications, and hence are not only deceivers, but deceived. But are they self-deceived? They rely on a power which influences them to write, speak, and act in a manner foreign to themselves. What is that power that enlightens, purifies, and refines those subjected to its influence?

11. Impossibility of moving Matter.

It is impossible for a human being to move physical matter without contact; and the moving of ponderable substances, without such contact of the medium, settles the question of self-deception and collusion. A rap, or the playing of a musical instrument at a distance from the medium, is conclusive on this point. The movement of a table, while the hands of the circle rest on its surface, of itself is not satisfactory; but it becomes so by the intelligence of its answers. If it answers in such a manner as to identify the controlling force with the departed whom it purports to be, imparting facts unknown to the medium or circle, the cause, whatever it may be, is removed outside of the circle.

The facts which prove that matter has been moved without contact, musical instruments been played, and intelligence manifested superior to the medium, are so common for the present we take them for granted. Volumes might readily be filled with them; but skepticism, to be thoroughly convinced, must witness for itself, as belief cannot grow out of the statement of what others have seen.

12. Are the Senses Reliable?

If the medium does not deceive, perhaps the circle are self-deceived: perhaps their senses are unreliable. Nowhere else are they so deceptive as in the border-land lying between the known physical realm, and what has been called the supernatural. It has become fashionable to ridicule everything of a spiritual character as miraculous, and hence unworthy of credence. Because the senses are sometimes deceived, their evidence is entirely discarded unless susceptible of proof. This is by no means justifiable. All knowledge is referable to them; and we, in the end, are compelled to accept their testimony.

They often become deranged. The ear hears, the eye sees, when there is nothing external to produce sight or sound, the cause residing in organic changes in the nerves or brain. The deaf hear roaring or whistling sounds, as of the wind, or falling water, or rush of steam; the abnormal action of the auditory nerves simulating the effects of sounds naturally produced. This does not prove that there is no reliability in hearing. Two deaf persons listening for the same sound would not receive it alike. Hissing to one would be roaring to the other, proving that neither heard an external sound. The normal ear would hear no sound, and its evidence would be receivable. The records of insanity furnish innumerable instances of the deception of the senses, which have been employed to account for spiritual phenomena. If the senses are not to be trusted, if the normal cannot be distinguished from the abnormal, it should be known, and distrust awakened.

The *savants*, who annually publish "expositions" of Spiritualism, talk as if the world was a world of hallucinations, — an unreliable, phantom existence. It is true all are liable to hallucinations; and such liability does not necessarily indicate insanity. Disease often produces hallucinations; as in delirium tremens, fevers, and fasting.

Among the sane, sight, and, among the insane, hearing, are oftenest imposed upon. Brierre states, that, out of sixty-two patients in his asylum, thirty-eight had hallucinations: of sixty-six cases admitted into the Bicetre, thirty-five had hallucinations. The fiends and reptiles of delirium tremens are reproduced in the maniac who fancies himself pursued, or wild beasts ready to devour him.

"A patient in the York Dispensary used to complain bitterly of a voice repeating in his ear everything that he was reading; and, on one occasion, he distinctly heard the same voice commanding him to throw himself into a pond in his garden. He obeyed the voice; and when removed from the water, and asked why he had done so rash an act, he replied that he much regretted it, but added, 'He told me that I must do it, and I could not help it.'"

"The poet Cowper was distracted by hallucinations of the sense of hearing. 'The words,' says his biographer, 'which occurred to him on waking, though but his own imaginations, were organically heard; and Mr. Johnson, perceiving how fully he was impressed with their reality, ventured upon a questionable experiment. He introduced a tube into his chamber, near the bed's head, and employed one, with whose voice Cowper was not acquainted, to speak words of comfort through this contrivance. The reality of his impressions is shown by the remarkable fact that he did not discover the artifice. His attendant, one day, found him with a penknife sticking in his side, with which he had attempted suicide, believing he had been ordered to do so by a voice from heaven."

Hallucinations of the sense of touch exist but rarely among the insane. Haslam records a case of a man who fancied himself pursued by a gang of villains, learned in the secrets of pneumatic chemistry, who used their knowledge to inflict punishment on him. They would draw out the fibres of his tongue; stretch a veil over his brain, and thus intercept the communication between his mind and heart; or, by means of magnetic fluids, almost squeeze him to death.

Berbiquin believed that hobgoblins were constantly coming to and leaving his body, supporting themselves on him in order to fatigue him, and oblige him to sit down. These invisible enemies traveled over him day and night; and their weight was sometimes such that he was afraid of being smothered.

Hallucinations of smell are of rare occurrence, or are complicated with those of other senses. "Patients do, however, complain of very bad odors, and, at other times, of very pleasant ones, when neither have any existence. We had a very good example of the former in an insane patient, who complained exceedingly of the injury done to her health by the sulphurous fumes with which some one, as she believed, continually filled her room."

The same author describes a lady with disordered mind, in whom all the senses were abnormal. She heard a voice from her stomach continually tormenting her, and directing her actions, and at length made her believe that she was possessed. She saw fearfully distorted forms in her room, defiling before her. Her food tasted like vinegar, or other things which she detested. When walking, she felt drenched with ice-water; and she was frequently annoyed with disagreeable odors.

The author previously quoted thus presents a succinct view of this subject: " Hallucinations may be continuous, remittent, intermittent, or periodical. They may, although rarely, be at the will of the individual, so that he can recall them at pleasure. They may have one character to-day, and another to-morrow. In some cases, in which the sense of sight is hallucinated, closing the eyes will dispel the affection. Sometimes the patient hears sounds through only one ear, or sees imaginary objects through one eye; the other eye or ear being unaffected. Again the number of voices will vary. In some instances, an animated dialogue is sustained with all the force of reality; in others, two or more distinct voices are recognized by the patient; and a linguist will occasionally hear voices in different languages."

13. WHAT IS HALLUCINATION?

Hallucination is the perception of the sensible signs of an idea: "illusion is the false appreciation of real sensations." "Either may exist (the former rarely) in persons of sound mind: but, in that case, they are discredited in consequence of the exercise of reason and observation ; or, if credited, they do not influence the actions."

14. SPIRITUAL PHENOMENA HALLUCINATIONS.

It is said that those who witness spirit-manifestations are hallucinated, and the facts of Spiritualism are thus summarily classed with those of insanity.

A proper understanding of both series of facts shows the puerility of this assertion. If a score of persons subject to illusions were in company, no two would be hallucinated alike. If one saw the table move, there would not be another to corroborate him. If two should see the table move, it would be presumptive that their sense of sight was normal; and, if three, it would be positively certain.

At circles, all the members see, feel, and hear alike. How, then, can it be called illusion or hallucination? The facts presented show many points of resemblance to those of Spiritualism. How far departed minds may influence the insane is a question Spiritualism only can solve. The ancients believed insanity wholly caused by spiritual obsession, and they had a shadow of the truth. But any one experienced in spiritual manifestations can draw a sharp line between the narrow hallucinations of the insane, or illusions of the sane, and the ever-changing, broad, and characteristic facts of Spiritualism.

If it is considered probable that the members of a circle are hallucinated, that thousands should be so is not only improbable, but impossible. Wise and learned men have unqualifiedly endorsed its facts, and bravely announced their belief. It is not a single case of insanity, but of millions, all infatuated alike, if they are infatuated; and, as the quoted facts show, rarely, if ever, are two individuals contemporaneously alike,— the chances of their being so become infinitely improbable.

A list of the names of those who have embraced Spiritualism would include the leading men of the nation,— statesmen who wield the most power, scientists, and almost all the advanced and radical thinkers. Dare any one brave the sneers of coming ages by declaring all these hallucinated? If the senses are valueless in informing as to a table's moving, how can they be trusted as to its not moving? If twenty persons think they see it move when it is stationary, who is to judge whether it be stationary or not? Then we float into a sea of unreality, and science itself has no basis. If the senses of sight, hearing, touch, are unreliable, presenting what is false, then there is no certainty anywhere. But this once favorite theory is thrown aside by more enlightened opponents, but is still urged by those who have not taken the trouble to acquaint themselves with the phenomena.

15. Is it Evil Spirits, or the Devil?

The opposers of Spiritualism have each a favorite theory, which they maintain with dogmatic complacency. There is a respectable party, who have at once fallen on a sure and perfect method, which quiets their nerves, and satisfactorily explains the whole subject. When Luther lit the fires of the Reformation, and Catholicism saw the fierce flames rise high, and lap its most cherished institutions, the priesthood mounted the summits of their grim towers, and shrieked, in one long, wild refrain, " The Devil! the Devil!"

When England threw off the Catholic yoke, and became spiritually free, there came across the wide sea, and echoed along the shores of the channel, that awful, sullen, and portentous growl, " The Devil!"

When a comet's glare flashed out on the evening sky, and shook out its fiery train, the Pope prayed to be saved from the arch-fiend, the Devil!

When a concussion, manifesting intelligence, is heard, and a table moved by invisible power; when individuals fall into an unconscious state, and have the realities of the future life revealed to them,— the clergy mount their pulpits, and shriek, "The Devil!" Ah! Satan, you are much abused. You are the scape-goat for all the folly and ignorance of the world.

The party who receive this theory is large, and headed by strong leaders. Whether referred to the Devil or evil spirits, this important question arises: If evil spirits can communicate, why not the good? Ah! here is an unfortunate dilemma. Can a benevolent God let loose on mankind an innumerable host of demons, and allow them to delude the children of men, and obstruct all avenues by which the good and loving ones can hold the same intercourse? Such a conclusion would be a profanation of Deity, contradictory to the Bible by which the theory is supported. Take the parable of Dives and Lazarus. Dives was an evil spirit; but he could not return to earth, and hence requested Lazarus to bear a message to his brethren. The Bible thus proves that the good spirits, if they desire, can communicate; but the bad cannot.

"The tree is known by its fruit. The good tree cannot bring forth evil fruit, nor the evil tree good fruit." Spiritualism makes men better. It teaches a sublime code of morality. It destroys infidelity. It inculcates virtue, goodness, and purity. It holds out the greatest inducements for right doing. It destroys oppression. It gives assurance of an afterlife, and the presence of loved ones gone before. It threatens a terrible retribution on those who do wrong. Can such sweet waters flow from a bitter fountain?

16. Is it Electricity?

Static electricity, as generated by an electrical machine or other means, is always detected by electrometers. When of any degree of tension, it gives a spark; but even when accumulated to the extent of human means, as in the Leyden battery, it does not move objects in the manner that tables are moved. It can only affect objects directly in its path, and that for an almost infinitely short space of time. Wheatstone calculated that it would pass around the globe in the tenth of a second. How instantaneous must be its passage from one neighboring object to another! In electricity generated by a machine or battery, perfect insulation is requisite, as in telegraphic apparatus.* In a circle, as usually constituted, there is no insulation, no generating battery, not a single condition necessary for the production of an electrical effect; and the most delicate instrument science can devise for the detection of that force gives not the least indication of its presence. Lightning might rend a table into splinters, if in its path; but it could not rock it to and fro. The snapping sound of the electric spark is entirely different from the rappings.

17. Is it Magnetism?

Those who understand the laws of the magnet well know that a table, however violently it may move when subjected to magnetic tests, gives not the least indication of magnetic attraction. There are extremely few substances in nature capable of

* The "wise men" who illustrate this theory by instancing the electrical eel as producing electrical shocks, and the cases where individuals have been in an electrified state, yielding sparks, forget to mention that the human organism has no special electrical apparatus, like the gymnotus; and the electrified condition is rarely met with in circles or mediums. If the moving object is electrified, every floating shred of dust will indicate the fact; and laying the hands of the medium or circle on a table, so far from "charging" it, would instantly *discharge* it, however strongly electrified.

exhibiting this property. Iron is the principal one; and it has been questioned whether the others do not derive the slight magnetism from a trace of iron they contain. Wood may be termed the antipode of iron, magnetically. An iron article moves no better than one of wood. The table, when moving, will not attract the smallest iron filing, any more than, electrically, it will attract a pith ball. It sounds exceedingly wise to refer a fact to electricity or magnetism, and has been quite the fashion. The human body cannot charge a table electrically or magnetically. It never exhibits the latter force. Both these hypotheses are untenable. The *odic force* is equally so. In none of Reichenbach's experiments, did he find *odic force* capable of moving a particle of matter. Acting on the nervous system, it attracted or repelled persons susceptible of its influence. It acts entirely and exclusively on living beings, and has not the least effect on inorganic bodies. This theory flourished for a time, made popular by its sounding name, and the ignorance of those who received as well as of those who taught it. *Od force* has no more intelligence than iron or lime or heat. How, then, account for intelligent communication? Does it absorb them from the minds of the circle? How account for its intelligence transcending the knowledge of the circle?

18. Mental Phenomena.

So theorists attempt to account for the mental manifestations, as trance, writing, etc., by mesmerism or psychology. Here, there is a show of argument for impressibility,—allowing a spirit freed from the physical body to communicate is the same which allows a mesmerizer to impress his thoughts on the mesmerized subject. The spiritual and mesmeric are mixed, because they depend on the same laws and conditions. It is probable that much that is received as spiritual might be readily traced to special mesmeric causes. But mesmeric impressions do not go outside of the person or objects *en rapport* with the subject. They never reveal what is unknown to those in connection. Spiritual impressibility reaches outside of surroundings, and reveals the thoughts of the spirit who is *en rapport*. No one pretends psychology moves articles of furniture without physical contact. It can be employed only in the domain of mind, and fails even then of a complete explanation.

How can the following fact be explained by any law of psychology? I state it because of the authority, not because it is unique. It is related by Dr. Hare ("Spiritualism Scientifically Demonstrated," p. 171).

"I was sitting in my solitary, third-story room at Cape Island, invoking my sister, as usual, when, to my surprise, I saw 'Cadwallader' spelled out on the desk. 'My old friend, Cadwallader?' said I. 'Yes.' A communication of much interest ensued; but, before concluding, I requested him, as a test, to give me the name of the person whom I met in an affair of honor, more than fifty years ago, when he was my second. The name was forthwith given, by pointing out on the desk the letters requisite to spell it. Now, as the spirit of General Cadwallader, during more than fifteen months that other friends had sought to communincate with me, had never made me a visit, why should his name have been spelled out when I had not the remotest idea of his coming, and was expecting another spirit,— the only one who had been with me at the cape? Further, the breakfast-bell being rung, I said, 'Will you come again after breakfast?' I understood him to consent to this invitation. Accordingly, when afterwards I reseated myself *in statu quo*, I looked for him; but, lo! 'Martha,' my sister's name, was spelled out."

19. Position of Scientists.

Scientific men have generally been the most unfair and prejudiced opposers. They are quick to say that they are the only class capable of investigation. They scorn the idea that ordinary persons can make close observations. In every experiment, they know certain well-determined conditions must be fulfilled; and nature, not themselves, determines these conditions. When these *savants* attempt to investigate, they invariably reverse this axiom; and, if they are not allowed to enforce conditions, at once discard the whole. They are moral cowards, who, daring not to acknowledge the truth, avail themselves of this means to extricate themselves. Sir David Brewster, seeing a table rise into the air, said, "It seems to rise." He did not believe his eyes, or else did not say that he did. When Faraday was told that his table-turning theory had failed, that tables actually rose into the air, he dared not go and see for himself, but expressed himself "heartily tired of the whole matter." To honestly investigate the phenomena is to become a believer. This is the invariable result. Those who oppose them are unexceptionably those who know nothing about them.

It is the misfortune of theorizers that there are two classes of phenomena to account for,— the physical and the mental; and a theory, however nicely adjusted to one, is sure to be overthrown by the other. It has been a favorite hobby with many to say, with a wise accent, "It results from some unknown law of mind." If the mental phenomena were alone, this might satisfy superficiality; but is not the rising of a table into the air a wonderful feat for an "unknown law of mind"? So account for the physical phenomena, and there lies an immense field of mental manifestations wholly beyond explanation.

Many of the theories advanced require a much greater stretch of credulity than the acceptance of the one of its spiritual source.

20. THE INTELLIGENCE MANIFESTED IS HUMAN INTELLIGENCE.

It is conceded that the communicating power, whatever it be, manifests intelligence. It is of the same order as our own. It is human intelligence, partaking of all its qualities.

21. IT IS NOT DERIVED FROM THE MEDIUM OR CIRCLE.

This intelligence is not derived from the circle or the medium. Volumes of facts might be introduced in proof of this point. It is not derived by absolute knowledge, nor clairvoyantly.

This conclusion, sooner or later, must be reached. The bigoted churchmen, who attempt an explanation on any other ground, little understand the dangerous weapons they handle. Admit that these manifestations are explainable by "unknown laws of mind," by "odylic force," or electricity, will not the same explanation apply to the records of the Bible? Christ becomes a poor deluded, biologized person; the miracles, only feats of "odylic force." Let the doctors of divinity take this ground, and they proclaim Christianity a despicable sham, and themselves arrant deceivers.

22. BUT ONE RECOURSE.

There is but one recourse,— the acceptance of its spiritual origin; and then Christianity becomes spiritualized, and the so-called supernatural in Hindostan, China, Persia, Europe, and America, at once becomes amenable to law, and order is discernible amidst even the confusion of dogmatic beliefs.

23. Identification of Spirits.

The strongest arguments in favor of the spiritual origin of the manifestations are found in the physical phenomena. The independent moving of inanimate objects, sounds produced beyond the reach of the medium, are entirely outside of the laws of mentality. Let us suppose a concussion is produced: how can it be identified; how proved of spiritual origin; how referred to a certain individual? If a friend was concealed in an adjacent room, and the only means of communication was by his rapping on the door, how would you proceed to identify him? Would it not be by his correctly answering questions which none other could answer? And, if he thus answered you, would you not consider his identification complete?

It is precisely in this manner that spirits communicate by rappings, and in this manner can they be identified. When identified, the real cause of the manifestations is determined.

III.

EVIDENCES OF SPIRITUALISM.

WHAT was I before I was born? What am I now? What shall I be to-morrow? — GREGORY OF NAZIAN.

The world will perish; but the soul of man is immortal. — GREGORY OF NYSSA.

/ It (Spiritualism) has more evidence for its wonders than any historic form of religion hitherto. It is thoroughly democratic, with no hierarchy; but inspiration is open to all. It is no fixed fact; has no *punctum stans;* but is a *punctum fluens.* It admits all the truths of religion and morality in all the world-sects. — THEODORE PARKER.

24. MATERIALISM.

WE have learned to discard the supernatural and miraculous. Even the churches have become skeptical; and their great leaders scoff at the spiritual. What Hume wrote in the last century, and which branded his name with infamy, has now become, in reality, a part of their belief.

This skepticism and materialism is a natural reaction against the superstitions of the dark ages, as Spiritualism is a counteraction against its darkness.

25. THE IMPOSSIBLE.

In producing proof in favor of spirit-communion, we are necessitated to use the evidence of others.

Those who have never seen objects move say it is an impossibility. That is a word of ready use, but is an expression of conceit and ignorance. The wise will rather acknowledge that he knows too little to say anything is impossible. Of the laws which operate in the vast unknown, we know not; and it is puerile to draw positive conclusions from the little that is known. Columbus and Harvey, Kepler, Galileo, and every one who has given expression to a new thought, has been met by the "impossible." After a time, their truths become possible enough; and the present always smiles at the positive expressions of past ignorance.

26. The Positive.

There are few things which are positive. Mathematics is the only science which we can regard as fixed. A problem in geometry, as that the square formed on the hypothenuse of a right-angled triangle is equal to the sum of the squares formed on the other two sides, depending as it does on the unvarying relations of numbers, can never change, and is a positive expression. Outside of mathematics, the positive realm is very narrow, although daily enlarging with the acquisition of knowledge. If an object has never been observed to move, the evidence of witnesses may yield an infinitely probable proof. Circumstantial evidence in law rests on this principle.

It is considered, if several witnesses of known

veracity agree in their statements, it is morally certain that they speak the truth. Thus, if a witness is of sufficient veracity and clearness of sight to speak the truth ten times out of eleven, then there are ten chances to one that any statement he may make is correct. If another witness, of equal reliability, aver to the same, the chances are ten times ten, or one hundred. If a third testify to the same, the probabilities are ten times one hundred, or one thousand.

27. THE SENSES.

The testimony of the senses is received in law as *prima-facie* evidence. No judge would suppose that he was imposed upon, and no counsel argue that witnesses should be set aside because no faith can be placed in the eyes or ears. Life and death are made dependent on the senses: otherwise all received rules of evidence must be set aside. We live in a dream-world; and so hallucinated are we, that there are none to tell us of our hallucination. We receive Berkeley's idea, that the external world is only a fancy of the mind without any real existence.

When thousands of reliable witnesses testify that they have seen objects moved without contact, the probabilities are infinite that they have done so. No amount of negative testimony is of any avail. That a thousand individuals have not seen a table move, does not invalidate the testimony of one who has.

28. Belief Educational.

We place the greatest reliance on the evidence of our senses; and, although we say we take that of others reported to us as equally valuable, practically we do not believe until we have seen, especially that which is unusual, and out of the common order. Our egotism makes us consider ourselves the best judges in the world. Belief is very much a matter of education; and we have little hope that all the argument possible to produce will be of any avail. Hence we rely on facts. The advent of Spiritualism is through facts, and not theories. Its purpose is to destroy theories, and place positive knowledge in their stead.

29. Spirit is Individualized Force.

It is in the invisible, the intangible, not in the external and tangible, that force resides. Power must be an attribute of spirit, and spirit only; for the gross external, what in common speech is called matter, is nothing without life.

30. One Fact is of more Value than a Thousand Theories;

And, if it can be proved that spirit can move matter, its *modus operandi* is of secondary consideration.

31. Why not given to the World before.

Had it in any former age assumed its positive, rationalistic character, the world would not have been ready to receive it. Mediums would have been destroyed as wizards and witches, and darkness would have been triumphant.

Spirits cannot exceed, in their communications, the intellectual temperature of the age; nor can man. The most exalted genius is chained by the demands of his time. He cannot far exceed it: neither can spirits; else, as is expressed in a homely proverb, they will be casting pearls before swine. This objection can be made against every system in the world. Why was not Christianity introduced before? Was it not needed as imperatively three thousand years ago as now? There is a repugnance, in some quarters, to the doctrine that spirits return to earth. The old mythological idea, that they slept until the resurrection trump, or went direct to a place from whence they could not escape, has secured such a strong hold that it is difficult to eradicate it. The objection has been ably met by a distinguished writer.

32. How is it possible for Spirits to return?

By the same method by which they leave the world. How do they leave? Let the skeptic answer. If it be asked, "How can they converse?" we reply, "How can men converse, thousands of miles apart, by an earthly telegraph?" We are told, by the medium of electricity. You have, then, our answer; and we would press the inquiry by asking if men, by a knowledge of the eternal principles of nature, can daguerreotype a human countenance upon a metallic plate, think you it must be impossible for spirit-friends to stamp an idea, a thought, a sentence, a book, upon the human intellect? Which is the more reasonable to suppose, — that God, in the constitution of his universe, left no means of communication for his children, or that he has given to all the agencies of reciprocal approach and friendship.

33. NOT NEW.

Although greatly developed in the present, spirit-communication is by no means new. The world was not prepared to receive the phase they have taken now; but history is filled with accounts of spirit-manifestations. Poets have sung of it in all ages. It has entered into the sacred and current literature of all races. The Old Testament is filled with it: it is the warp and woof of the sacred books of all nations. So far from being new, it is as old as mankind.

In the year 364 of our era, or fifteen hundred and five years ago, in the reign of the Roman Emperor Valens, mediums conversed by means of rappings, and employed the alphabet. The spirit-pendulum, almost exactly in result like the dial, was then in use. It consisted of a ring suspended by a thread over a bowl of water, around the margin of which the alphabet was arranged. By successively swinging to the desired letters, words and sentences were spelled. Numa Pompilius used it in this manner in augury. Such a pendulum has been used by modern mediums successfully.

The subject passed into disrepute as a black art, and dealings with the Devil. Learned men scoff at the dial as a new trick. If it be one, it is fifteen centuries old.

34. First Manifestations.

In the little village of Hydesville, N. Y., stood a small, unpretending dwelling, temporarily occupied by an honest farmer and his family, — a wife and two daughters. He removed to it on the 11th of December, 1847; and, from the first, the manifestations began. "The noises increased nightly; and occasionally they heard footsteps in the rooms. The children felt something heavy lie on their feet when in bed; and Kate felt, as it were, a cold hand passed over her face. Sometimes the bed-clothes were pulled off; chairs and dining-tables were moved from their places. Mr. and Mrs. Fox, night after night, lighted a candle, and explored the whole house in vain. Raps were made on the doors as they stood close to them; but, on suddenly opening them, no one was visible." They were far from superstitious, and still hoped for some natural explanation, especially as the annoyance always took place in the night.

35. They assume a new Character.

In March, 1848, they assumed a new character. The children's bed had been moved into the room of their parents; but scarcely had Mrs. Fox lain down when the noises became as violent as before. The children shouted, "Here they are again." Their father shook the sashes to see if they were not moved by the wind, when the lively Kate observed that the sounds were imitated. She then snapped her fingers, and asked it to repeat, which was done. She then simply made motions with her thumb and finger, and the rap followed. The invisible power, whatever it was, could see and hear. Mrs. Fox's attention was arrested. She asked it to count ten, which it did. "How old is my daughter Margaret?" Twelve raps. "And Kate?" Nine. "How many children have I?" Seven. "Ah! you blunder," she thought: "try again." Seven. Then she suddenly thought. "Are they all alive?" No answer. "How many are living?" Six raps. "How many dead?" One rap. She had lost one child. She then asked if it was a man. No answer. Was it a spirit? Raps. She then asked if the neighbors might hear it; and Mrs. Redfield was called in, who only laughed at the idea of a ghost, but was soon made serious by its correcting her about the number of her children, insisting on one more than she counted. She, too, had lost one; and, when she recollected this, she burst into tears.

36. THEY EXTEND TO OTHER LOCALITIES.

It is needless to recount the numerous investigations that were made, and how the little girls always escaped suspicion of imposture. Having become intelligible, the spirits determined to improve their opportunity; and rappings were heard in the house of Mr. Grainger, a wealthy citizen of Rochester, and in that of Dr. Phelps at Stratford, Conn. In the latter, they became very destructive; cut the clothing off his boy, broke windows, threw down glass and porcelain. He says, "I have seen things in motion above a thousand times, and, in most cases, when no visible power existed by which the motion could be produced. There have been broken seventy-one panes of glass, more than thirty of which I have seen broken before my eyes."

Such was the advent of the mighty spiritual movement. If it had not been discovered that the sounds were intelligent, and the discovery followed out, the old house might have been considered as haunted, deserted; and nothing more resulted. But the time had arrived for this development; and, seized by the powerful and flexible American mind, it has, in a score of years, become the spiritual life of millions.

37. Advent of Spiritualism in France.

About the time Spiritualism was first introduced into the United States, or somewhat previously, M. Cahagnet, a working-man of France, had, by means of clairvoyance, solved the great problem of spiritual existence, and the possibility of intercourse with spirits.

When perusing his book, "The Celestial Telegraph," every one must be forcibly struck with his candor, his honesty of purpose, untiring zeal, and general accuracy. We can only regret, that, in his ardor, he admitted statements without sufficient circumspection, which weaken rather than strengthen his positions. His magnetized clairvoyants taught him almost all the great principles of spirit existence, as believed by Spiritualists at present. The identification of spirits was well understood by him; and his best clairvoyant rarely failed to give accurate descriptions of spirits that she said were present.

A few instances of this result illustrate the countless facts narrated by this author.

"M. Renard, of whom I have already spoken, — a a man to whom I am indebted for the little knowledge I possess in magnetism, — being called to Paris on business, begged me to send Adele to sleep, and give him a sitting similar to what he had read of in my journal. I was most happy to comply with the wishes of so sincere a friend, and so judicious and well-informed a man. Scarcely was Adele asleep, when he called for a person named Desforges, an old friend of his, who had been dead fifteen years. Desforges appeared. M. Renard had so accurate a description given him of his friend, that left no doubt as to the reality of his apparition. A dispute took place between him and Adele (though he was not *en rapport* with her) as to the dress of this person, — Adele maintaining that he appeared to her in a blouse slit in front; while M. Renard declared that he had never seen him in such an article of dress, and usually wore a jacket or round vest. After puzzling his brains for some time, M. Renard recollected, in fact, that, some time before he left his friend, people began to wear, in his part of the country, blouses of this kind; and he wore such a one as Adele described. It would be useless to mention the minute details, attitudes, language, &c., with which Adele persuades persons consulting her on such a point."

"Up to this day, I had never desired that any of my clairvoyants should see any of the deceased members of my own family, for a reason that will be appreciated; viz., that they might have depicted to me an image engraven on my memory. I had a mind to try Madame Gouget. I asked for my mother by her Christian name, and also by her maiden name, and was very much surprised when Madame Gouget told me she saw a very old woman. After a minute description, and particularly as to a mark that she told me she perceived on the left cheek of this woman, I recognized in her my grandmother, who was precisely as Madame Gouget described her to me. This apparition, uncalled for, and which I was far from expecting, was owing to the resemblance of the names of my mother and grandmother. I ought not to have asked for my mother by her maiden name. I had already fallen into a like error with Adele, when several members of the same family presented themselves on account of the resemblance in the names. To make sure whether Madame Gouget really beheld my grandmother, I put to her questions the answers to which removed all my doubts in this respect. My mother appeared at the same time; and the portrait she painted of her was quite true."

"Louise, Adele's niece, comes in haste to tell her that her brother is about to appear to her. 'Oh, here he is! It is my brother Alphonse, who died in Africa.'—'When?'—'Four years ago.'—'On what day?'—'I don't know.'—'Ask him.'—The 11th of August.'—'How is he attired?'—'In the uniform of a dragoon.'—'Is that his dress in heaven?' —'No: it is that of the corps in which he served before his death; and it was in this costume that I saw him on earth.'—'Why is he dressed thus?'— 'Spirits must surely appear in the costume and condition by which they were known on earth: otherwise we should be unable to recognize them.'— 'Since you did not ask for him, who told him to come and see you?'—'My little niece.'—'Is she with him at this moment?'—'Yes; and how beautiful she is! Her fine black hair falls in ringlets on her shoulders, as on the day of her first communion.' —'And Alphonse—does he appear to you handsome?'—'Oh, indeed he does. His forehead, which was, however, very dark, appears to me as white as snow. He tells me that it will not be long before I see my mother, father, and brother-in-law. I have no wish, however, to see the last-named one: he was too wicked on earth.'—'If in heaven there is no wickedness, you must not think of the past.'—

'I won't see him!' Adele stretches out her arm to detain her niece, who has just quitted her, despite her efforts. It is surprising to see the mimicry, the apparent mutual understanding, the contrariety. One cannot doubt the reality of the scenes in which the imagination, as we may believe, is not always strongest; for nothing appears to respond to the caprices of the clairvoyant."

The way was thus prepared in France, where Spiritualism has made a rapid but singular growth.

38. Unexpected Report.

The often abrupt and unlooked-for message from a spirit-friend is conclusive evidence that it does not originate in the minds of the circle or medium. Prof. Hare records some interesting facts bearing on this subject.

"Agreeable to my experience in a multitude of cases, spirits have reported themselves who were wholly unexpected, and when others were expected. When I was expecting my sister in Boston, my brother reported himself. Lastly, when expecting her, 'Cadwallader' was spelled out, being the name of an old friend, who forthwith gave me a test proving his identity. As this spirit had never visited my disk before, I had not the smallest expectation of his coming."

"Being at Cape May, one of my guardian spirits was with me frequently. On the third instant, at one o'clock A. M., I requested the faithful being in question to go to my friend Mrs. Gourlay, in Philadelphia, and request her to induce Dr. Gourlay to go to the bank to ascertain at what time a note would be due, and that I could be at the instrument (his dial) at half-past three o'clock to receive the answer. Accordingly, at that time, my spirit-friend manifested herself, and gave me the result of the inquiry. On my return to the city, I learned from Mrs. Gourlay that my angelic messenger had interrupted a communication which was taking place through the spiritscope, in order to communicate my message; and, in consequence, her husband and brother went to the bank, and made the inquiry, by which the result was that communication to me at half-past three o'clock by my spirit-friend."

In the experience of Mrs. Gourlay, a medium relied on by Prof. Hare, many interesting facts are stated. Among others, the following:—

"While spending the evening of Jan. 21, 1854, at the house of a friend, it was proposed by the lady and her husband that we form a circle. We had not been long seated at the table, when three ladies, two of whom I had never seen, favored us with their company, and took their seats at some distance from the circle. They had been seated in the room but two or three minutes, when the following was given through the table:—

"'MY DEAR MOTHER,— In love I meet you this evening. O mother! why do you mourn my death? I have just begun to live. Grieve not for me. I wish my husband to investigate Spiritualism. I will communicate to him. Why should you erect a monumental slab to my memory? Let me live in the hearts of my friends!

"'SARAH NORTH.'

"When the gentleman who took down the communication read it, I was surprised at hearing the name, 'North,' that being my maiden name. As there was no Sarah in our family, I asked the spirit, 'Who is Sarah North?' Before it had time to reply, one of the ladies referred to approached the table in tears. She said, 'That is from my daughter Sarah. I have been engaged to-day in the solemn duty of erecting a tombstone to her memory.'"

39. VALUE OF DARK CIRCLES.

As an incentive to investigation, dark circles have their uses; but they are usually of far greater disadvantage than benefit. The cause of Spiritualism is the worse for what they have done. The opportunities for trickery and deception are so great, and the chances for detection so small, that it is difficult to distinguish the true from the false. They should be discouraged by Spiritualists. The amusing feats of rope-tying and ledgerdemain, at best, are the work of earthly spirits, and without instruction. There is no spiritual phenomena that cannot occur in a room sufficiently lighted to allow objects to be discerned as well as in absolute darkness; and the medium who refuses to submit to conditions which do not conflict with those necessary for the manifestations should be mistrusted. So far as true spiritual phenomena are concerned, tying the medium with thread or twine or tarred cord, or confining with handcuffs, is as well as with ropes. It is by pretense to the contrary that charlatans flourish, who insist that a rope, easily slipped and untied, is essential. They flourish because, whenever proper safeguards are used, no manifestations occur, the "conditions" not being right; and, when these are removed, they give "astounding manifestations," because there is no chance for detection. The time is not far distant when all those who have been convinced by "dark-circle manifestations," or have been connected with and upheld them, will suffer deepest disappointment.

The faith based on such "tests" constantly seeks new wonders, asking for greater and still greater; and the believer thus brought into the fold is not of value in extending the influence of Spiritualism. These manifestations have given no positive evidence in favor of Spiritualism. They are impossible of demonstration, and the most exact so liable to error as to be valueless as proof.

40. MOVING PHYSICAL OBJECTS WITHOUT CONTACT.

The only physical phenomena from which all sources of error are eliminated are the moving of physical objects without contact, and the identification of spirits by means of the intelligence manifested by the movements. This is the absolute test of Spiritualism.

Prof. Hare, in his careful and extended experiments, recognized the value of such manifestations, and invented an apparatus which rendered deception impossible. His researches are the most perfect scientific demonstration of Spiritualism yet produced, and, if made in any other field, would have been received without question. Prof. Hare's method is purely scientific. His experiments, instituted with great philosophic ingenuity, can be submitted to the test by any one, and, if acknowledged as correct, are perfectly demonstrative.*

Of the several contrivances he employed, only two need be mentioned. The first isolated the medium by mounting a small board on balls, resting on the top of the table. The medium's hand resting on the top of the board, of course, at the slightest movement, the balls would roll. Valuable

---

* "The most precise and laborious experiments which I have made in my investigation of Spiritualism have been assailed by the most disparaging suggestions as respects my capacity to avoid being the dupe of any medium employed. Had my conclusions been of the opposite kind, how much fulsome exaggeration had there been, founded on my experience as an investigator of science for more than half a century!" Speaking of the above apparatus, "It was on stating this result to the Association for the Advancement of Science, that I met with much the same reception as the King of Ava gave the Dutch ambassador who alleged water to be at times solidified in his country, by cold, so as to be walked upon."

communications were received by the movements of tables thus situated. The second apparatus was more ingeniously contrived. "A board is supported on a rod, so as to make it serve as a fulcrum, as in a see-saw, excepting that the fulcrum is at the distance of only one foot from the end, while it is three feet from the other. This end is supported by a spring-balance, which indicates pounds and ounces by a rotary index. Upon this board, at about six inches from the fulcrum, is placed an inverted glass vase nine inches in diameter." Into this vase a wire cage or basket is let down so as to approach within an inch of the brim. The vase is filled with water. Now it is apparent that any pressure on the board will be indicated by the balance; but the medium's hands placed in the water cannot give that pressure, as the cage effectually cuts them off from contact with the vase. If manifestations are obtained in this manner, they cannot be referred to human agency. Yet Prof. Hare obtained not only movements of the balance, but communications, in presence of his scientific friends. The balance indicated a pressure of eighteen pounds, and "would probably have been depressed much more, but that the water had been spilled by any further inclination of the vase."

Manifestations thus obtained are no more positive than the movement of a table without contact; but errors are more readily detected and guarded against.

If Prof. Hare's investigations be received, it must

be admitted that spiritual beings do communicate, or that there exists an unrecognized force, possessing intelligence, and capable of identifying itself as being that of our departed friends,—a conclusion requiring far greater credulity than the first. The moving of tables is the most common of manifestations: but I introduce the following statement from Owen as a representative of its class; and, if admitted, it at once silences all theories yet advanced by scientific men to explain the phenomena.

"*The imposition of hands is not a necessary condition.* In the dining-room of a French nobleman, the Count d'Ourches, residing near Paris, I saw, on the first day of October, 1858, in broad daylight, a dinner-table seating seven persons, with fruit and wine on it, rise, and settle down, while all the guests were standing around it, and not one of them touching it at all. All present saw the same thing. Mr. Kyd, son of the late Gen. Kyd of the British army, and his lady, told me (in Paris, in April, 1859), that, in December of the year 1857, during an evening visit to a friend, who resided at No. 28 Rue de la Ferme des Mathurins, at Paris, Mrs. Kyd, seated in an arm-chair, suddenly felt it move, as if some one had laid hold of it from beneath. Then slowly and gradually it rose into the air, and remained there suspended for the space of about thirty seconds, the lady's feet being four or five feet from the ground; then it settled down gently and gradually, so that there was no shock when it touched the carpet. No one was touching the chair when it rose, nor did any one approach it while in the air, except Mr. Kyd, who, fearing an accident, advanced, and touched Mrs. Kyd. The room was, at the time, brightly lighted, as a French *salon* usually is ; and, of the eight or nine persons present, all saw the same thing in the same way. I took notes of the above, as Mr. and Mrs. Kyd narrated to me the occurrence ; and they kindly permitted, as a voucher for its truth, the use of their names.

Here is no drawing-up of a heavy object, without effort, with the fingers, the concomitant which Mr. Faraday speaks of as indispensable. And the phenomenon occurred in a private drawing-room, among persons of high social position, educated and intelligent. Thousands in the most enlightened countries of the world can testify to the like. Are they all to be spoken of as "ignorant of their ignorance"?

41. THE EVIDENCE OF PSYCHOMETRY.

Since the application of the impressibility of mind to the delineation of character, and its extension by experimental research by Mr. Denton, few doubt the truth of psychometry, as the new science has been named. It is found that an autograph placed on the forehead enables a sensitive person to delineate perfectly the character of the writer.

If the mind so affects the paper that the character of the writer be obtained, it is a matter of just inference that a spirit's autograph, if truly originating from a spirit, would not give the character of the medium through whom it was written, but of the spirit-writer. If this be true, it goes a great way in the support of Spiritualism. It is the next thing to an absolute demonstration. My experiments on this subject have been various and successful. I first procured an autograph letter from the medium. This gave, by psychometry, his true character, which was as follows: —

"This is a very passive organization. This person could be easily molded to the influence of others. Naturally is very pure in thought, yet adapts himself to the company he is in. In matters of right, could meet tremendous opposition unflinchingly; yet would repine at his lot. Is very susceptible. Natural powers not large; yet there appears a degree of activity or excitement in the mind produced by apparently foreign agency, — I can't understand it. There seems a contradiction, as of two minds; but it is certain his natural powers are not as large as they appear to be. They are very active. This person has large spirituality; is refined and spiritual in his thoughts; is rather cast down by the things of this world, too much for his own good. The animalities are all small; and he lacks energy and decision; is not persevering." I here asked if he could be impressed by spiritual agency. "Yes; but it would be by an inferior order of spirits, unless he wrote mechanically." — "What organs induced him to take the stand he has in regard to Spiritualism?" — "Approbativeness, or that peculiar organization which had rather be talked badly about than not at all. There is not enough depth about him for a Spiritualist; and he can do that cause no good, but would be apt to bring it into disrepute by the unsatisfactory communications he is liable to receive, and the manner he relates them, and the explanations he attaches."

This delineation was very satisfactory. The following autographs were obtained through this medium, being written mechanically. The difference between the influence they gave, and that of the medium, is remarkable. The first was derived from the autograph of President Taylor.

" This is a stern, resolute man. His will and his energy are predominant. He never stops to examine the right of the cause in which he is engaged, but does his work as he is commanded. He is not consecutive, nor has he given the subject sufficient thought to be liberal. He would be an infidel, or, at least, inclined that way. There is no order about him. His pride is in being slovenly. He never stops to consider the justness of his cause, but how he may accomplish his end; is jesuitical, considering the cause as justifying the means. Would make a good warrior as regards courage and perseverance, but would be deficient in the qualities which make a great commander. He would not be apt to see the traps a wily foe might lay for him, if not reminded continually of it. He would be a good Indian warrior, to command a few hundred or a thousand men, but would be incapable of a greater command."

— "What kind of a statesman would he make?" — "Indifferent. He was never designed for any civil office. He could not stand the necessary mental labor and anxiety of mind. He requires a great deal of bodily exercise, and can bear little mental toil. His thoughts have been revolutionized; and he has become progressive and hopeful. It appears that he has entirely changed his mode of life, his occupation, and that his mind does not act in its old and accustomed channel. There is a great agitation of feeling, a retrospective on past incidents, regrets for deeds committed in former years, for which I am unable to account. Spiritual feelings seem to be slowly awakening."

The reason for the last remark will be seen when it is known that the psychometrist first obtained impressions of the earthly character, and, lastly, of the spiritual.

The next autograph was one of Lord Bacon.

"This is a character which looks deeply into the philosophy of things. His mind is contemplative and reflective. He would be liable to be led into the fields of philosophical inquiry: if so, his philosophy would be inductive, and deal in facts and causes. I cannot express, by words, the depths of mind. It seems as if this was a mind that had been years and years maturing, yet possessing all the vigor and strength of youth, — so mature in its wisdom, so laborious in its research. It is a wonderful mind, — one of giant powers, of capabilities sufficient to grasp the ultimate of causes, and solve the vastest problems of nature. It has wonderful powers,—an intellect like a God; and over that intellect sits a superior and pure morality, unlike that which controls the actions of other men. There is ethereality of thought, a boundlessness of desire, a mighty grasping after the great truths which lie beyond the sphere of human knowledge, that I cannot express. The influence is cheerful, hopeful, loving, angelic."

This delineation ascribes far too pure a morality to Bacon. It represents his present rather than his earthly life.

42. Spirit Identification by Psychometry.

Admitting the truth of Spiritualism, it has been said that it was impossible to identify our friends; but here we have the key which unlocks all the mysteries that lie in the invisible domain beyond the senses, and a complete identification of our spirit-friends. We have also a test for the truthfulness of the medium: for, if he writes himself, it will give his own character; while, if a spirit writes, it will give the character of the spirit. We also have the truthfulness of the communication determined by the character of the spirit-author. A test of identity has been asked for; and here it is given. Spiritualists will do well to subject communications to this test, and demonstrate, to their own satisfaction, their correctness. I ask the skeptic to answer, —as the two last-given delineations could not have been derived from the medium, whose character, as given, is so decidedly different, and as the psychometrist knew nothing of the character of the writer, — from whom could the last delineations have been derived? Until this is satisfactorily answered, this test must be considered as a demonstration that the spirit exists, and holds intercourse with earth.

These two delineations are not given as sufficient, of themselves, to prove beyond a doubt the value of psychometric delineations. They are taken from a mass of similar readings, as illustrations as well as proofs. The experiments are so easily tested that any one may prove the position for himself. A hundred illustrations would not set the principle before the mind more distinctly.

Following this method, the autographs of spirits may be employed for their identification, and that even when they are executed by impressions. The influence of the latter is more mixed, partaking of the character of the medium, but always reveals its spirit origin.

It is not our intention to give a compilation of the facts, but an outline of the philosophy, of Spiritualism. Facts have already been compiled, and volumes innumerable might be written. Little is gained by them, except as they excite inquiry; for no amount of written statement can equal a single *séance* with a truthful medium. Spirit communion must be brought in direct contact with our reason, we must receive the direct words of our dear departed friends, to have the reality of their existence become to us, not only a belief, but absolute knowledge.

43. WHAT GOOD.

It is often asked, "What is the good of spiritual communications?" The question is urged as if it really was an argument. We might as well ask, "What is the good of the stars shining, or the rising of the sun? What is the use of human existence; of life in any of its multitudinous forms?" To answer would extremely perplex the most astute metaphysician. We take existence as a fact, nor can we answer wherefore. The world exists, and man exists; but who can tell what good is to grow out of that existence?

Whether Spiritualism is moral or immoral in its tendencies; whether we understand its uses or not, — affects not the grand question at issue. On other grounds, how can this heartless question be asked? Is it not a good to us to know that our loved ones exist on the other side of the grave; to have all doubts and misgivings swept away by their sweet voices speaking to us of an infinite future? Christianity is of little worth compared to this beautiful demonstration. Prostrated though we are at the side of the cold grave, through our blinding tears, and the night of our sorrow, we see the loved forms of our departed angels; and their words of cheer sound sweetly over the agitated ocean of our grief. *Cui bono?* The value of all we possess, though it were the oceaned world, would be freely given for one single word from their angel-life.

44. Personal Experience.

In the "Banner of Light," 1865, might be noticed an obituary. That short paragraph related an event which overwhelmed us, and gave us to drink of the bitterest cup of grief.

Aggie, a sister adopted in our family circle as our child, and, under our care, matured into the fulfillment of the brightest destiny, went from us a perfect representation of health. We answered the telegram that said she could not live, but too late. Even the poor consolation of a parting word was denied us. Her beautiful features still showed marks of terrible pain, — that was all. She was frozen to marble.

I had thought that the spiritual philosophy would sustain one in this trial; that, knowing the spirit existed, the keen edge of our grief would be taken off. For the time, this was not so. We are accustomed to form our judgment by the senses.

As we stand before the corpse of our departed friend, our grief overwhelms our intuitions, and darkens our spiritual perceptions. When we cry in our agony, the waves of feeling deafen our ears to the sound of spirit-voices. Our eyes meet the wreck of the beautiful, inanimate, still, cold, dead, and, with the heartlessness of our materiality, tell us there is nothing beyond. Soon will the elements claim their own from the sleeping; and a year shall suffice to dissolve the being which for a time cheered us by her winning ways, and scatter her ashes to the winds.

Thus Materialism, stifling, dark, and dreadful, took the place of Spiritualism, and was sustained by the senses, and unopposed by spiritual perceptions too lacerated to feel. The days came, and went: slowly our minds assumed their normal condition; and the desire to communicate with the departed remained to be answered.

Then began the most complete and satisfactory series of communications I have ever witnessed. They were free from any collusion on the part of any one outside of ourselves, as Mrs. Tuttle and myself were usually the only persons at the table or in the room.

We had often endeavored to have the table tip, but had failed. Now, however, we had a spirit in the shadow, in unison with ourselves; and the gateway of communication was opened.

I had previously seen her clairvoyantly, but so dimly, so shadowy, I doubted whether it was not a conjuration of a disturbed mind. Those doubts have been removed. It was before her funeral; and the attractions of earth remained unimpaired. She was sad, and unable to speak. Her spirit-mother was with her; and, in thought, I asked her if she intended to remain, and witness the painful ceremony of the morrow. She answered, "I would not have my child see it: we go away, not to return until all is over."

We held a *séance* nearly every evening; and she was always present, and gave us some word of assurance. Sometimes she failed to answer correctly, the table being uncontrollable. At other times, all her answers were perfectly correct for an hour's questioning. We soon learned to discriminate; and, so far from supposing that undeveloped spirits came at those disturbed *séances*, we knew the fault lay in our own organizations. The details of these *séances* are very interesting to us, but not to the public. I shall relate but one incident, as it illustrates the spirit's power of prophecy.

Shortly after her departure, and at our *séance*, she informed us that her father, who was slightly ill, could not recover. This was against our reason; for his sickness was not considered serious. Two weeks afterwards, she fixed the day of his death at nearly three months ahead. About two weeks previous to the time she had fixed for that event, she came, and, by the tedious process of spelling by the alphabet, gave the following communication to her sister:—

"Emma, prepare to go to Braceville. Father has dictated a letter to-day, wishing you to come. He is not yet ready to die; but, if you do not go, you will not have an opportunity to enjoy his society on earth again. The letter will reach you on Thursday; and, on Friday, you must go."

The letter came, and the spirit-voice was obeyed; and if conferring happiness on those who are dear, during the last days of their mortal life, be a life-long comfort to us, we are thankful for that thoughtful admonition.

Her father lived twelve hours past the time she had appointed; but, at the very time he sank away, so completely that all thought he had breathed his last, he recovered, and exclaimed, —

"What a beautiful scene! I saw"—

He could not complete the sentence. He struggled through the night; and just as the sun arose in the east, and the birds awoke the earth with song, his spirit arose into heaven, and awoke to the song of angels.

I often asked her to go to the "Banner" circle-room, and communicate; but she said that she could not approach on account of the number of strange spirits congregated there. She said that she could do so, however, if I went with her.

At length the opportunity offered. I met Mrs. Conant several times; but I did not urge a *séance*. I too well understand the laws of spirit-communication to think satisfactory results can be *commanded:* they must flow voluntarily. I almost became assured not to expect anything through Mrs. Conant; but one evening, as we were engaged in conversation, she suddenly became entranced. Her manner, her tears, identified the controlling spirit. Aggie, in broken accents, said that this first direct contact with earth completely overpowered her; and she could only say how much she loved us all, how sad our grief made her, and that we must not mourn for her any more.

To a skeptic, there was furnished no test; but that was to come. She remarked that she had found a medium through whom she could write all she desired, and I must meet her at Miss S——'s at eleven o'clock on the next day.

I met the engagement punctually. I had never seen the medium before, and did not give her my name. I simply told her I had called for a *séance*. We sat down on opposite sides of a table; and she told me I could write whatever questions I desired, and, after folding the paper tightly, lay it on the table. I wrote, "Will the spirit who made this engagement write her name?"

I rolled the paper closely, and laid it on the table. Immediately the medium wrote, "Maggie." This was written, as is all she writes, reversed; so that it must be held before a mirror to be read. I wrote, "That is wrong." Instantly the medium's hand was again influenced; and the "M" was stricken off, leaving the name correctly spelled,—"Aggie." Then I wrote, "I do not want to ask questions: write whatever you please."

To this, the following was the reply; and, considering that to the medium I was a total stranger, the accuracy with which the names were given is astonishing. Aggie's guitar had been left at a friend's, and had not been touched by any one, remaining exactly as she left it, leaning against the wall. She alludes to it, as well as to the favorite horse "Bill;" and both allusions are tests of identity.

"Dear Hudson and Emma,— I am with you, as I promised last evening; but I cannot control this medium as readily as I supposed I should be able to. But I shall improve, and shall be able to control yourself so perfectly that you will be compelled to acknowledge my presence. I have the same affection for you as while on earth. I shall never change. I am with you, in spirit, always, and hope to control Emma so perfectly that I can fulfill my imperfectly performed mission on earth. I am very happy: do not grieve for me.

"Dear Emma! dear Emma! I am very near you. How I do want to give you proof of my identity!

"Bring my guitar home, and lay it on the table: perhaps I can play on it.

"Do you remember I loved to see Emma ride? but I was afraid of 'Bill.'

"Dear little Rosa and Carl! you miss me, don't you? but I am still with you, and will lead you to truth and right, if you will be patient and unwavering."

I received other answers equally correct, but of too personal a character to insert here. There was no failure. Every question written, and rolled into a ball, and placed on the table, was answered in less time than I have occupied in writing this. But here let me insert a word of caution, for I would not convey the impression that such is invariably the result; for the next day I called for a *séance*, and did not receive a single answer to my written questions.

By our daily converse with this beloved spirit are we strengthened in our knowledge of spirit-life. We know that she exists as a bright immortal in the spirit-land; and daily our prayer, carved in the marble headstone over her grave, ascends:—

> "Wait, darling, wait!
>   You have reached the heavenly strand;
> But those you love are toiling up
>   To the heights of a better land.
>
> "Oh, pause by the shining gates of pearl,
>   Look down the narrow way;
> And guide us, by your angel-hand,
>   Into a perfect day."

IV.

MATTER AND FORCE: THEIR RELATIONS TO SPIRIT.

> IN the study of nature, questions of force are becoming more and more prominent. The things to be explained are changes, active effects, motions in ordinary matter; and the tendency is to regard matter, not acted upon, but as itself inherently active. . . . The study of matter resolves into the study of forces. Inert objects, as they appear to the eye of sense, are replaced by activities revealed to the eye of intellect. The conceptions of gross, "corrupt," "brute matter" are passing away with the prejudices of the past; and, in place of a dead, material world, we have a living organism of spiritual energies. — YOUMAN.

45. TO COMPREHEND SPIRIT,

THE laws of the physical elements must be understood. The moving powers of the universe reside within the atom. These can only be studied by their effects, and must be pursued through long and intricate mazes of investigation. The following pages, though seemingly foreign to our subject, will, in the end, be found to have a most important bearing on the correct comprehension of the source of power, and even the intelligence of the spirit-world.

The new theory of force has been triumphantly arrayed against the possibility of immortality. This theory is here presented, and its relations to spiritual existence examined. Wonderful and beautiful is the correlation presented, and broad as the universe the field of investigation.

46. Ancient Science.

The science of the ancients, if they can be said to have possessed a science, was an evolution from the mind independent of facts. The Greeks were impatient of the study of external phenomena. They set the intellect entirely above facts, and supposed that it was capable of working out a system of nature from itself. Aristotle, perhaps, departed from this method; but it remained for modern science to establish its firm basis directly on observation. In this consists the difference between the ancient and modern methods. One reasons from within outward; the other, from the external to the internal. Locke's sensuous theory is scorned; but it is the sheet-anchor of science, and every one of its inductions presupposes its truthfulness. Hence the inductive method has been accused of materialism; a charge certainly merited, and from which it cannot escape. Locke's method is correct, and the inductive method is correct; but neither have the whole and complete truth. Because we derive knowledge from the senses does not prove that all our knowledge is thus derived. Beyond stands the unexplained and unexplainable I. Smelling, tasting, seeing, hearing, feeling, one or combined, never yield reason. Because by the inductive method we arrive at truths does not prove that it is the only channel to truth. The mind capable of understanding phenomena by observation of facts should be able to evolve the laws of those or other facts.

47. Present Tendency of Thought.

The present tendency of thought is material, so far as abolishing miracles, and the determination of phenomena by laws, are concerned; but, in another direction, it has an opposite tendency. The laws themselves assume a spiritual outline. Scientists are throwing aside matter, and applying themselves to the study of force. Here they find the bridge spanning the chasm between matter and spirit; and each day they approach nearer the latter unseen and mysterious realm. Each day the existence of gross matter becomes more doubtful. It is asked, "Is an atom more than a centre for the evolution of forces? And what assurance is there that such centres will not instantly dissolve, fading into some other forces?" When a stone is dropped into water, its surface is thrown into waves. Now it is a serious question of science, one of vast importance, "Is not an atom like the central portion of those waves, — a vortex from which waves of force are constantly thrown?" Then arises the question, "Is there any matter, is there anything, but *force?*" But we cannot divest ourselves of the idea of substance; the testimony of the senses of the existence of matter, the body of the universe, to which force holds the relation of spirit.

48. Progress.

This tendency is observable in all departments of science, but more particularly in astronomy. From the cumbersome crystalline spheres of Ptolemy to the epicircles of a later date; from these to the subtle vortices of an electrical medium wafting the planets on their swift currents, as set forth by Descartes, — lengthy steps were taken: but, from the latter, the domain of force was at once revealed by Newton in his incomparable doctrine of gravitation.

In the same manner, at the close of the last century, chemistry made a great advance by the discovery of the indestructibility of matter. The intellect, befogged by educational prejudice, could never have arrived at this fact, except by mechanical means. The balance of Lavoisier was more penetrating than the minds of the most astute philosophers. His balance proved that matter, however changeable in form, in weight is unchangeable. The invisible gas pressed downward as much as the heavy, black coal from which it escaped. The escaping smoke was as heavy as the burned wood. Matter might be converted from a solid to a fluid or a gas, or from a gas to a solid; but nothing is lost by the protean metamorphosis.

49. Force.

Similar is the step now taken in regard to force. Force is never lost. There is just so much in the universe, and none is destroyed, as there are so many atoms; and there is no less, no more. Heat, light, magnetism, electricity, from their discovery, treated as subtile, imponderable fluids pervading matter, have been proved to be forces, propagated by determinate laws, mutually convertible into each other, and all capable of being produced by motion. From a given amount of electric force, a definite magnetic power, heat, light, or motion may be obtained, or *vice versa*. When one of these expends itself, and cannot be discovered in its original condition, it can always be found in one of its other forms. This definite quantitative change has received the name of "*correlation and conservation of forces.*"

50. EXPLANATION OF FORCE.

It must be held in remembrance, that, by the term "force," nothing is explained. It is used in the sense of power to produce an effect; but, of the cause of the individual phenomena, we are just as ignorant.

Our actual knowledge results from comparison of the phenomena to which the term is applied. If a piece of caoutchouc be stretched by an application of weights, it will yield in proportion to the weight applied; and, when the weight is removed, it will recoil with exactly the amount of force which was applied. This power is held by each of its component particles, and is a striking illustration of the conservation of force. The term may be objectionable, but is less so than any other, and expressive of the meaning implied. Force is indestructible and uncreatable. A spring pressed downwards by a weight of a hundred pounds will recoil with the force of a hundred pounds when the weight is removed. The pendulum of a clock continues to swing until the original power used in winding up the weight becomes exhausted, and not a moment longer. If a thousand oscillations equal a power of an ounce, then an ounce is subtracted from the original force which was applied by that number of movements. This is a cardinal principle, equally important with the eternity of matter, and should be thoroughly understood. To turn a wheel, the water must fall: every pound of power gained by the wheel, the water must lose. The stroke of the wheel consumes a definite quantity of steam. The labor of man consumes muscular power.

51. MOTION.

The first idea of force is motion. The gross idea of motion is change of matter in space. The more subtile conception fades into vibrations of matter without any relative change. Thus we have a glimpse of an impalpable something transmitted, which operates powerfully, but changes not the substance in its path. Thus sound is motion: it is nothing but motion. If the ear be placed at one end of a long metallic rod, and the other end be struck, it shortly receives an impression of sound conducted through the rod. The rod has not moved: it has only allowed something to pass through it.

That something is vibration, capable of exciting the auditory nerves producing hearing. Motion only has passed.

52. RESOLVABILITY OF MOTION.

Motion is resolvable into heat, light, magnetism, electricity, and what may be called, for want of a better name, spiritual power. The production of heat by motion is among the most common occurrences. Wherever there is friction between moving surfaces, heat is produced. In machinery, oil is applied to all the irregularities of the surfaces so that they may slide freely over each other. In heavy machinery, there is great difficulty in preventing the rapidly revolving parts from burning. Car axles often take fire from this cause. By roughening the surfaces, greater friction is produced, more heat, and consequent loss of power. What becomes of this lost power? Is it annihilated? No. The precise amount of power absorbed by friction is reproduced as heat. Friction results from the tearing asunder of the inequalities of the opposing surfaces; and the force necessary to tear these asunder is equivalent to the heat produced. In other words, if this heat was applied to convert water to steam, the steam would tear off precisely as many particles. Of course no allowance is here made for waste.

53. EQUIVALENT OF MOTION.

The equivalent of one degree Fahrenheit, expressed in motion, has been approximately determined, by Mr. Joule, as seven hundred and seventy-two pounds, falling one foot. Other experimenters have arrived at widely different results; but his computations are made with so much care and nicety that they are generally received.

54. Light.

Light often, and electricity always, accompanies friction, when the opposing surfaces are different. If they are homogeneous, heat results; if not, electricity. The intense electricity of the electrical machine is derived from the friction of the rubber against the glass wheel.

55. Affinity.

By means of an electrical current, decomposition can be effected, or *chemical affinity* evoked. By means of heat or electricity or affinity, the circle is completed by the production of motion. All of these are motions of atoms; and all that is required is their proper direction to produce motion of masses.

56. Exceptions.

There are apparent exceptions, readily explainable; but it is a general truth that heat expands all bodies. Every increment of heat widens the distance between the component atoms, and weakens their attraction, until the latter becomes so small that the body assumes a fluid state, or becomes gaseous. A gaseous body may be considered as holding a large portion of heat as a force necessary to preserve its gaseous form. Mechanical pressure can wring this heat from it; or, in other words, the capacity of the condensed gas for heat is not so great as in its expanded state. Heat and cold are relative terms. When a body is said to be heated, the meaning is that it is so in comparison to other bodies. As there is a tendency to equilibrium, to heat one body, we employ another having the required temperature. Thus we understand that a fluid or gas is such from heat alone.

57. Heat and Cold.

The experiment of compressing air beautifully illustrates this. If air be confined in a tube, and forcibly compressed, a flash of light is seen; and, if tinder be placed in the tube, it will become ignited: the reverse of this occurs when compressed gas is allowed rapidly to expand. Then it absorbs heat, and produces the phenomenon of cold. When carbonic-acid gas is allowed to escape from a narrow orifice, from great condensation, its expansion, on meeting the air, is such that it is frozen, and falls in a shower of snow. So cold is this frozen carbonic-acid gas, that, if a closed vessel, filled with water, be surrounded with it, and thrown into a red-hot crucible, the water will be almost instantly frozen. A little thrown on mercury will congeal it into a solid which can be hammered out into bars. If, when the mercury begins to melt, it be allowed to drop into water, it will form tubes of ice in passing through it, it is so intensely cold. In this experiment, a portion of the gas obtains the heat necessary to convert it into a diffused gas; but, by so doing, it takes so much from another portion that the latter becomes solid.

When the piston of the tube before mentioned is pressed downwards, a soft and elastic cushion arrests its progress. In common terms, it is said this is the air; but it is not. It is heat. The atoms of air do not touch each other. They are surrounded, and held apart, by heat. The piston meets with this resistance, which cannot be overcome more than the power of gravitation.

58. Transformation of Force into Heat.

The power applied to the piston is converted into heat; and, if the compressed vapor is allowed to expand, it does so with precisely the same force with which it is compressed, and the heat disappears. It is the same with steam. It expands, and forces the piston forward; but loses, in the same ratio, its apparent heat. So slight is the quantity used, compared with the whole amount of heat which steam contains, that it is scarcely appreciable. If the whole amount could be used, the power of the steam-engine would be multiplied indefinitely. As at present constructed, the steam is rejected while at a high temperature; and thus a major portion of the power is lost. This presupposes the waste of fuel.

59. Force in Animals.

If the full capacity for power substances offered be wanted, it is supplied by the animal frame. The most careful experiments show that a pound of carbon in the animal system will produce more heat than twenty pounds burned in the most economical furnaces. If this heat be converted into motion, we find the animal has the advantage. Mettucci found, that, by applying an electric current to the limbs of a frog, notwithstanding the defects of the apparatus, a much greater power was obtained than by any artificial apparatus.

60. Electricity.

The friction of similar bodies produces heat; that of dissimilar bodies, electricity. The old explanation, of positive and negative fluids, is utterly baseless; and that of a single idio-repulsive fluid has been discarded. The terms "positive" and "negative" have served, for a long time, to conceal ignorance, and show learning, and are without meaning when applied to two suppositional fluids.

Perhaps not many will dissent in the end to the statement that electricity is the polarization of ordinary matter, — a force propagated in waves, and only varying in a few particulars from heat.

61. Conduction.

With the exception of fused metals, it is almost certain that no body conducts electricity without decomposition. It is conducted because chemical affinity is annulled, and the particles become polarized. The phenomenon of induction is opposed to the theory of a fluid, and favorable to that of polarization. When, for example, the air becomes what is termed positive to the earth, it is found that any part of the atmosphere is negative to that above, and positive to that below. This is experimentally illustrated by placing thin plates of mica on each other, like a pack of cards; placing the pile between two metallic covers, and charging the latter like a Leyden jar. Upon separating the plates of mica, it will be found that the surface of one side is positive, and the other negative; each plate being thus polarized.

This polarization enters into the structure of the plate itself. If a coin be placed on a pile of thin plates of glass, and electrified, on removing it, and breathing on the plate, an image of the coin is discernible. Even when the plate is ground and polished, the image can be reproduced; so that we may suppose that the image can be produced by each lamina of particles. If the plate is exposed to hydrofluoric acid, the design is beautifully etched. Or if the plate be coated with collodion, and be passed through the usual photographic processes, the image appears on the collodion surface. The glass is not only polarized, but induces its peculiar state in other bodies with which it comes in direct contact.

The brush flame of an electrical discharge has been employed as an argument in support of the actual emission of a fluid; but the variation, according to the material of the discharging point, is an unanswerable objection. The flame results from a vaporization and combustion of the conducting material. This is shown by collecting the vapor in a tube over the flame. Iron which is fused at a high temperature can thus be vaporized and condensed. This wonderful phenomenon furnishes a clew to the formation of mineral veins, which, as a general rule, run in the direction of what may be called the great magnetic currents of the earth. Metals can be taken up, and conveyed to remotest distances, by electric currents; and their deposition produce astonishing crystalline forms of beauty.

62. Sound.

We may safely state, although there are cases where it is not yet proved, that electric currents always produce change by transmission. Even in muscle, they induce a certain change, as is proved by their influence ceasing after a time, and renewing after a moment's cessation. The external portion of muscle is always in a positive state to the internal; that is, the component atoms are polarized. It is far more reasonable to refer electrical effects to a force than a fluid. We do not call to our assistance anything but force to account for the phenomenon of sound; yet beautifully parallel are the two classes of phenomena. Electrical discharges will break glasses; so will sound. They may become sonorous like the latter. Some bodies readily conduct sound; while others arrest it, or are non-conductors. The same distinction holds in regard to electricity. It has even been proved by Becquerel that some compounds may be decomposed by sound, just as all can be by electricity.

Electricity produces heat and light of the greatest known intensity, and is readily converted into magnetism; and, lastly, it produces chemical affinity, organizing and disorganizing in so powerful and delicate a manner as to be the most serviceable of chemical agents.

63. Light.

Light is the most intricate and least defined of the imponderables or forces. So incalculably extended and intricate are its relations, that, in its chemical activity, it is difficult, or, rather, impossible, to determine where its action leaves off, and that of chemical affinity begins. In its optical relations, it follows determinate, mathematical laws. Refraction, reflection, polarization, and absorption are precisely like similar phenomena of rays of heat. Conduction of heat, and transmission of light, are similar. Heat intensifies chemical affinity; but light is essential to a great majority of chemical actions.

64. Analogy to Sound.

Light and sound present many striking analogies. They progress in straight lines. When they meet an impenetrable body, they are reflected in the same manner. When they pass into a medium of different density, they are alike refracted; and, lastly, sound can be polarized in a similar manner to light.

Light acts as a chemical force. Its power to change the salts of silver is shown in the beautiful art of photography.

65. Magnetism.

Magnetism can be produced by, and can produce, electricity; and electricity produces heat, light, and chemical affinity. Perhaps one of its most curious effects is its disturbance of rays of light or heat when passing its influence. A ray of polarized light can be made to swerve from its course by the attraction of a magnet. The direction of chemical force is in like manner effected.

66. Affinity.

The attraction of atoms is called chemical affinity; that of masses, gravitation. Wonderful are the effects produced by this force, many times inexplicable. If electricity produces it, it is the inexhaustible fount of electricity. All the various forms of batteries depend on chemical action; and, could the electricity generated by combustion of coal or wood be secured, it would afford a power incalculably greater than that of the engine in the furnaces of which they are consumed.

67. Quantity of Electricity.

The amount of electricity depends invariably on the amount of chemical action. If the electric current be employed to decompose a fluid, as water, it will be found that precisely the same amount of oxygen unites with the zinc in the battery as is set free at the terminal, or pole in the fluid; and the quantities of hydrogen are equal. If different fluids are acted on from those in the battery, then the relations of the element united with the zinc, and set free in the fluid, are as their equivalents. Thus if hydrochloric acid be placed in the battery, and the poles be immersed in water, for every thirty-six parts by weight of chlorine united with the zinc, eight parts of oxygen would be liberated from the water; for such are their combining weights or equivalents.

68. Heat.

Chemical affinity never occurs without evolving heat. It is the source of all our artificial heat and light. The flame of a candle or of gas, the heat of the grate, comes from the clashing particles uniting in new gaseous compounds. The relations of heat, light, electricity, magnetism, and chemical affinity are thus intimate; and they are all resolvable into motion, and can all be evolved from motion. Whenever any of them produce motion, they lose precisely so much of their individual characteristics as there is motion produced.

69. Theories.

It is indifferent what theory we advocate, — the theory of vibrations in an ether, or of matter itself, or of emission: this inter-relation, or correlation and conservation, holds good of one as well as the other.

Force is as indestructible as matter; and the imponderables are only various manifestations of force. The present tendency of scientific thought is towards the theory of vibrations of matter itself, and perhaps the weight of argument is on that side: but it fails to explain many phenomena; and the action of gravitation across planetary spaces calls to aid, if not a universal ether, something very similar. The theory of emission has been discarded long since. The "imponderables" must be regarded as forces, not as matter. As there is so much matter in the universe, and not a particle can be lost or destroyed, there is so much force, and not the sufficiency to float a down on the wind can be created or destroyed.

This resolution of "imponderables" into motion solves some of the greatest cosmical problems. Motion being an indestructible attribute of matter, the revolution of worlds falls into its province. The original heat which once diffused the planetary bodies as vapor through space calls for no other explanation than is furnished by conservation of force.

When the exact numerical relation of heat and motion is determined, the calculation is very simple to ascertain how much heat the velocity of a planetary body represents. The moment the particles of cosmical vapor met and united, — in other words, condensation began, — heat was generated. It was the great obstacle in the way of condensation. From the amount of heat represented by the present motion of the earth, the degree of heat of the original chaos can be determined. It is found that only the four hundred and fifty-fourth of the original force remains; but if this remainder were converted into heat, as it would be if the planets were all to fall into the sun, and the whole system suddenly be brought to rest, it would raise the temperature of the entire mass to twenty-eight million degrees centigrade, or fifty million degrees Fahrenheit. When we consider that the highest temperature we are capable of attaining is by the oxhydrogen blow-pipe, and that this does not exceed three thousand six hundred degrees Fahrenheit, but is sufficient to not only melt, but vaporize, platinum, the most infusible of metals, we can at once learn the incomprehensibleness of fifty million degrees, or more than thirteen thousand times that number. If the entire mass of the system were pure coal, and at once lit up in terrific combustion, only the thirty-five hundredth part of this heat would be generated.

A simple calculation affords us a view of the result if the earth were suddenly stopped in its orbit. The momentum of a ponderous ball, eight thousand miles in diameter, hurled sixty-eight thousand miles an hour, is at once converted into heat. A rifle-ball arrested becomes too warm to touch.

The earth is raised to sixteen thousand five hundred and sixty degrees Fahrenheit, a temperature sufficient to convert its most obdurate minerals into vapor, into a vast cometary chaos. If arrested, it would fall into the sun; and the degree of heat developed by such a catastrophe would be four hundred times greater, or six million six hundred and twenty-four thousand degrees Fahrenheit.

70. THE SUN THE FOUNTAIN OF LIFE.

The heat of the sun's surface — the great perpetual fountain of life — has been estimated, from what appear to be correct data, to be from seven thousand to fifteen thousand times greater than the oxhydrogen blow-pipe. This incomprehensible temperature is maintained invariably, and an immense flood of light and heat radiated into space. Meeting the surface of the planets, it warms, enlightens, and sets at work the processes of life. It is the origin of living beings, who derive from its exhilarating rays all their motion, or living force, which stands directly correlated to sunlight and heat.

We are all children of the sun, from the humblest worm to the divinest man. All are storehouses of these forces, which can be at any time called forth. When wood is burned, it is not newly created heat we produce, but the light and warmth of the sun exerted in building up the cells of the wood.

A diamond shines in the dark, after exposure to the sun's rays, from the absorption of those rays.

Wonderful thought! when we burn the dark and shining coal, we set at liberty the sunlight and sun-heat treasured up by plants in the dark age of mythically gigantic vegetation flourishing in the marshes of the coal period! We create nothing. The coal is simply a treasury of the heat and light of the sun.

71. Beautiful is this Circle of Transformation.

The heat of the sun builds up a plant. It is a storehouse of these forces to the animal that eats and digests it. The original heat is liberated by the chemical action in its system; and it is warmed thereby, and tremendous muscular power derived. The same chemical processes occur when wood is burned in the furnace of an engine. The treasured heat is reconverted to the original motion of the chaos of the beginning. Thus the force of the animal frame and of the engine are reproductions of the primal forces of the planetary bodies.

72. The Realm of Life.

Ascending in this generalization, we inquire if this correlation holds in the realm of life; if the aggregate motions we call life may not be transformations of the terrible forces of nature.

73. Wonderful are the Motions of Living Beings;

So mysterious, they seem to spring directly from the will, and at once to be connected with a forbidden domain lying outside of matter. But careful study finds that the circulation of the fluids in the animal frame, and the motions of their organs, differs not from the motion observed in the cascade, the rush of winds, or the orbs of space. Motion cannot be produced without the consumption of force. A pound of carbon in the furnace yields a certain amount of power.

74. FORCE AND CHEMICAL CHANGE.

Chemical decomposition yields, according to conditions, electricity, light, heat, magnetism, or motion.

75. VEGETATIVE LIFE IS PURELY OF GROWTH: ANIMAL LIFE EXPENDS ITSELF IN RESISTANCE TO EXTERNAL AGENCIES.

Thus, in plants, a certain amount of the force derived from their food is employed in resisting the causes of decay; but the balance is entirely used in growth. The materials of which they are composed are of so fixed a character that little force is consumed in opposing their oxidization. We see however, in the compounds forming the flower and fruit, an instability held in equilibrium only by a strong effort, and which invariably exhausts the vitality of the plant. As soon as the connection of fruit or flower ceases with the parent stem, vitality no longer resists, and decay at once commences.

76. New Direction in Animals.

In animals, the forces of the system are also used in growth, but another direction is given to them. The animal has a nervous system, which the plant has not, by which its various parts are brought in unison. In both is observed what has been called vital force.

What is this vital force? Consider an organized being. It is a representative of all the forces and conditions which have ever acted on it, or on its remotest ancestors. It is the concrete expression of all these. In it, these forces have acquired a momentum. They are not wholly dependent on external circumstances, but are able to re-act on surrounding conditions. The sum of forces thus individualized, the momentum of force thus represented, is what is called vitality. Whatever power a being gains from its food or otherwise, not expended, is so much gained by vitality.

It is not an original force imported from ancestors, which weakens as it departs from the parent stock, as has been argued. This is refuted by the propagation of plants by cuttings, or the embryonic growth of animals. The bud or the sperm-cell can only give direction to the causes of growth, which yield vitality as the surplus of the force extracted from the sustaining material.

77. Use of the Nerves.

By means of the nerves, all the organs of the body are brought into harmony. They are the conducting wires by which the forces generated in the system are kept in equilibrium. Where they do not exist, there is no motion. They convey the excess of force existing in one organ to another when it is deficient, or to organs which do not generate the force which they need.

As force cannot be created nor destroyed, its manifestations depend on chemical changes within the organism. This is true of the force used in the voluntary and involuntary motions of the body. Even the movement of a finger, or the exhalation of a breath, necessitates consumption of material in the body. That is, every motion requires force, which is derived from some of the component particles of the organism entering into new combinations, and thereby becoming effete, and rejected by the system. They cannot be used a second time.

The vital force stands in direct relation to chemical force, or, in other words, to the amount of destructions of tissues. It is precisely parallel to the results obtained by a galvanic battery. An atom of acid unites with an atom of zinc: the attached wire transmits force by which we can separate the most firmly united compounds, produce light, heat, or magnetic force; but we can never obtain any more force than that afforded by the original attraction of the atom of acid and zinc.

Thus it is that force is derived from the oxidation effected in the body, which must be proportional to the material consumed. In fevers, where the waste is great, the production of heat is correlated with motion.

78. Oxygen the Creator and Destroyer.

The oxygen of the atmosphere that bathes us constantly is the natural agent of change, which, while it stimulates the living organism, seizes its particles at death, and hurries them to swift decay. It is only because the organs exposed to its action constantly present substances for which it has a greater affinity that they are preserved. Thus the living lung has as much attraction for oxygen as the dead; but it presents, spread through its countless capillaries, the blood, for which oxygen has a greater attraction. It is thus controlled by vitality. The same may be said of the mucous membrane and gellatinous and cellular tissues: they readily combine with oxygen, and are protected by the substances they present to take up oxygen. In case where such substances cannot be presented, as in starving, they yield at once to the action of oxygen.

79. Compensation.

There is absolute compensation in the organic system. It has a certain amount of force, which, if used in one direction, cannot be in another. If the involuntary motions are increased, the voluntary are weakened; if the voluntary are violently overtasked, the involuntary are weakened, sometimes to such an extent, that, no force being left to carry on the vital processes, death results.

The force which in plants is applied to unlimited growth is employed by animals in motion. This is effected through and by the muscles. Muscular *growth* does not imply the exertion of force: for the conversion of blood into muscle is only a change of form, their composition being the same; and change of form does not require expenditure of force, only proper condition.

80. CORRELATION OF MIND.

Arising to the lofty regions of the intellect, this correlation still holds. If man puts forth intellectual effort, it is so much force taken from some other direction, and is measured by organic change in the body. This by no means explains the phenomena of mind, as is claimed by the too ardent advocates of materialism. If standing alone, it may appear to do so; but, if the evidences of continued existence furnished by Spiritualism are sufficient, then a higher correlated power is introduced, and finite man must rest on the borders of the infinite. Spiritual beings are composed of higher forms of matter; and hence immortality does not present the impossibility of forces isolated, and the materialist has no room for his objections.

We have pushed this investigation to its extreme limit, and direst conclusions, that we might show more vividly how beautifully the ultra-material philosophy blends with the spiritual, as illustrated in the succeeding chapters.

V.

PHYSICAL MATTER AND SPIRIT.

MATTER and force are inseparable. We know nothing of force except through matter, and nothing of matter except by its forces. — YOUMANS.

81. THE OLD PROBLEM.

PHILOSOPHERS, from the earliest times, have attempted the solution of the question, if the substances with which our senses are brought in contact are capable of an indefinite division, or whether a point is reached — the ultimate molecule — where division can go no farther. No arguments can reach, nor experiments solve, the problem; and, from the idle conjectures of Democritus and Leucippus to the experimental researches of Wollaston and Faraday, there is no advancement except in the form of the investigation.

Matter, infinite space, and infinite duration, are the elements of creation. That space and time are infinite, we pause not to prove. The eternity of matter requires consideration. We have no proof to the contrary. That it is not is an assumption, and the affirmer must first produce evidence. Our senses never yielded us knowledge of the creation or extinction of matter. All the deductions of science are based on its eternity. We see it change form, — it becomes solid, liquid, or gaseous, but never diminishes in quantity. The candle burns, yielding light; it is consumed, apparently destroyed: as a candle, it exists not; but, as gaseous products floating in the air, every atom remains, and, if subjected to the test of the balance, would exactly poise the candle. So of the coal and wood in our grates: it is destroyed as coal and wood, but not as matter.

82. ETERNITY OF MATTER.

We cannot imagine either the extinction or the beginning of matter. We contemplate nature, not as having beginning nor end, but as an infinite series, a few of whose members only are brought before us. It stretches before us like an endless way, up and down which we can travel, but never to either termination; and having no data, nothing positive, we cannot judge whether the path has or has not termination. So far as we know, it has not. Here is an end to all speculation; and, until something more than the idle conceits of men are produced, we are obliged to rest content with the apparent eternity of matter. I say apparent, because such are the teachings of our senses. Forms perish with appalling rapidity; death vying with life, and resurrection triumphing again and again over the power of dissolution: yet the atoms of which all these countless swarms of existences are formed remain unchanged. Compared with the fleeting existence of animated nature, or even with the durations of the worlds of space, which grow old and are absorbed, matter is eternal. So let it rest until proof to the contrary is produced. I disturb not its repose. Nothing in sacred volumes, more than in the walks of nature, contradicts our conclusion. Nowhere do they teach that God created matter.

83. What is Matter?

It is an aggregation of atoms. What is an atom? It is the type of the universe; for in it are concentrated all the laws and principles in nature. Is it a real, tangible existence? or is it, as taught by some philosophers, a mathematical point, from which, as a centre, forces are manifested? This question is difficult to decide; and in this, as in all others, we are compelled to fall back on the evidences of the senses, and, until the production of proof, abide their decision. It is difficult to conceive of the propagation of force from a mathematical point, or rather a centre, where nothing exists. It is wide of the spirit of our system of philosophy, which refers all productions of force to matter. It is, at most, but a flight of imagination; but, let it be decided as it will, force must be referred to the atom, — to matter. The atom exists because this force is present. The force is a part of the atom. In other words, and as a general expression, the attributes of matter are co-existent and co-eternal with it.

84. DEFINITIONS.

By attributes, I mean direct manifestations of the primary force into which the phenomena of the atom are resolvable.

Principles are combinations of these.

Properties are primary results.

All of these are the means by which the existence of matter is manifested to our senses; and without them we could not conceive of its existence. I have neither space nor inclination to enter into a metaphysical discussion of this question. I refer to this plain statement.

85. AN ATOM WITHOUT ATTRIBUTES.

How could the atom exist without extension and attraction and corresponding repulsion? Vigorous, indeed, must be the imagination which can build a world of such atoms. Robbed of its attributes, the atom has no tangible existence. Here, resting our deduction on the basis of facts, the testimony of sense, we conclude that the atom, and the forces which it manifests, are co-eternal, co-existent. Their relations we cannot conjecture.

86. RESOLUTION OF PHENOMENA.

All the phenomena presented by matter appear to be resolvable into the forces of attraction and repulsion. This is opposed to the received idea, that inertia is its characteristic. Matter is supposed to have no internal force. If it is not acted upon from without, it remains forever at rest. If it is possible for matter thus to remain, we never see it in such a condition. A post planted by the roadside is at rest compared with the objects around it: but it is not really at rest; for, not to mention the internal changes in its structure by which it shortly is reduced to dust, each day it makes the circuit of the globe, and yearly journeys around the sun. Does the globe move, and compel it to move? What moves the globe? Ah! now we arrive at the end. Every atom the globe contains exerts its influence, and their combined force is the motion of the globe.

87. THE ATOM.

To the microscope, the finest powder to which a substance can be reduced presents all the aspects of the entire body. Gold may be hammered so thin that one grain will cover fourteen hundred square inches. A microscope can detect the gold on the thousandth part of a linear inch; so that gold may at least be divided into particles a fourteen hundred millionth of a square inch in size, and still retain its character. Coloring substances, such as indigo, show an almost incomprehensible divisibility. A single drop of strong indigo in solution can be shown to contain at least five hundred thousand distinctly visible portions, and will color a thousand cubic inches of water. As this mass of water is at least five hundred thousand times larger than the drop, it is certain that a particle of indigo must be smaller than the twenty-five hundred billionth part of an inch. A fragment of silver a hundredth of an inch in size, when dissolved in nitric acid, will render distinctly milky five hundred cubic inches of common salt. Hence the size of a particle of silver thus dissolved must be less than a billionth of a cubic inch. The attenuation presented by solutions are far exceeded by the complex beings revealed by the microscope. Atomies are revealed no larger than the particles of dissolved indigo, living, moving, having organs of prehension, digestion, and assimilation, and a circulating fluid or blood, with globules bearing the same comparative size to them as ours do to us.

Millions of these beings heaped together would be scarcely perceptible to the unassisted eye. Every advance made in the perfection of the microscope reveals grades of animalculæ hitherto unseen; and these feed on still more minute forms. These examples only show the possible division, but do not touch the question of infinite divisibility. The definite extension of the atmosphere, showing the limitation of the repulsion existing between its gaseous atoms, appears to settle the question; for, it is argued, were the particles infinitely divisible, their repulsion would be infinite. This conclusion is not inevitable; and doubts have also been cast on the determination of the limits of the atmosphere.

88. THE CHEMICAL ATOM.

The chemical atom may be regarded as formed by a group of smaller particles; and the number uniting to form a group is what we call the combining number: but this is conjectural. There then remains but one theory; and that is the one advanced by Boscovitch, or some one of the modifications of which it is susceptible. We must confess that we know of force; but, of matter, we know nothing. What we call matter — that which we see, feel, taste; which manifests gravity, impenetration, &c. — is not matter, but the forces which surround and conceal something beyond. This something lies beyond our ken; and all we know of it we learn from its phenomena. It is difficult for the mind to grasp the idea of substance without atoms, and there is a necessity of employing the term; yet all we know of it may be expressed by a centre radiating force. Whether that centre is a mathematical point, or occupied by a determinate atom, we cannot ascertain; though the latter inference is most consonant with the finiteness of our minds. This point, this something, around which the forces of the universe cluster, and from which they radiate, is called an atom. It is uncreatable and indestructible. On this basis, all positive science rests; and, without it, its inferences would be wholly unreliable. It may change its form, from solid to liquid, from liquid to gas; it may be apparently dissipated, as wood in a grate, as food in the animal body: but it always re-appears. The

Physical Matter and Spirit. 123

atom is eternal, whether a particle, or a centre of force.

There is a great difference between the theory of atoms and the theory of forces. The former explains, satisfactorily, but few phenomena; while the latter adjusts itself to all. Certain inferences suggest themselves, when the latter is received, which generalize the most diverse phenomena.

89. DOCTRINE OF IMPENETRABILITY FALSE.

The facts presented by the combinations of potassium and sodium overthrow the long-held statement that matter is impenetrable. The mutual diffusion of gases, the contraction in bulk of liquids when employed as solvents, confirm the idea that matter is highly penetrable. If the component atoms are considered as widely separated, we may consider foreign atoms as introduced in the interspaces, and affording no proof of penetration. But we cannot, from the foregoing facts, consider such to be a correct view of the constitution of matter. As space cannot be a conductor and a non-conductor, there must exist some bond of union between the particles so remotely situated. Take the theory that an atom is a centre of force, it occupies all the space over which its force is propagated. When aggregated into masses, they fill all the area of the substance. The influence of force, which is all we know of matter, must extend to infinite distance. Matter, thus considered, fills all space; for all space is filled with the gravitation of atoms, and gravity is a constituent part of matter. Suns and worlds are but central condensations rotating in the midst of matter. Every atom, while it constantly retains its own individuality, extends throughout all space, penetrating and being penetrated by all others.

90. Form of the Atom.

The shape of the primary atom, so often conjectured, and conceived in the manner one would fancy the outline of a mathematical point, becomes clearly defined. Its form depends on the manner in which the force is propagated from the centre. If by consecutive waves, it assumes the powers of a sphere; if with greater strength in the direction of an axis, of an oblate spheroid; if it circulate around the axis in the manner electric currents are supposed to do around a magnet, polarity may be manifested. Its form would depend on the disposition of force.

91. Atom a Centre of Force.

When two atoms having affinity, as an atom of metal and an atom of oxygen, unite, the Newtonian theory regards them as simply arranged side by side in a manner easily conceived, and often forcibly represented; but why such a union radically changes the properties of the constituent elements, why an atom of acid uniting with an atom of alkali produces a neutral substance, is not explained. On the other hand, if an atom be regarded as a centre of

Physical Matter and Spirit. 125

force, when two unite, they mutually penetrate to the very centres of each other, forming one molecule with powers determined by the new combination of forces. The manner in which two or more atoms unite or separate under the influence of stronger forces, may be illustrated by the union of sea-waves, and their subsequent separation into the original waves.

92. IS THERE SUCH AN ENTITY AS SPACE PENETRATING THE PORES OF ALL SUBSTANCES?

It is difficult to understand its want of properties; more difficult to understand those which it apparently possesses. If we consider matter as an objective substance acted on by forces, then the atoms of gas, fluid, or solid, cannot touch each other, but are separated by intervals of space. Space penetrates all substances with a fine network of cells. The component atoms of a body have been likened, by these atomic philosophers, to the stars scattered in the vaults of the sky, being comparatively equally far removed from each other. There can be nothing continuous in the universe but space. Every substance must be broken and limited. How does this agree with the conducting and non-conducting properties of bodies? A stick of shellac, penetrated by space, and having its particles far asunder, is an insulator. If space was a conductor, it could not be; for there could be no such thing as insulation. Hence space is an insulator. A pile of loose, dry sand is a non-conductor; but fill its pores with water, and the mass becomes continuous and a conductor. In the same manner, if space were a conductor, penetrating all bodies, not the least insulation could be effected.

Conducting bodies have their atoms widely removed from each other, and are penetrated by space. If space is a non-conductor, these atoms are in the condition of metallic dust stirred into melted resin. As each particle is surrounded by an insulating film of resin, the mass is a non-conductor; so, each atom being enveloped in non-conducting space, the mass becomes a non-conductor. Hence, as space is the only continuous portion of bodies, it must be a conductor.

But it cannot be both a conductor and a non-conductor. According to the atomic theory, if the specific gravity of the metals be divided by their atomic numbers, the result is the number of atoms in equal bulk of the metals. It would be presumable that the metals containing the largest number of atoms — that is, having atoms nearest together — would have the greatest conducting power. This is not, however, the fact. Iron, containing nearly three times the number of atoms of gold, is only one-sixth as good a conductor. Copper, containing nearly the same number of atoms, is a sixfold better conductor; being nearly equal to gold, the best of all metals, although containing the fewest atoms. Silver, having the same number as gold, is only three-fourths as good a conductor. The results are reversed in lead, which contains almost the same number of atoms as gold, but is only one-twelfth as good a conductor.

These facts are very perplexing, and difficult to harmonize with the atomic theory; and the difficulty is augmented by those presented by the alkalies and their compounds. As an example, take potassium, the metallic base of potash. We shall find, by comparison of its specific gravity and atomic weight with that of its hydrate, that the same bulk of metal potassium containing forty-five atoms will contain seventy atoms of the metal, and two hundred and ten atoms of oxygen and hydrogen. In other words, the same space which contains four hundred and thirty atoms of potassium, when that metal unites with two thousand one hundred atoms of oxygen and hydrogen, can not only contain them, but two hundred more atoms of potassium. So it is possible that a piece of potassium contains less potassium than an equal part of potash formed by its union with oxygen and hydrogen. If the bulk occupied by the atoms of potassium can contain not only two-thirds more atoms of potassium, but nearly five times as many atoms of oxygen and hydrogen, its atoms must be very wide apart, occupying, considering the compounds thus produced as absolutely solid, but one-sixth of the area. That potassium is a conductor, implies that this intervening space is a conductor, which it is not. Other compounds show similar results. Thus the volume containing five hundred and thirty atoms of metal potassium will, in the state of nitre, contain four hundred and sixteen atoms, and two thousand nine hundred and twelve atoms of nitrogen; and, as carbonate, the volume of four hundred and thirty atoms will contain two hundred and fifty-six more atoms, and two thousand seven hundred and forty-four atoms of oxygen and carbon, or three thousand four hundred and thirty atoms.

In adding water to sulphuric acid, and in most solutions of salts, there is contraction of bulk. There is not only penetration, but a clear space formed by penetration. It is thus evident that the *impenetrability* of matter must be discarded.

If atoms are so remote from each other, it is easy to account for the entrance of other atoms between them. It is also evident that little is known of the atom. The equivalent number, which chemists consider as expressive of the number of atoms, cannot express that fact, but rather the relative cohesive attraction, or weight of the atom.

93. Change of Properties.

Having received these views, it is easy to understand why such radical changes in properties occur by the union of different elements. The compound atom, as long as the conditions of its creation hold, is in every respect a new element. No one would infer beforehand, that the union of the intense alkali, caustic potash, with the powerful acid, sulphuric, would produce a salt having the properties of neither. The union of potash with nitric acid yields nitre, or saltpetre; of sodium, a beautiful metal, with poisonous chlorine, common salt, on which life and health depend. How can we suppose such changes to occur by the placing of particles side by side? Very simply, if these particles penetrate each other, and for the time become one, with properties produced by the sum of the forces of both.

94. OBJECTIONS.

It will be said that the impenetrability of matter is demonstrated by the senses, and has been held as an axiom in natural philosophy. "Whatever occupies space, and is revealed to the senses, is termed matter." A bar of iron is felt by the hand, and is impenetrable to it. It is seen by the eye because it reflects light; it has weight; we say that it is absolutely impenetrable. This is only true when affirmed in respect to the human body. It may be very penetrable to other substances. Beneath the elements known to the senses may be an innumerable number of other elements, not recognized by the senses, because not holding the proper relations to them.

95. WE THUS LEARN THAT THE ATOM IS OF LITTLE MOMENT: THE FORCES WHICH EMANATE THEREFROM ARE THE ESSENTIALS.

Whether we regard it as a particle, or as a centre of force, changes not the result. If a particle, we can never know anything of it except by means of the attributes or forces flowing from it. We never see, feel, hear, taste, nor touch matter: it is its properties and its atmosphere which affects us. All visible effects are produced by invisible causes. Cohesion, which unites atoms into solid masses, or gravitation, chaining world to world, does not result from external pressure, but internal force. All the forces of nature act from within outward. The most materialistic philosophers admit this; and, in the study of nature, questions of force "are becoming more and more prominent. The things to be explained are changes, active effects, motions in ordinary matter, not as acted upon, but as in itself inherently active. The chief use of atoms is to serve as points, or vehicles of motion. Thus the study of matter resolves itself into the study of forces. Inert objects, as they appear to the eye of sense, are replaced by activities revealed to the eye of intellect. The conceptions of 'gross,' 'corrupt' 'brute matter' are passing away with the prejudices of the past; and, in place of a dead, material world, we have a living organism of spiritual energies."

This is the highest ground taken by philosophers at present; and, while they congratulate themselves on their Positivism, they really are entering the vestibule of Spiritualism.

When the mind is freed from the ideas created by the senses of physical matter, and, with intellectual vision, understands that what it calls fixed and unchangeable are fleeting shadows of unseen, spiritual energies, it is ready to comprehend how this force can be immortalized in specialized forms and spiritual beings.

96. Perfection of Man.

The rudiments of the organs of sense appear low down in the scale of being. If we receive the theory that living beings were created by the forces of matter, and not for them, it is probable that there is a sense for every order of manifestation of which matter is susceptible. In man, all the organs, of which rudimentary indications are given in the lower order of beings, are perfected; and we have thus a right to suppose him to be susceptible to every sensation matter is capable of imparting. Were it otherwise, he would possess some rudimentary sense for future ages to perfect. Sight, hearing, taste, touch, are all as perfect in animals as in man, and, in many, even more perfect; but he surpasses them in nervous sensibility, — a faculty dimly seen in the animal world, and reaching to the spirit realm.

This may almost be called a new sense, and must be regarded as still rudimentary. A dim shadow of its capabilities is revealed by the clairvoyant. In its direction more than in any other, are we to expect progress. Through it, matter reaches up to spirit; and, by it, we learn the laws of that mystic realm.*

* I here cannot refrain from alluding to the corroboration of the principles laid down in the first volume of the " Arcana of Nature." When it was written, years ago (1858), I searched in vain for the least scientific testimony confirming its statement of principles. I was impressed that there were persons in Europe holding nearly the same views, but could not procure their works. I wrote as impressed, with faith in the utterance of the controlling power: "The power which wafts suns and worlds on their orbits must reside in themselves." "Motion belongs to the atom." "Motion is ever the same, directed in different channels, and fulfilling different missions, nevertheless the same." "Life is born of motion" (p. 20). "Life, then, is the specialization of the living principles of matter." And it is there held that intelligence is specialized through life from the intelligence organizing creation. The theological press sent up one long hiss: the most dignified of its journals said it was good pantheism. Now, as I write, this very doctrine, that matter is nothing but force (being, in its various manifestations, but a modification of motion), is everything, is scientific orthodoxy. In the "Arcana," it is stated that there is no *inertia*. The statement was ridiculed; but, now, the idea of "inert, brute matter" has passed away, and many works have appeared, extending over the whole ground, from physical motion to intelligence. (See compilation by Youmans of the essays of Joule, Mayer, Helmholtz, Carpenter, and Faraday, — "The Correlation and Conservation of the Physical Forces.")

It is notable that the first volume of the "Arcana," having been translated into German, should be repeatedly quoted by the learned and fearless Büchner, in his work on "Matter and Force," in proof of Materialism.

VI.

SPIRITUAL ATMOSPHERE OF THE UNIVERSE.

> An atmosphere more sublimate than air
> Pervades all matter, be it here or there:
> No finite power its wrappings can disperse;
> For its thin billows lave the universe, —
> Each portion linking to all other parts,
> Whether stars, blossoms, or responding hearts
>
> EMMA TUTTLE.

97. THE INSTRUMENT EMPLOYED IN INVESTIGATION.

AS the investigator reaches the threshold of the domain of spirit, he meets phenomena protean in form and expression, but having a common family type. The object of the present chapter is to attempt, from observed facts, a generalization which shall unite the strangely diverse phenomena of impressibility. In the study of this subject, we have a perfect instrument ready formed for our purpose, — the sensitive brain. Through its impressibility we become cognizant of spiritual forces, and, by its aid, are enabled to enter the secret courts of the spirit.

98. THE IMPRESSIBILITY OF THE BRAIN.

The faculties of man may be usually traced in rudimentary form in the lower animals; and the impressibility of his nervous system forms no exception. Its presence can be seen in the lowest zoophytes or plant-animals. They seek the darkest places, and shrink from the influence of the light. This is the only sense they manifest. It is possessed by all animals; but the experiments of Spallanzani on bats show that they are possessed of highly somnambulistic faculties.

99. IMPRESSIBILITY OF ANIMALS.

"Completely blinded bats were not in the slightest degree obstructed in their motions. They flew about by night and by day with their wonted rapidity, avoiding all obstacles which lay, or were intentionally placed, in their way, as dexterously as if in full possession of their sight. They turned around at the right time when they approached a wall, rested in a convenient situation when fatigued, and struck against nothing. The experiments were multiplied, and varied in the most ingenious manner. A room was filled with thin twigs; in another, silken threads were suspended from the roof, and preserved in the same position at the same distance from each other by means of small weights attached to them. The bat, though deprived of its eyes, flew through the intervals of these threads, as well as of the twigs, without touching them; and, when the intervals were too small, it drew its wings more closely together. In another room, a net was placed, having occasional irregular spaces for the bat to fly through, the net being so arranged as to form a small labyrinth; but the blind bat was not to be deceived. In proportion as the difficulties were increased, the dexterity of the animal was augmented. When it flew over the upper extremity of the net, and seemed imprisoned between it and the wall, it was frequently observed to make its escape most dexterously. When fatigued by its high flights, it still flew rapidly along the ground, among chairs, tables, and sofas, yet avoided touching anything with its wings. Even in the open air, its flight was as prompt, easy, and secure as in a close room, and, in both situations, altogether similar to that of its associates who had the use of their eyes."

It is this impressibility that enables animals to influence each other, man to influence man, or *vice versa*. That such influences exist, there can be no doubt. The few facts I relate are representative of volumes which might be collected. The tiger shows the faculty of "charming," with the other members of the feline family. An interesting instance of its exertion is recorded by Lieut.-Col. Davidson.

"My detachment, after passing through several low forests, was one morning encamped at Gorapichar, on a somewhat cleared spot, but still completely surrounded by jungle, reputed to be swarming with tigers and all other wild animals. I issued orders that none of the Europeans should lose sight of their tents: but they were all wild lads, desperate after sport; and one of them, named Skelton, walked away from camp, with fusil in hand, and the honorable company's ammunition in his pocket, eager to distinguish himself by the death of a tiger.

"The consequence was, that, had it not been that he was soon missed by his comrades, he would undoubtedly have been eaten up by a tiger for his disobedience of orders.

"He was reported absent; and I ordered a strict search to be made for him. A party of the Europeans immediately issued forth, and soon found the sportsman, standing, musket in hand, wholly immovable and stupid, eagerly staring at a bush about thirty yards in advance. They spoke to him; but he could not answer. They rushed up, and tried to rouse him; but his eyes continued fixed. And then they observed the head of a tiger, with his brilliant eyes riveted on the intended victim, while his long curly tail was gracefully waving over his back in fond anticipation of a bloody feast. They shouted; and the tiger speedily vanished. Skelton was conveyed back to his tent; and so great was the shock given to his brain, that many days elapsed before he recovered his usual vivacity: and there was no more tiger-shooting during the remainder of the march to Asseer-Gurh.

"I was, in the year 1831, executive engineer of the province of Bundlecund, and dwelt within the forests of Calpee, in a stout, stone building on the margin of the precipice, about sixty feet above the waters of the ancient river, the Jumna, and within a few yards of that classic spot at which one of the incarnations of Crishna made his appearance on earth.

"While within the building, my attention was drawn, one morning, to piercing cries of great distress, which I knew proceeded from one of that beautiful species of squirrel called 'gillairy,' or striped Barbary squirrel. I quickly ran to the spot whence the sound proceeded, which was at the very edge of the precipice, then covered by many stunted bushes and trailing plants; and there I observed the gillairy about four or five feet from the bank, leaping backwards and forwards, with his tail erect, upon a slender branch overhanging the river. The animal paid no attention whatever to my presence; and I could not, for some time, discover the cause of his outcries. On looking more carefully, I observed the head and about a couple of feet of the body of a large snake. The body of the reptile continued to undulate in a very gentle manner: but the head seemed to be almost on fire, so very brilliant were the almost fire-shooting and triumphant eyes, that seemed to anticipate his victory over the helpless squirrel, which seemed absolutely spell-bound; for it made no effort to escape, which, under any other circumstances, it could have done with facility, by dropping down on a protruding part of the precipice, a few feet below the bough on which it traversed. Its cries became more and more urgent and piercing; and, moved by compassion for suffering, I shot the serpent. The squirrel's cries instantly ceased; and it dropped down, and disappeared."

The influence of this subtle power of animals on man has been recorded by the eminent and bold Dr. Caldwell.

"We knew a gentleman, who, in the largest chamber, covered with a carpet, in the midst of deep darkness, could tell if a cat entered it with her stealthiest tread, and in perfect silence. Nor could he tell in what way, or through which of his external senses, he made the discovery. When interrogated on the subject, his only reply was that he experienced a peculiar and disagreeable feeling, which told him that there was a cat in the room. Nor could he look on one during daylight without experiencing a sense of horror."

100. Sympathy a Form of Impressibility.

This sympathy is strongly marked between intimate friends and relations, and gives the philosophy of the old saying, "The Devil is always near when you talk about him." Some interesting cases have been recorded by Dr. Pratt.

"A lady residing in my family, an invalid, under medical treatment at the time of this occurrence, was seized suddenly with what appeared to be an apoplectic fit, about two o'clock P. M. The fit continued till the next morning, the patient being perfectly insensible to all surrounding friends and influences: after which she aroused to consciousness, stating that she had received a severe blow upon the forehead, in the region of the organ of benevolence, which had deprived her of her senses; that her head now ached severely; that she felt faint, &c. She had no recollection of the time passed in the fit.

"Three days after this event, the cause of the fit was satisfactorily explained to my mind, as follows: The lady's 'other half' arrived, an invalid, having been struck down about two o'clock P. M., three days before, by the fall of a tackle-block from a mast-head, the blow being on the frontal portion of the head, scalping his forehead, and stunning him for nearly twelve hours, and rendering his life extremely doubtful.

"CASE 2D. A lady with whom I conversed last winter, whose husband was an itinerant clergyman, informed me that she had repeatedly risen from her bed late at night, and prepared for the reception of her husband, whom she had no reason to expect home at that time, only from vague impressions. 'For two years,' said she, 'I have been in the habit of doing this; and I have never once been mistaken in my impressions. My husband would often exclaim, "Why, Mary! what made you think I was coming?" I could only answer that I *thought so.*'

"CASE 3D. A gentleman in the State of New York, while plowing in the field, was suddenly shot through the heart, — at least this was his impression. His sensations were such that he could not work; and he put out his team, and returned to the house, stating that he believed that his brother, who was then a soldier in the Mexican war, had been shot through the heart, or had fallen in battle. Two months after that, the news arrived of his brother's death in battle, by a ball through the chest, occurring on the same day and hour of his impression.

"From these examples it appears that there is such a phenomenon in the mental constitution as communication between mind and mind, not only among friends present, but even sometimes when absent, however distant.

"This is an effect of sympathy. Every one has heard, in his own circle, of numerous instances of it. I am informed for example, by a lady nearly related to me, that her mother always had such a warning at the time any near and dear friend died. This occurred so often as to leave no doubt whatever of the fact. It happened that this lady, more than once, made the voyage to and from India; and that, during the voyage, she, on several occasions, said to her daughter and to others, 'I feel certain that such a person is dead.' On reaching port, these impressions were found to be true."

Referring such astounding phenomena to sympathy is far from furnishing an explanation. What is this sympathy? It must have a cause; and from its universality and resemblance among all races of men, and between every form of animal life, its cause must be universal, held in common, binding together all these diverse phenomena.*

* For more extended evidence on this subject, see chapters on Spirit.

101. INFLUENCE OF THE EXTERNAL WORLD ON THE NERVOUS SYSTEM.

The experiments of Reichenbach not only prove the sensitiveness of the nerves, but the kind of influence exerted by the inorganic and organic worlds. His experiments, instituted with the most consummate care, had they been made in an orthodox channel, would have been considered conclusive. The day of his honor is in the future; for, although stumbling in many of his conclusions, the noble stand he assumed for the sake of truth is worthy of all praise. The results obtained from organic life are no less apparent, and confirm his conclusions.

102. REICHENBACH'S EXPERIMENTS.

The requisite sensitiveness to see and feel the magnetic flame in a marked manner seems to accompany diseases of the nervous system. Such is the case with most of the subjects introduced by Reichenbach in his attempt to establish the fact of such influence. It is not, however, wholly dependent on disease for its manifestation, sometimes being possessed by persons enjoying perfect health.

103. INFLUENCE OF MAGNETS.

The exaltation of nervous sensibility in the daughter of the tax-collector, Nowotny, was wonderful. "In her, all the exalted intensity of the senses had appeared, so that she could not bear the sun nor candle-light; saw her chamber as in twilight in the darkest night, and clearly distinguished the colors of all the furniture and clothes in it. On her the magnet acted with extraordinary violence, in several ways; and she manifested the sensitive peculiarity in all respects in such a high degree that she equaled the true somnambulist (which, however, she was not) in every particular relating to sensory irritability.

"She perceived a distinct luminosity as long as the magnet remained open; but, on placing the armature on the poles, the light disappeared. The flame seemed to be somewhat stronger at the moment of lifting up the armature; then to acquire a permanent condition, which was weaker. The fiery appearance was about equal in size at each pole, and without perceptible tendency to mutual connection. Close upon the steel from which it streamed, it seemed to form a fiery vapor; and this was surrounded by a kind of glory of rays. But the rays were not at rest: they became shorter and longer without intermission, and exhibited a kind of darting ray and active scintillation which the observer assured us was uncommonly beautiful. The whole appearance was more delicate than common fire: the light was far purer, almost white like the sun's rays, mingled with iridescent colors. The distribution of light in rays was not uniform: in the middle of the edges of the magnet they were more crowded than at the corners, where they formed little tufts."

Spiritual Atmosphere. 143

The case of Miss Sturmann, daughter of an inspector of farms in Prague, is still more curious.

"She was suffering from tubercular affection of the lungs, and was subject to somnambulism in its slighter stages, with attacks of tetanus and cataleptic fits. When I stood in a darkened ward, holding a ninety-pound magnet open at a distance of six paces from her feet, while she was perfectly conscious of what was going on around her, she ceased to answer, and fell into tetanic spasms and complete unconsciousness from the influence of the magnet. After a while she came to herself again, and said that at the moment I had removed the armature she had seen a flame flash over it, about the length of a small hand, and of a white color, mingled with red and blue. She had wished to look at it more closely, when she became unconscious from its influence."

104. AN ELECTRO-MAGNET

Presents the same appearance as a steel magnet, showing that it is really the magnetic force that is observed.

When the poles of an electro-magnet were brought near those of a steel, the flames from the latter were repelled as by a strong wind.

Subjected to purely physical tests, the magnetic flame is found to be devoid of heat, and, when applied to a delicate daguerreotype plate, to yield only dubious traces of light. No degree of condensation by a lens renders it visible to common eyes.

105. Influence of Crystals.

After many and carefully repeated experiments, it is found that natural crystals possess a power equal to that of magnets. Amorphous bodies are without influence; but crystalline, with few exceptions, manifest this property.

"It has never yet been observed, in ponderable matter, that the form, the arrangement of the molecules, can be the cause of new forces acting at a distance." — *Pouillet in Muller's Physics*, 167.

Reichenbach concludes that the influence of a crystal on a sensitive, while the same substance in an amorphous state has no influence, contradicts this statement. But it does not necessarily. The minute crystals of such bodies are opposed one to the other, just as if it was formed of minute magnets indiscriminately aggregated, so that their poles would mutually neutralize each other. Remove one of these crystals, and indefinitely enlarge it, it is then free from neutralizing influences: its force acts in certain defined directions, and can be felt. There is no new force: it only becomes appreciable.

A crystal of quartz is a fine substance with which to experiment. When drawn down the inside of the hand of the subject, it produces the same feeling as a magnet. The sensation is like that of a pleasant, light, cool breeze. When the motion is reversed, passing the point of the crystal from the hand upward, the sensation becomes disagreeable. From the many experiments recorded by Baron Reichenbach, one is selected as an illustration. At the University Hospital, the experiment was made on Miss Sturmann.

"I made a pass over her hand with the apex of a rock-crystal six inches long, and two thick. The effect ensued immediately: the patient felt the warm and cool sensations very sensibly when the passes were made over her hand. When I applied the magnet in the same manner, the sensations were of the same kind, but weaker and reversed. The action was so strong that it affected the whole arm as far as the shoulder, the warm and cold sensations being prolonged all the way up. When I subsequently applied a crystal three times as large, it acted so powerfully upon the hand, immediately upon the first pass, that her color came and went suddenly, so that I did not venture on a second experiment with her. . . . Finally I tried the same on Miss Maix. On this very sensitive patient — who, however, always remained fully conscious — the crystals acted, not merely on the line of the pass, but over a broad strip up and down the hand, which action ascended the arm. Miss Reichel, to appearance a healthy and strong girl, possessed such sensibility to the crystal pole, that she perceived its approach even at a considerable distance. Like her predecessors, she found the pass downward cool, and upward warm. Lastly, I became acquainted with Miss Maria Atzmannsdorfer, and found her to feel the pass of the crystals strongest of all. Even little crystals of fluor spar, &c., an inch or so long, produced a sensation of cold when passed down the hand. With rather thin, acicular crystals, I could, so to speak, describe lines upon the hand; but the pass upward produced warmth of the hand, and so adversely upon her that it affected her whole body unpleasantly, and began to produce spasms as soon as I repeated it."

These results were tested, not only on cataleptic patients, but many prominent physicians, physicists, and chemists; and especially were the results remarkable on the naturalist, Prof. Endlicher.

The peculiar force is exerted in the direction of the axis of the crystal; is strongest at the two poles, and of opposite effects, agreeing in this with the positive and negative poles of the magnet.

The force of the crystal, however much it may affect the nervous system, is not of a magnetic character. The largest and purest crystal of quartz or lime will not attract the minutest dust of iron; has no directive tendency, like a magnetic needle, if ever so delicately suspended. Nor can it induce magnetism in a steel bar, nor influence the polar wire when placed in the helix, producing no induced current. While the magnet and crystal are alike in their effects on the sensitive nerves, the magnet has properties which the crystal has not, such as directive and attractive qualities, and relations to terrestrial magnetism and electricity. These properties stand, in relation to the other force, as light does to heat in the burning of a taper. They can be separated, so that the magnet would have no directive tendency, but will affect the sensitive; as the light of a taper can be cut off by a screen of certain substances, and yet allow the heat to pass unimpeded. The crystal is built up by the operation of definite chemical forces, but of too low an order to yield magnetic force. They act on *atoms*, magnetism on *masses;* herein being related to chemical affinity, which holds precisely this relation to gravitation. It resembles the magnet in having polarity to sensitives: it is quantitively different at the two poles. Cold is produced at the pole corresponding to the $-M$, and heat at that corresponding to the $+M$. The north pole is the stronger.

If crystals are brought in contact with amorphous substances, they impart their power; and the latter produce sensations as crystals do. The influence is not permanent, but rapidly disappears. It is transmitted through matter in the same manner as attraction, no intervening substance producing any more effect than air, except a slight retardation. Like the force of the crystal, this imparted influence is limited, and cannot be indefinitely accumulated. In crystals, it increases with their size; but varies in different substances. Thus a small crystal of cobalt is more powerful than a large one of quartz; and the influence of the minute crystals of morphine is distinctly felt.

106. CRYSTALLIC FLAME.

Of the result of experiments made to determine whether crystals yield a visible flame, Reichenbach gives a most convincing record.

"I instituted an experiment with the heightened vision of Miss Sturmann. A room was made as dark as possible: she entered, remained some time, till her eyes became accustomed to the obscurity, and then I placed before her a large watch-crystal. She actually at once perceived a flame-like light over it, half the size of a hand, blue, passing into white above, remarkably different from the magnetic light, which she described as much redder and yellower. The flame was movable, in a waving and sparkling condition; and then a light glare over the support on which the crystal rested, of the diameter of almost forty inches, just as a magnet had done when flame-like appearance and light radiating from it could be easily distinguished." Miss Reichel described the flames in the same manner. "She said that they were of peculiar, star-like forms, which assumed different shapes as the crystal was turned. It was evidently the crystalline structure of the stone, its combination in different directions, which caused the production of luminous appearances and internal reflections, such as could not of course exist in this way in a steel magnet." Is this light connected with that observed in the crystallization of many substances? Probably it is. It is proved by Prof. Rose that crystallization is entirely free from heat and electricity. The polarity of crystals, their access of growth, conclusively prove that the production of their beautiful forms is the result of magnetic forces.

A bar of soft iron, when applied to a magnet,

becomes itself magnetic, and so remains as long as held in contact, but not a moment longer. Magnetism then is destroyed; but that peculiar force recognized by the sensitive remains much longer, and therefore acts on them precisely as a magnet.

Cataleptic persons readily distinguish water to which a magnet has been applied; and whatever substances the magnet may have recently touched produce on them impressions almost as strong as the magnet itself. They are also affected by water, or other substances which have been electrified by having a current of electricity passed through them.

107. IMPARTATION OF INFLUENCE.

When a magnet is passed over a person, he becomes temporarily endowed with magnetic properties. When Prof. Endlicher passed the magnet over himself, "to his surprise, he now, as had never happened before, could attract the hand of the patient with his hand; cause it to attach itself, and follow everywhere, just as the magnetized glass of water had done. He retained this power for nearly a quarter of an hour: by that time it had by degrees disappeared. The same unknown something which had been left in the iron rod by the magnet, and had likewise passed into the water, must therefore have been conveyed into the whole person of the physician. It manifested itself, from the same cause, to the same effect in his fingers." This experiment was subsequently repeated in a variety of forms. In particular cases, this physician let his hand lie in Miss Nowotny's, while he rubbed the back of it with a strong magnet. The patient here said that she felt the force increase in the hand of the physician, by starts, with each pass of the magnet. It is a remarkable fact that this force can be transferred from the magnet to an individual, enabling that individual to exert a powerful magnetic influence which he did not previously possess; in fact, placing him in the exact position occupied by the strong natural magnetizer. Here the chasm between magnetic and crystallic influence, the force of the inorganic world, is bridged, and, with the power of animal magnetism, proved identical. Water can be magnetized with the hand as well as the magnet; and the force of the hand is conducted and retained in precisely the same manner.

108. POLARITY OF THE BODY.

Such being the case, we ask, "Are we endowed with polarity, like a crystal or magnet?" Experiments show that we are. Our dual structure — two hemispheres of brain, double organs of senses, two hands, two limbs — points to this fact. Sensitives at once detect the difference between the hands. They describe the current as passing up the right, and down the left, arm. This difference can be nothing else than polarization such as is seen in the magnet. Of one of the baron's patients, he remarks, "She found, not only her right hand, but the whole right side of her body, opposed to her left: nay, the mere approximation towards her of my right or left hand affected her in a very different manner." This patient observed that the fingers were always tipped with light in the same manner as the poles of a magnet or crystal. This is confirmed by repeated experiments; and I have often observed the same. If a small magnet, or a crystal a few inches in length, can exert such an influence on a sensitive, causing even cataleptic spasms, agreeable sense of coolness, or disagreeable warmth, how much greater the influence of that vast magnet, the earth, with its tremendous polar attraction, and rivers of electric influence! The planetary bodies, the sun and the moon, must also exert a strong influence. This conclusion may excite a smile of derision in those who have foregone conclusions, and class such ideas with the absurdities of astrology. To them we have nothing more to urge than the simple facts. The conclusions towards which they lead are inevitable, and wide of the vagaries of astrology.

109. Abnormal Sensitiveness of the Diseased.

The concealed processes of nature account, when understood, for many of the vagaries and inconsistencies of men, especially of those rendered peculiarly sensitive by disease. Sometimes there seems to be a kind of polarity developed, so that the individual is restless when lying in any other position than that with his head to the north. The painful sensations so often experienced by those suffering from disease can be often dispelled by placing them in this position, and their restoration to health be greatly accelerated. These statements are confirmed by the following facts recorded by Reichenbach:—

"Mr. Smith, a surgeon of Vienna, had received a chill of the right arm, and had for some time suffered from acute rheumatism, with the most painful cramps running from the shoulders to the fingers. His physicians treated him with the magnet, which quieted the cramps; but they always returned. I found him lying with his head to the south. On my remarking this, they brought him in direction of the magnetic meridian, with his head to the north. Directly after coming into this position, he uttered expressions of pleasure: he declared he felt refreshed and strenthened. A pleasant uniform warmth diffused itself in the chilled part; he felt the pass of the magnet incomparably more cooling and agreeable than before; and, before I came away, the stiffened arm and the fingers became movable, and the pain had wholly disappeared."

The sensitive Miss Nowotny had sought a position exactly corresponding to the direction of the needle: she found any other insupportable. Whenever she was placed in any other, her pulse rose, her face flushed with increased flow of blood to her head, and she became restless and uncomfortable. Of all positions, that of having her head to the west was most unbearable, being much worse than that of south-north position. While in that position, her sensations to external things became strikingly changed. The usually agreeable passes of the magnet became unpleasant, and large ones insupportable. Substances, as sulphur, before disagreeable, were almost indifferent; and others, like lead, were agreeable. The results of experiments on eight different subjects were the same. These patients recalled to mind how uncomfortable they always were in church, without understanding the cause. The Catholic churches are all built from west to east, so that they had to take the west-east position, the worst of all for a sensitive, and often fainted from exhaustion.

110. DISEASE AND SLEEP.

Thus it is observed that terrestrial magnetism is appreciable by sensitive persons, modifying sleep, "disturbing the circulation of the blood, the functions of the nerves, and equilibrium of the vital force."

These facts bear strongly on magnetism as applied to the cure of diseases. Processes which will cure if the patient be in one position will only aggravate the disease if in another. They unravel the mystery which has shrouded the domain of mesmerism, and account for failures under seemingly identical circumstances. In one case, the magnetizer has the powerful influence of the earth working with him; in another, against him.

Of the influence of the sun, moon, and planets, we

have all to learn. Undoubtedly, with their light and heat, is emanated the subtile force which is measured only by sensitive nerves. When any substance is exposed to the sunlight for some time, it becomes luminous to the sensitive, and exerts a magnetic influence. This influence is conductible. When the patient, remaining in a dark room, takes hold of a wire passing out into the sunshine, he at once experiences the cooling sensation of magnetism. With the sun's rays, water can be magnetized, a weak magnet strengthened; and, when an individual exposes himself for a brief time in the sunshine, he becomes capable of exerting a strong magnetic influence.

111. INFLUENCE OF THE MOON.

The moon's rays afford the same results; but they seem to have a stronger attractive power, drawing strongly the subject's hand towards the object from which they emanate.

112. INFLUENCE OF THE SUN.

Here is the key to the relation of sunlight to physiology. It is well known that many diseases are aggravated when night approaches, while others are more severe during the day. All varieties of nervous pains are generally more unbearable at day than at night. This fact has been observed, but, by the materialism of modern science, referred summarily to imagination. The silence of the night gave free reign to fancy; and small aches became unbearable. During the day, the half of the earth illuminated is positive to the other illuminated hemisphere; and, when darkness reigns, the transition from one state to the other is as certain as that of the exchange of light and darkness.

The sensations of evening are different from those of morning. We have enjoyed the light, and been positive, during the day. When night advances, we are to sink into its negative embrace. We are to become passive in the enveloping darkness, and enter a state "twin brother to death." At morning we arise from invigorating rest to meet the positive day. It is more restorative to sleep during the night. It is then the subtile magnetic forces are in harmony with that state. Sleep during the day, in the most secluded apartments, is restless and feverish. This distinction is recognized by animals of all species, and by plants. The former, during the presence of the sun, absorb oxygen, and throw off carbonic acid: plants, on the contrary, absorb carbonic acid, and yield oxygen. During the night, the vital powers of the former are reduced to their lowest ebb; and the latter reverse the process of combination, and throw off carbonic acid, and absorb oxygen. Night is no more terrible than day; yet the mind, overcome by the negative condition imposed then on all things, peoples it with fancies. It is the established season for ghosts, especially the hour of midnight. Night, too, is the wakeful season for the author and thinker: they find it more fruitful of original thoughts; for their minds are then passive, and can drink truth through their intuitions. After being in the intense sunlight for a length of time, how agreeable is the shade, or a darkened room! The effects are remarkably intense. In negative diseases, the effect of sunlight is wonderfully beneficial; and, in positive diseases, darkness is equally so. Cataleptic persons, in whom it may be thought the normal condition of the faculties is so vitiated that they are not reliable, are not the only ones affected; but often the nerves of persons in health become susceptible to such delicate influences. The magnetic flames arising from almost all bodies, especially those undergoing chemical change, are by such discernible, and probably the prolific cause of ghost-seeing. It is said that only nervous, and hence unreliable, persons see ghosts: but this is not as strong an objection as has been supposed; for it is possible only for those with a delicately vibrating nervous organization to perceive what is unperceivable to common eyes. As illustrations, a volume of evidence might be compiled.

113. INFLUENCE OF LOCALITY.

"An occurrence which took place in Pfeffel's garden at Colmar is tolerably well known, and has appeared in many published accounts. I will briefly mention some of the most important points. He had appointed a young evangelical clergyman as his amanuensis. The blind German poet was led by this person when he walked out. This occurred in his garden, which lay at some distance from the town. Pfeffel remarked, that, every time they came to a particular spot, Billing's arm trembled, and he manifested uneasiness. Some conversation about this ensued; and the young man unwillingly stated, that, as often as he came over that spot, certain sensations attacked him which he could not overcome, and which he always experienced at places where human bodies were interred. When he came to such places at night, he usually saw strange sights. With a view to cure this man of his delusion, Pfeffel returned with him to the garden the same night. When they approached this place in the dark, Billing at once perceived a weak light, and, when near enough, the appearance of a form of immaterial flame waving in the air above the spot. He described it as resembling a woman's form, one arm laid across the body, the other hanging down, wavering, erect, or at rest; the feet elevated about two hands'-breadths above the ground. Pfeffel walked up to it alone, as the young man would not accompany him; struck about at random with his stick, and ran across the place; but the spectre did not move nor alter. It was as when one passes a stick through flame, — the fiery shape always recovered the same form. Many things were done during several months, parties taken thither; but the matter remained always the same, and the ghost-seer always held to his earnest assertion, consequently to the supposition that some one must lie buried there.

At last, Pfeffel had the place dug up. At some depth, a solid layer of white lime was met with, about as long and as broad as a grave, tolerably thick; and, when this was broken through, they discovered the skeleton of a human body.

"It had been covered with a layer of quick-lime, as is the custom in time of pestilence. The bones were taken out, the hole filled, and the surface leveled. When Billing was again taken there, the appearance was gone, and the nocturnal spirit had vanished forever." — *Dynamics, p.* 142.

114. OF CHURCH-YARD GHOSTS.

When the baron conducted some of his sensitives to a church-yard, they at once recognized a similar appearance over all the graves, especially the more recent ones; and they at once referred them to the same class as that of the magnet or crystal. Although this flame has been a prolific source of ghost-stories, we need not call ghosts to our aid to furnish an explanation. We know that this flame is produced by chemical change. All bodies undergoing change exhibit it. Of course the decomposition occurring in a grave furnishes an abundant source; and, as these gaseous products slowly arise, so will the flame.

It is said truly, that not to all is given the sight which enables them to see the ghosts which hover around church-yards; for all are not sufficiently sensitive: but many are, and are derided as cowardly or fanciful, when the objects they perceive are realities to them, as much as the tombstones are to others. It requires no stretch of fancy to shape the upright, waving, luminous cloud into human form. Educational prejudice, the horror of the place, the dread season of night, generally beget sufficient fear to at once so shape the clouds much more distinctly than those we form into angels and beasts as they float through the sky.

These ghosts are nothing more than the luminous flame produced by the chemical changes always accompanying it; and it can be seen by the sensitive. It is strange that this fact of chemistry should have given rise to the most unbelievable stories of goblins and ghosts, having no more existence than a wisp of flame, or fog-like cloud.

115. THE IMAGE SOMETIMES REMAINS.

Sometimes the image of a thing remains impressed in the place where it has stood. M. Teste, in his journal, cites, with respect to this, a curious experiment. A female somnambulist enters the room, and exclaims, "What a pretty girl is sitting on that chair!" At this exclamation, M. Teste observes to her that she is mistaken; that no pretty girl is there. Far from giving in to this declaration, she sees one on each chair; and there were six of them. Unable to account for this hallucination, he contented himself with gathering exact details of the dress of these little girls, and confessed that a little girl precisely similar had been playing there for a moment before the somnambulist entered, and had jumped upon the six chairs, one after the other, sitting down on them. "I have often recognized that the image of natural objects, set in a certain place, remained there for a long time."

Mrs. Denton, an extremely sensitive person, relates, that, on entering a car from which the passengers had gone to dinner, she was surprised to see the seats all occupied.

"Many of them were sitting perfectly composed, as if, for them, little interest were attached to this station, while others were already in motion (a kind of compressed motion), as if preparing to leave. I thought this somewhat strange, and was about turning to find a vacant seat in another car, when a second glance around showed me that the passengers who had appeared so indifferent were really losing their identity, and, in a moment more, were invisible to me. I had had sufficient time to note the personal appearance of several; and, taking a seat, I awaited the return of the passengers, thinking it more than probable I might in them find the prototypes of the faces and forms I had, a moment before, so singularly beheld. Nor was I disappointed. A number of those who returned to the cars I recognized as being, in every particular, the counterparts of their late but transient representatives."

116. Psychometrical Dream.

The explanation of the following dream may seem incredible; but, after a thorough understanding of the vast generalization we are attempting of mental and physical phenomena, it may cease to appear so.

"Several years ago, during a severe winter, the Schuylkill River, near Philadelphia, became thickly bridged over with ice; and thousands of persons resorted thither for the purpose of skating, sliding, &c. Among other inventions for the amusement of those visiting the place, there was a post sunk through the ice, at the top of which there was a point, and a horizontal revolving arm attached to it. To the end of this, the drag-ropes of sleds were attached; so that, by pushing the shaft, the sleds, with persons on them, might be made to revolve swiftly in a circle upon the ice. Among the rest, a negro got upon the sled; and the person in charge of the shaft caused it to revolve so rapidly that the negro was thrown outward by the centrifugal force, and, striking violently against a large, projecting piece of ice, was killed instantly.

"This occurrence was witnessed by a physician, a friend of my informant, who happened to be present. On that very evening, the physician had occasion to prepare a dose of pills for one of his patients, a lady extremely susceptible to magnetic influences. As he was mixing the ingredients of the pills, and rolling them in his fingers, he related in all its particulars, to persons in the office, the occurrence he had witnessed on the river during the day. The pills were afterwards despatched to the lady by another person. The next day, the physician, seeing one of the lady's family, inquired concerning her health. In the answer that was returned, it was stated, among other things, that she had had a singular dream the night previous. She dreamed that she was somewhere on the ice, where many people were sliding and skating; that she had there seen a negro thrown, from a revolving sled, against a cake of ice, and instantly killed, &c. Her dream, as related, was an exact reproduction of all the essential statements of facts which had, without her knowledge, been given by the physician while he was preparing the medicine, and concerning which facts she had received no information from any quarter."

The physician imparted his influence to the medicine, which, acting on an impressible mind, reproduced his thoughts in the form of a dream.

So the mechanic imparts a portion of himself to his wares; and the various articles of food are impregnated with the spheres of their producers. Dwellings partake of the influence of all those who have once entered them. Garments reproduce the character of their wearers. Dwellings wherein countless persons enter, and the products of various climes are stored, are always pervaded by innumerable influences. These affect all more or less, but only the extremely sensitive in a marked degree. Many who are not susceptible while oppressed by the cares of the day are highly so during the negativeness of night, and the passivity of sleep. These surrounding influences, blending, often re-appear in dreams.

117. INDIVIDUAL SPHERES BLENDING

Produce the distinctive characters of communities and cities. The emanations from the earth,— which Reichenbach terms "odylic,"— which all minerals exhibit, also exert an influence in the determination of the character of the people dwelling on its surface. Sometimes persons feel this subterranean influence keenly, although, in ignorance of its cause, they fail to understand why they are disagreeably or agreeably affected.

118. CONCLUSIONS.

The preceding facts lead to two conclusions,— first, the impressibility of the nervous system, not only of man, but of all animals; second, that emanations capable of exciting influence on the nervous system are thrown off from all organic and inorganic substances.

Granting these, no matter what theory of transmission we receive, that of pulsation, or of simple force, there must exist a bond or medium of communication. A brain in England, to affect a brain in America, must do so through a connecting substance. Admitting the facts of impressibility, the existence of a spirit-ether, universal and all-permeating, becomes self-evident.

VII.

RELATION OF THE SPIRITUAL TO THE ANIMAL IN MAN.

> NOT that I think their sense divinely given,
> Or prescience theirs to mark the will of Heaven:
> But still, through Nature's vast and varied range,
> The airs, vicissitudes, and seasons change;
> New instincts sway; and their inconstant mind
> Shifts with the cloud, and varies with the wind.
> VIRGIL.

Brahma inscribes the destiny of every mortal on his skull; and the gods themselves cannot avert it. — HINDU MAXIMS.

Man is a civilized animal.

119. THE BRAIN.

THE brain is the organ of the mind in animals as well as in man. Its different sections manifest different faculties. The passions reside in its base; the intellect, in its front; and the moral and spiritual, at its summit. Although the mapping of its surface, as practiced by phrenologists, may be regarded as in a great measure visionary, and far from scientific, these great divisions are recognized by all. Animals have the base of the brain as fully developed as man; but in them the frontal portion is defective, and the upper region almost wanting. In savage man, the latter is scarcely more expanded than in the animal. In proportion as the front and coronal portions of the brain expand, man becomes civilized, and removed from the animal world. The manifestation of mind in the animal has been called instinct; in man, intellect; and an impassable gulf is said to exist between the two by those who study the subject in the fog of metaphysics. Anatomy, however, is the umpire, and decides that the difference is in kind, not in degree. Intellect is instinct, modified by the development of faculties before latent. The passions of man, considered purely by themselves, are the same as those of animals. With them, they constitute nearly their whole mentality; with him, a minor part, — the base on which his superior intellectuality rests.

120. INSTINCT.

If the actions of animals are observed, all the faculties which connect man with physical matter can be unerringly traced. Their possession is a necessity. Desire for food, the sexual instinct, love of offspring, gregariousness, the dawn of friendship, constructiveness, exist in all the mammalia. In them, these traits are, as it were, concreted, and are exhibited in their pure, unadulterated form, going straight to their mark, unguided by reason. In man, their office is the same; but they are controlled by superior faculties, which have become active. They are the motive power; but are guided, instead of rushing blindly to their object.

121. REFLECTIONS.

It may pain us to contemplate this connection, by which our immortal nature dips into the stratum of materiality; but it should rather elevate our conception of the harmony and divine order of nature. From this lower stratum, the spirit draws its life; and, how high soever may be its future flight, it will hold to this connection.

Does the noble tree, throwing aloft its branches, swayed by storms, and fanned by zephyrs, despise its roots, winding through rugged ways in the dark recesses of the rocky earth? Does it consider their office an ignoble one? There must be roots before an oak; and those roots are of the dark and material soil. Far above, the flower may fill the air with fragrance, or the mature fruit tempt the passer-by; but they remain steadfastly grasping the material world.

So with the spirit, expanding upward into the light of the divine. Its progress is accretive: it loses nothing. The passions are roots by which it takes hold of the physical world, and is sustained.

122. THE SPIRIT LOSES NOTHING.

As the tree loses not its leaves when it expands its blooms, but profits by them continually, the spirit throws away none of its faculties.

It is a strange philosophy which teaches that spirit does not retain its propensities after the dissolution of the body. It is a theory belonging to the time when the definition of spirit was the best that could be given of nonentity, — without emotion or love, retaining only the susceptibility of enjoyment and suffering.

What is it that sends the Howards, the Nightingales, the Dixes, on their visits of mercy to the suffering and needy? We say it is their benevolence, the warm sympathy they feel towards the sufferers. This is true; but it is also true, that, without decision, firmness, and combative energy, — the forces of the lower brain, — they would not stir from their own comfortable firesides. They would feel deeply for misery; but theirs would be a passive sympathy, never putting itself in action.

The engine may be ever so well constructed in its mechanism; but if water is withheld from the boiler, and fire from the grate, it is useless. I would not be understood as advocating the supremacy of the basal brain. Far from it: I only say that its office is important and necessary, when confined within proper limits. It should never dictate to the spiritual perceptions; but, as the steam of the engine is controlled by the power it itself evokes, so should the energy of the passions be governed. If otherwise, and the motive power be allowed to guide itself, there is explosion, collision, and ruin.

123. No Perversion in Animals.

Concrete and intense as are the basal faculties in animals, they are rarely, if ever, misdirected or perverted. They go straight to their object, and no farther. To provide themselves with food, and care for their offspring, are their ruling motives. They experience none of the insatiable desires which elevate or degrade mankind. They are content, because all the materials which their natures demand are found in their sphere of action.

Their appetites require only materials wherewith to build up their bodies; and these the herbivorous animals find in the grass of the field, and the carnivora in the flesh of the inoffensive herbivora. Their passions are included in the circle of increasing their species, and defending themselves and offspring from danger. The imperfect affections lead them to supply the necessities of their offspring for a short time only, and perhaps give them the gregarious tendencies by which some species are always herded together.

124. The Result.

The result of this combination is perfect selfishness. The care of its selfhood is the perpetual effort of the animal: only when caring for its young, does it, for a moment, depart from its selfishness. If it sees danger, it flies; or, if it thinks itself able, it defends itself: but it never becomes a conqueror. Selfish as it is, throughout the extent of the animal world there is not an Alexander nor Napoleon. Many lay by a winter store; but an Astor or Girard they have not. Their appetites are greedy; but no epicure disgraces their ranks.

125. Perversion — its Cause.

Seeing this, men often allude to it, and hold it up as an example worthy of imitation; but it does not prove the animal anywise superior to the man. The animal, finding all its desires gratified, has no need of violating its constitution. Not so with man. With him, the animal nature becomes the slave of a superior. It is the force by which that superior manifests itself on the material world. Man being far from perfection, his uneducated intellect often mistakes its wants; and, hence, perversions and abuses. The instinctive qualities of the appetites and passions are lost in the blaze of intellect; often in ignorance, a worse guide.

126. Man's Intellectual Nature.

Having considered man in his connection with the inferior world, let us view him under the new aspect bestowed by the addition of the above-named higher attributes. At once, he becomes another being. Here he is joined to the Infinite. Here gleams the light of his immortal nature, and, as we shall show in another place, rests the strong philosophical proof of his immortality. This nature bends every appetite and passion. It is restless, insatiable, striving after the unattainable. We see here glimmerings of an immortal nature, with cravings unsatisfied by the best the physical world can bestow.

127. Desires Insatiate.

The conqueror, the epicure, the drunkard, each seeks, after his own misguided fashion, to answer the demands of his nature. They mistake those demands, and are plunged in mire. The hero marshaling Greece, subjugating Persia, and rushing from the Mediterranean, past Babylon and Tyre, to the confines of India, grasped the sceptre of the world. His immortal aspirations were not appeased by the control of empires, but increased: for it is a law with our desires, if we pervert them, the greater the perversion, the more ardent they become; for we ever give them food of which they cannot partake. The whole realm of the world satisfied not the conqueror. He paused, red-handed, sick-hearted, by the ocean shore. He gazed off at its illimitable space, dimly shadowing his own soul, and wept that there were no more worlds to conquer. The coveted prize turned to dust in his grasp. It was not conquest the soul of Alexander wanted. His combativeness mistook the spirit's desires for infinite perfection for infinite conquest, and drove the mad man on. Napoleon, breathing his regrets to the desert air of St. Helena, is a type of the happiness bestowed by misguided ambition.

Nor does the acquisition of wealth bestow more happiness. Astor's millions made him their slave, as immense wealth always enslaves its possessor. Out of it he received the necessaries of life; and the remainder was a useless toy. Yet he was close in calculation, and strove to increase his millions, dwarfing his mentality in direct proportion as he increased his wealth. He found that there is little happiness in riches: they did not still the cravings of his soul. The drunkard thinks happiness can be obtained by the cup. His love for the pure beverage distilled from heaven mistakes the desire of the spirit, and drinks the distilled poison. That never appeases: the more given, the greater the demand, until the body breaks down under the burden. With all the animal faculties the amount of happiness yielded is very limited, being only sufficient to insure their activity.

The amount of pleasure the epicure enjoys is of a base kind and evanescent quality. So of the others. There is nothing permanent nor enduring in their character. They yield no pleasure after their gratification. They who expect to find happiness from them will be disappointed; for it will be so brief, and so coarse in quality, as not to be worth its cost. The spirit is unsatisfied with these. Immortal and infinite in capabilities, it demands expansion in the spiritual, not physical, realm. The happiness bestowed by them is only sufficient to insure the performance of their appropriate functions, and no more. Not one iota more can be wrung from them. If pressed to yield more, they recoil on their possessor, and either compel him to desist, by the pangs of disease, or, if he persists, by the dissolution of the physical body.

Mentally their gratification yields nought but dissatisfaction; physically, disease and death. Ah! it is a loathsome train that follows their paths. See their bloated forms, their haggard countenances, as they groan beneath the smarting lash of their own misguided passion! Theirs is the way of death,—death that comes to them a ministering angel of mercy, throwing from their immortal spirits the crushing weight of their physical deformities.

128. Moral Aspect.

The animal faculties are not necessarily sinful. Their functions are as holy as those of the intellect. Sin is the result of over-action, misdirection, or unguided activity. (Man's salvation depends on his intellectual and moral faculties, which overlie, and should control, his being.) To effect this desirable end is the chief object of education. In olden times men fled to the wilderness, and secluded themselves in the solitudes of mountains, that, by contemplation and humiliation, they might obtain this mastery of their passions.

They regarded their voice as sinful. We regard their licence as sinful, but their natural functions as right. Blind, and purely selfish, they rush to ruin unless controlled. They are not subdued by allowing them unlimited sway. They cannot burn themselves out; for use permanently increases their power. Give them free rein? As soon open the throttle-valve of a locomotive, and allow the monster to rush along the track without the guiding intelligence of the engineer. They are not the equals of the intellect, and, unrestrained, are always destructive.

129. IN THE IDEAL MAN,

All faculties are so perfectly balanced, that the spirit is free from the strife of untoward desires. This lofty ideal may be seldom attained, amid the cares and perplexities of earthly life, where it comes in rude contact with materiality; but it is possible.

130. THE MANDATE OF CONSCIENCE.

It is not desirable to trample the desires with haughty pride beneath our feet; to fast on a tower, or to lacerate our flesh. Far preferable to say to these terrible forces which hold us to organic existence, "So far as you subserve the maintenance, growth, and development of my spirit, it is well; but trespass not one step farther."

131. THE TEST OF CONDUCT.

Man is a half-civilized animal; and often the genii of his wild nature show their terrible forms, or refuse obedience to the voice of conscience. Is there ever a doubt whither to go; which to allow guidance? Ask which is the highest motive of conduct, and give that the preference.

VIII.

ANIMAL MAGNETISM, — ITS BOUNDARIES, LAWS, AND RELATION TO SPIRIT.

THE occult science, designated by the ancient priests under the name of regenerating fire, is that which, at the present day, is known as animal magnetism, — a science, that, for more than three thousand years, was the peculiar possession of the Indian and Egyptian priesthood, into the knowledge of which Moses was initiated at Heliopolis, when he was educated; and Jesus, among the Essenian priests of Egypt or Judea; and by which these two great reformers, particularly the latter, wrought many of the miracles mentioned in Scripture. — FATHER REBOLD.

132. NECESSITY OF INVESTIGATING THE LAWS OF MAGNETISM.

IT is so common for Spiritualists to refer everything of a psychological character to spiritual influence, that it seems necessary to enlarge on the facts of animal magnetism, or mesmerism. Being similar, and governed by precisely the same laws, the phenomena are intimately blended; and it becomes necessary to study the subject fully to determine what are and what are not of spiritual origin. I have not sought to present a compend of facts, but to give one or more as representing each class.

133. THE NAME.

Dissatisfaction has been repeatedly expressed at the term "animal magnetism;" and "mesmerism," "neurology," "patheism," and "psychodunamy," employed. All of these terms are more objectionable than the first. With proper definition, no confusion can occur by confounding with magnetism (and its simulate phenomena those observed in magnets) living bodies attracting or repelling each other. The adoption of the name of Mesmer has been the means of bringing the subject into disrepute. He knew nothing of the true method of determining truth; and, ecstatic from his discovery, he made such wild conjectures and improbable claims that even the friends of the measure became disgusted. Had he possessed a calm and reflecting mind, his statements would have been quite differently received.

It at once fell into the hands of selfish men, who sold it for money. Mesmer, himself, led in this movement; and, ever since, it has been its fate to be the stock in trade of charlatans and impostors. The early decision of the French Academy has been taken as conclusive; and men capable of investigating it have not been attracted towards an unpopular field. But, aside from Mesmer and his prolific brood of charlatans, there is a truth, which, from most ancient times, has been recognized. Mesmer simply gave his name to facts thoroughly known to the ancients, and grouped them under a wild hypothesis.

134. ANIMAL MAGNETISM AMONG THE ANCIENTS.

To Apollonius of Tyana must be given the palm of mesmerizers. He seems to have been a man of prodigious fascinating power, and was not only famous for curing diseases, and his powers of clairvoyance, but also for foretelling events. While delivering a public lecture at Ephesus, in the midst of a large assembly, he saw the Emperor Domitian being murdered at Rome; and it was proved to the satisfaction of all, that, while the murder was performing, he described every circumstance attending it to the crowd, and announced the very instant in which the tyrant was slain. It is recorded, that, so great was his nervous influence, that "his mere presence, without uttering a single word, was sufficient to quell a popular tumult." As we are thus drawing examples from antiquity, we might mention the narrative recorded in the Holy Writ,— the case of Saul when he entered the woman of Endor's house. She knew not who he was; but, when her spiritual powers were excited, she immediately recognized him. Swedenborg gives a striking illustration of the development of this sense. By its aid, he seemed to become *en rapport* with the spheres.

Once, while dining with a company of friends some miles distant from his own town, he became greatly agitated, arose, walked out, but soon came in composed, and informed the company that there had been a great conflagration in his town; that it had spread nearly to his residence, but had there been extinguished, while within only a single door of his house. This was all true.

Innumerable anecdotes might be related to prove that the mind, when in a peculiar state, receives knowledge of things of which none of the senses can be the channel of communication. I call this a sense. Perhaps "impressibility of the brain" would be a better term; but it is certain this sensibility differs from, and cannot be referred to, any one of the senses.

Animal magnetism was acknowledged in very ancient times. Thus it has been recorded of Pythagoras, who flourished five centuries before Christ, "that his influence over the lower animals was very great. He is said to have tamed a furious bear, prevented an ox from eating beans, and stopped an eagle in its flight."

135. MAN POSSESSES THIS INFLUENCE OVER ANIMALS.

The power of man over the horse is well known. Rarey became famous for his magnetic force, which inspired him with such confidence that he fearlessly met the most vicious animals.

According to Bruce, the African traveler, all the blacks of the kingdom of Sennaar are completely armed against the reptiles of their clime. "They take horned serpents into their hands at all times, put them into their bosoms, and throw them at each other, as children throw apples or balls; during which sport, the serpents are seldom irritated, and, when they do bite, no mischief ensues from the wound. He positively affirms that they sicken the moment they are laid hold of, and are so exhausted by this power as to perish. "I constantly observed, that, however lively the viper was before, upon being seized by these barbarians, he seemed as if he had been taken with sickness and feebleness, frequently shut his eyes, and never turned his mouth towards the arm that held him."

We see the same power in the influence housebreakers possess over the most savage of watch-dogs, and showmen who enter the cage of fierce lions.

136. Animals can influence Man.

This influence may be exerted in an opposite direction; and well-attested anecdotes are extant, showing that man may become fascinated by the lower animals.

A gentleman once walking in his garden accidentally saw the eyes of a rattlesnake; and, by watching it closely, he found to his dismay that he could not withdraw them. The snake appeared to him to swell to an immense size, and in rapid succession assume the most gorgeous colors, rivaling the rainbow in beauty. His senses deserted him, and he grew dizzy, and would have fallen towards the snake, to which he seemed irresistibly drawn, had not his wife, coming up at the moment, thrown her arms around his neck, thereby dispelling the charm, and saving him from destruction.

Two men in Maryland were walking along the road, when one, seeing something by the way, stopped to look at it, while his companion went on.

But the latter, perceiving he did not follow, turned around to know the cause, when he found that his eyes were directed towards a rattlesnake, whose head was raised and eyes glaring at him. Strangely enough, the poor fellow leaned as far as possible towards his snakeship, crying piteously all the time, "He will bite me! he will bite me!"

"Sure enough he will," said his friend, "if you do not move off. What are you standing there for?" Finding him deaf to all his entreaties, he struck the creature down with his cane, and pushed his friend from the spot. The man thus enchanted is stated to have been sick for several hours. But we cannot multiply cases of this description, which are common fireside anecdotes.

137. ANIMALS CAN INFLUENCE EACH OTHER.

Cases of snakes fascinating birds are common.

Prof. Silliman mentions, that, in 1823, he was proceeding in a carriage, with a friend, along the banks of the Hudson River, when he observed a flock of small birds, of different species, flying hither and thither, but never departing from the central point. He found that this point of attraction was a large snake, which lay coiled up, with head erected, eyes brilliant, and incessantly darting its tongue. When disturbed by the carriage, he went into the bushes, while the birds alighted on the branches overhead, probably to await the re-appearance of their deadly enemy.

A man from Pennsylvania, returning from a ride, saw a blackbird flying, in lessening circles, around the head of a rattlesnake, uttering frightful screams all the time. He drove the snake away, and the bird changed its note to a song of rejoicing.

Newman relates an anecdote of a gentleman, who, while traveling by the side of a creek, saw a ground-squirrel running to and fro between a brook and a great tree a few yards distant. The squirrel's hair looked extremely rough, and showed that he was much frightened. Every return was shorter and shorter. The gentleman stood to observe the cause, and soon discovered the head of a rattlesnake pointing directly at the squirrel, through a hole in the great tree, which was hollow. At length the squirrel gave up running, and lay down close by the snake, which opened his mouth, and took in the squirrel's head. The gentleman gave him a cut with the whip, which caused him to draw back his head, when the squirrel, thus liberated, ran quickly to the brook.

Such curious phenomena have long been observed and speculated upon. To extend the list is unnecessary; for almost every one has observed the facts for themselves.

They establish the conclusion that this influence or impressibility is not the result of sympathy or imagination; for it is experienced by animals that cannot be said to have any great degree of either. It is a power possessed by animals as well as by man. Animals influence man; man influences animals; animals influence each other; and man controls man.

138. WHY DO WE THINK OF THOSE WHO ARE THINKING OF US?

How often do we think of those, who, while we know it not, are approaching us! So general is this experience, that it has passed into a proverb.

I find two facts, illustrating this, in the "Univercœlum."

"A clergyman informed me that his mother-in-law, Mrs. P——, residing in Providence, R.I., had a distinct consciousness of the approach of her husband, on his return from sea, although she had no other reason to expect his arrival at the time. This impression commenced several hours before he made his appearance; and she accordingly prepared herself for his reception. She knew the instant he placed his hand upon the door, and had arisen from her seat, and advanced to meet him, before he entered.

"The wife of a clergyman in Maine lately informed me that her father, while lying on his deathbed, had a distinct perception of the approach of his son, who resided in a distant town, though none of the family expected him at the time. When he mentioned that his son was coming, and near the house, they supposed him to be wandering in his thoughts; but, in a few minutes afterwards, the son entered."

The following is taken from the transactions of the French Academy, found in "Newman's Magnetism."

"On the 10th of September, at ten o'clock at night, the commission met at the house of M. Itardt, in order to continue its inquiries upon Carot, their mesmeric subject, who was in the library, where conversation had been carried on with him till half-past seven; at which time, M. Foissac, the magnetizer, who had arrived since Carot, and had waited in the antechamber, separated from the library by two closed doors and a distance of twelve feet, began to magnetize him. Three minutes afterwards, Carot said, 'I think that Foissac is there; for I feel myself oppressed and enfeebled.' At the expiration of eight minutes, he was completely asleep. He was again questioned, and answered us," &c.

Carot did not know that M. Foissac was near, and yet by some means the irresistible influence overcame him.

139. INFLUENCE OF MAN OVER MAN.

It has been an adage from all antiquity, that young people were not so healthy for living with the old. The Hebrews acted on this idea when they procured a young damsel for their old king David, that he might be invigorated by her strength. There is an anecdote extant of an aged female who compelled her servants to retire in the same bed with herself, that she might prolong her life thereby, and carried this horrid vampirism to such an excess, that, her maids all becoming sickly after a time, she could induce none to work for her, and, in consequence, expired.

An eminent physician states a fact pertinent in this connection.

"I was a few years since consulted about a pale, sickly, and thin boy of about five or six years of age. He appeared to have no specific ailment; but there was a slow and remarkable decline of flesh and strength, and of the energy of all the functions, — what his mother very aptly termed 'a gradual blight.' After inquiring into the history of the case, it came out that he had been a very robust and plethoric child up to his third year, when his grandmother, a very aged person, took him to sleep with her; that he soon after lost his good looks, and that he had continued to decline progressively ever since, notwithstanding medical treatment."

The boy was removed to a separate sleeping apartment, and his recovery was very rapid.

A case lately came under my observation, where a consumptive, on the very verge of the grave, expecting to die every hour, and of course too feeble to move, on being magnetized, arose under the influence, and walked about the room; yet, as soon as the invigoration became expended, she was as weak as previously, and, in the course of a few days, expired. She was too near death to recover; and though magnetism might protract life, and cause a momentary excitation, it could not save.

It is from this cause that magnetic practice exhausts the magnetizer; not from his exertion in making passes, but the drain of nervous force.

140. GENERALIZATION. SPIRITUAL ETHER.

Whatever this influence may be, it must pass across greater or less distances to produce the effects observed. It cannot be transmitted across a void: it must have its own means of conduction. What do the facts teach? They all point in one direction, and are susceptible of generalization, as flowing from one common source,—a universal spiritual ether.*

141. THE IMPRESSIBILITY OF THE BRAIN,

Discovered in 1842, by Dr. Buchanan, opened a new field for human thought. To his surpassing powers of research we owe the opening of the portals of a new science, comprising and generalizing all mental sciences. Psychometry is the key by which the mysteries of many of the most occult sciences may be explored. It gives the historian a barque which will conduct him safely down the stream of time, beyond all preserved chronicles, where his tattered manuscript becomes confused in dates, and records imperfectly, and wafts on the psychologist through millions of cycles, down, down to the beginning of life in this world, when desolation and raging ele

---

* For extension of this subject, see Chapter V.

ments made the earth a chaos of contention. It enters into, and supersedes, phrenology. While the latter deals with the external structure, — with the wheel-work and gearing, as it were, — and foretells what the action of the mind will be when the power is applied, the former enters and lays bare the most interior desires and most secret thoughts, and speaks what *is*, not what can be.

If by phrenology we would know the character of a friend, he must be present; but, for this "soul-measurer," only an autograph, a lock of hair, or piece of apparel, is requisite. Thus, not only in our scientific researches, but also in our business relations, it offers us a sure and unwavering guide.

This field, which promises, more than any other, to reward the explorer, is as yet not fully defined. So varied are the conditions to be determined and proven, and so much skill is necessary in instituting experiments, that one may almost be charged with presumption for making the attempt. Mr. Denton, following in the steps of Dr. Buchanan, has extended his experiments over almost every field of research; and so great are the number of the impressible, that the skeptic can easily convince himself of their truth.

142. PSYCHOMETRY APPLIED.

As previously stated, the reading of letters is not its only application. It is a good barque for the historian and antiquarian, carrying them down the stream of time, where the written account becomes confused and contradictory. How interesting would be the true character of Alexander, Cæsar, or Napoleon, obtained in this manner, free from the prejudices of their biographers or their times! The linen which shrouds the Egyptian mummy will yield a good delineation of the character of the class thought worthy to be embalmed. The relics from Herculaneum will give the character of Romans two thousand years ago. The character of those races that scattered mounds and fortifications over the American continent can be determined from their relics.

Nor does susceptibility rest here. It takes the paleontologist by the hand, and leads him down through the carboniferous shales and sandstones, and, by the aid of the smallest organic remain, gives him a perfect description of the world in its various stages of growth and development, describing the dark waters, the smoky atmosphere, and the huge and unique forms which peopled the ancient world. It revels amidst the extinct fauna and flora of the ages, and is the only method by which a correct idea of the aspect of this planet in its infantile state can be gained.

In magnetism, the aura reproduces the magnetizer's thoughts in the magnetized: so the invisible aura of the manuscript reproduces the precise action of the brain by which it was produced, and consequently the same thoughts, more or less distinct in proportion to the impressibility of the psychometrist.

This capability of a manuscript or a lock of hair to yield the character of the writer or owner is analogous to the phosphorescence of bodies exposed to light. When the sun shines on some substances, they will continue to shine for a length of time after the sun has withdrawn. They, as it were, partake of the nature of the sun.

Not that the individual while performing the experiments is magnetized; no trace of this can be discovered: but as it succeeds best with those who are easily influenced, and whose organs of impressibility are large and active, it must be admitted that the mind is influenced in precisely the same manner, though not to the same degree. The two influences are identical in their nature, varying only in quantity. In one, the whole energies of the mind are employed; while, in the other, the influence of a scrap of writing is all that can be used.

This is proved by an impressible person placing his hand upon the head of one whose character he wishes to delineate, and the influence will be felt sooner and with greater intensity than from an autograph. Impressibility is the best delineator. It enters into the depth of the mind, lays bare all its thoughts and emotions, and, from this deep, penetrating gaze, understands *Man*. It recognizes the mind itself, and hence can better give the methods of its just control.

As spiritual susceptibility increases, the influences

of the stars will be recognized; and from the emanations of light, leaving their twinkling orbs millions of ages ago, their history and composition will be determined.

143. Likes and Dislikes.

Impressibility may become so intense as to be very annoying. The spirit is constantly bruised by conflicting emanations. So great sometimes are the shocks thus received as to lead to disastrous results. Our likes and dislikes of persons, places, or objects, for which we can assign no reason, may be thus accounted for.

"In the town of North Walsham, Norfolk, 1788, the 'Fair Penitent' was performed. In the last act, when Caliste lays her hand on the skull, a Mrs. Berry, who played the part, was seized with an involuntary shuddering, and fell on the stage. During the night, her illness continued; but the following day, when sufficiently recovered to converse, she sent for the stage-keeper, and anxiously inquired where he procured the skull. He replied from the sexton, who informed him it was the skull of one Norris, a player, who, twelve years before, was buried in the graveyard. That same Norris was her first husband. She died in six weeks."

She was highly susceptible, and the shock produced by the influence from the skull, recognized by her to be so like that of her former husband, was too great for her to bear.

144. APPLICATION TO FORTUNE-TELLING.

Fortune-telling is an application of psychometry. It is easy for an impressible person to take another's hand, and narrate the events of their past lives. In this, fortune-tellers generally succeed. If highly impressible, they may receive intuitions of the future. There are many remarkable instances on record of persons who at once read the past lives of those with whom they come in contact, among whom the celebrated German author, Zschokke, is perhaps most conspicuous. He writes of himself as follows:—

"'What demon inspires you? Must I again believe in possession?' exclaimed the spiritual Johann Von Riga, when, after the first hour of his acquaintance, I related his past life to him, with the avowed object of learning whether or not I deceived myself. We speculated long on the enigma; but even his penetration could not solve it. Not another word about this strange seer gift, which I can aver was of no use to me in a single instance; which manifested itself occasionally only, and quite independently of my volition, and often in relation to persons in whose history I took not the slightest interest. Nor am I the only one in possession of this faculty. In a journey, I met an old Tyrolese. He fixed his eyes on me for some time, joined in the conversation, observed, that, though I did not know him, he knew me, and began to describe my acts and deeds, to the no little amazement of the peasants, and astonishment of my children, whom it interested to learn that another possessed the same gift as their father.

"I myself had less confidence than any one in this mental jugglery. So often as I revealed my visionary gifts to any new person, I regularly expected to hear the answer, 'It was not so!' I felt a secret shudder when my auditors replied that it was true, or when their astonishment betrayed my accuracy before they spoke. Instead of many, I will mention one example, which pre-eminently astounded me. One fair day, in the city of Waldshut, I entered an inn (The Vine) in company with two young student-foresters. We were tired of rambling through the woods. We supped, with a numerous company, at the *table d'hôte*, where the guests were making very merry with the peculiarities and eccentricities of the Swiss, with Mesmer's magnetism, Lavater's physiognomy, &c., &c. One of my companions, whose national pride was wounded by their mockery, begged me to make some reply, particularly to a handsome young man who sat opposite to us, and who had allowed himself extraordinary license. This man's former life was presented to my mind. I turned to him, and asked him whether he would answer me candidly if I related to him some of the most secret passages of his life, I knowing as little of him, personally, as he did of me. That would be going a little farther, I thought, than Lavater did with physiognomy. He promised, if I were correct in my information, to admit it frankly.

I then related what my vision had shown me, and the whole company were made acquainted with the private history of the young merchant, — his school years, his youthful errors, and, lastly, with a fault committed in reference to the strong-box of his principal. I described to him the uninhabited room, with whitened walls, where, to the right of the brown door, on a table, stood a black money-box, &c.

"A silence prevailed during the whole narration, which I alone occasionally interrupted by inquiring whether I spoke the truth. The startled young man confirmed every particular, and even, what I scarcely expected, the last circumstance. Touched by his candor, I shook hands with him over the table, and disclosed no more. He asked my name, which I gave him; and we remained together, talking, till past midnight."

145. ANIMAL MAGNETISM AS A CURATIVE AGENT.

Magnetism has been from earliest ages, and among all races, employed in the cure of disease. "The practice of rubbing or pressing or squeezing the limbs of a person suffering under pain or weariness is carried to a great extent in India. Even among the lower orders, the wife may often be seen employed in this soothing avocation, to the great relief of her fatigued husband. Females practice it professionally in most of the principal bazaars; and there are but few men or women of rank or opulence who are not subjected to the operation before they can procure sleep. Such is the fact. The mind of the operator is mesmerically fixed on the body of the patient, with the hope and view of removing pain ; and, by a series of the most powerful and continued grasping of the hands (used as indices to the will), this object is ultimately accomplished."

The cure which I shall now relate could not in any conceivable manner, nor with any candor, be attributed to the effects of imagination. It can only be explained by the action of mesmerism.

"The wife of one of my grooms, a robust woman, the mother of a large family of young infants, all living within my grounds, was bitten by a poisonous serpent, most probably by a cobra or *coluber naja*, and quickly felt the deadly effects of its venom. When the woman's powers were rapidly sinking, the servants came to my wife, to request that the civil surgeon of the station (Bareilly in Rohilcund), Dr. Grimes, might be called to save her life. He immediately attended, and most readily exerted his utmost skill ; but in vain. In the usual time, the woman appeared to be lifeless ; and he therefore left, acknowledging that he could not be of any further service.

"On his reaching my bungalow, some of my servants stated, that, in the neighborhood, a fakir, or wandering medicant, resided who could charm away the bites of snakes, and begged, if the doctor had no objection, that they might be permitted to send for him. He answered, 'Yes, of course : if the people would feel any consolation by his coming, they could bring him; but the woman is dead.' After a considerable lapse of time, the magician arrived, and commenced his magical incantations.

"I was not present at the scene: but it occurred in my park, and within a couple of hundred yards of my bungalow; and I am quite confident that any attempt to employ medicines would have been quite useless, as the woman's powers were utterly exhausted, although her body was still warm. The fakir sat down at her side, and began to wave his arm over her body, at the same time uttering a charm; and he continued this process until she awoke from her insensibility, which was within a quarter of an hour."

146. USE OF PRAYER.

Many miraculous cures are recorded, seemingly granted to the voice of fervent prayer. The explanation of such cures requires no miraculous interposition. A person actuated by blind faith, by prayer, concentrates his mind to a degree it is possible for him to do by no other method. His magnetic power is intensified, and directed on the patient. In this manner, prayer becomes a magnetic process; and the cure follows necessarily, not from any foreign interposition, but as an effect of an adequate cause. By thus accounting for the benefit sometimes derived from prayer, I by no means would be understood as referring all so-called miracles to that cause. Superstition, credulity, and design, have their full share in their production.

147. MAGNETIC HEALING AMONG SAVAGES.

This magnetic power is not unknown even to savage people; and they have, although ignorant of the law, complied with the essential conditions of magnetic induction. Thus the Indians of Oregon produce the trance by songs, incantations, and passes of the hand. The Dakotahs made the same manipulations; and, at a given moment, the novice was struck on the breast lightly, when he "would fall prostrate on his face, his muscles rigid, and quivering in every fibre."

The trance thus induced was lightly clairvoyant. Capt. Carver says that a medicine-man correctly prophecied the arrival of a canoe-load of provisions to his starving tribe. Such was the faith reposed in his prevision, that, at the appointed time, the village assembled to welcome the canoe, which arrived exactly at the mentioned hour.

The magnetic process of cure resembles the transfusion of blood from healthy veins to those which are exhausted. New life and vigor is transferred by means of nervous influence. The same may be said of spirit magnetism. transfused through mediumistic influence.

148. THE APPLICATION TO SPIRIT-COMMUNION.

A spirit, when controlling a medium, is governed by the same laws as the mortal magnetizer. It is for this reason that the resulting phenomena are mixed; and it becomes difficult to distinguish, in partially developed mediums, between the magnetism of the circle and that of the spirit attempting control. The utmost caution is requisite to prevent self-deception. If the medium is in the peculiar susceptible condition usual to the early stage of development, he will simply *reflect* the mind of the circle; and what purports to be a spiritual communication will be only an echo of their own minds.

The state which renders the medium passive to a spirit renders him passive to mortal influence in the same degree; and, from the similarity of all magnetic influences, it is difficult to distinguish spirit from mortal. Circles often, in this manner, deceive themselves by their own positiveness. They repel the approach of celestial messengers, and substitute the echoes of their own thoughts. They find contradiction and confusion, which they complacently refer to "evil spirits." Tread lightly and carefully this path, O lover of truth! for many are the by-ways of error.

Nothing can be gained to the cause of truth by misstatement, or exaggerating the importance of one fact to the detriment of another. Honest investigators of Spiritualism, coming to the task without previous knowledge of animal magnetism, refer every phenomenon they meet to spiritual agency, when it is probable that at least one-half of all they observe is of a purely mundane source. So far as healing by laying-on of hands is concerned, it has been shown to be of ancient date, and explainable by organic laws. There is no reason why a magnetizer should not cure disease, and relieve pain, as well as a disembodied spirit; and the probabilities of success are in his favor. If a spirit perform such cures, it is unquestionably by and through the same means.

All that we said at the commencement of this chapter, in regard to the selfish charlatanism of magnetizers, is equally true of spirit-healing. Good, true, and honest men there are whose nervous systems are strengthened by invisible friends to relieve suffering; but Spiritualism is brought to the very dust by the actions of others. The worst forms of empiricism, quackery, and humbug, are loudly advertised and extolled in its sacred name. The foul brood that were fostered in the field of animal magnetism almost bodily adopted the new and more startling system. They have brought shame to the hearts of true Spiritualists.

149. LET US NOT BE MISUNDERSTOOD.

Our object is to draw a sharp line between phenomena really of spirit-origin, and those referable to mortal action. We may possibly discard a half or two-thirds of all manifestations alleged to be spiritual; but the remainder will be all the more valuable. A cause is not strengthened by a mountain of irrelevant facts, but, rather, weakened. The refutation of a few of these is oft-times taken for the overthrow of all.

150. A Safe Rule

Is to refer nothing to spirits which can be accounted for by mortal means. Thus sifted, those that remain are of real value to the skeptic and the investigator.

Man in the body is a spirit as well as when freed from it. As a spirit, he is amenable to the same laws. The magnetic state may be self-induced, or inducted by a mortal or a spirit magnetizer. This is true of all its manipulations, whether in somnambulism, trance, or clairvoyance.

Fully recognizing this fact, it will be seen how exceedingly liable the observer is to mistake these influences.

When a circle is formed, and one of its members is affected by nervous spasms, it does not necessarily follow that such member is spiritually controlled. That cannot be certainly predicted until a spirit has identified its control. It is only by thus testing the phenomena, that a sound and accurate knowledge of spiritual laws can be gained. It may please the marvelous to refer to one source all manifestations, from the involuntary contraction of a muscle, the removing of pain by laying-on of hands, the incoherencies of a sensitive entranced by the overpowering influence of the circle, to the genuine impressions of spiritual beings; but it will not satisfy the demands of science, which ultimately will seek to co-ordinate all facts and phenomena.

IX.

SPIRIT — ITS PHENOMENA AND LAWS.

THE ethereal regions are like a populous city, filled with immortal spirits, as numerous as stars in the firmament. — PHILO.

Shall we know our friends again? For my own part, I cannot doubt it; least of all when I drop a tear over their recent dust. Death does not separate us from them here: can life in heaven do it? — THEODORE PARKER.

When a man is dead, the flesh and the bones are left to be consumed by the flames; but the soul flies away like a dream. — SHADE OF ANTICLEA.

151. NECESSITY OF IMMORTALITY.

WHO, when the great thinkers of earth perish, can but exclaim with Goethe, when his friend Wieland died, "The destruction of such high powers is something which can never, under any circumstances, come in question"?

> "Who builds on less than man's immortal base,
> Fond as he seems, condemns his joys to death."

An old author observes, "The very nerve and sinew of religion is hope of immortality." It enters into the fountain from which flow the great and exalted deeds of patriots, martyrs, thinkers, and saints. It elevates above the shadows of mortal life, showing that there is nothing real except in the eternal, and that the gratifications of the delights and passions of the present life are unworthy of an immortal being. This belief at once lifts the soul out of the slough of selfishness, and directs it to magnanimity and virtue. The various religious systems of the world, while based on, and seeking to unfold, this grand idea, offer little consolation to the reflecting mind. They yield no broad, universal philosophy in which we can feel secure, absolutely know that we shall exist in the beyond, and breathe the power and beatitudes of that existence. This is not written in disparagement of any of the countless religious sects. They are not useless in the economy of progress; but they have most signally failed in producing a philosophical and consistent system of immortal life. They all set out with the mistaken idea that heaven is to be gained by belief in certain creeds, and the admission of certain dogmas; whereas, if man is immortal, immortality is conferred on him as the highest aim of creative energy, admitting of no mistakes. His spiritual state must surpass his mortal, which is its prototype; extending, and carrying on to consummation, the outline sketched in mortal life. We exist — how or why, we cannot determine; and we can no more blot out our existence than that of the stars of heaven. What is the logical deduction from this fact? That the emotions, affections, and culture of this existence cannot be lost. The least fraction of our existence cannot be eliminated or destroyed.

152. Eternal Progress of Spirit.

What follows? That the imperfect attempts of this life will be perfected in the next, which is the reality of which this is only the shadow. Whether we die drawing our first living breath, or after a full century, has not the least weight in final growth and development of the spirit. Eternal progress is written in the constitution of nature; and man, as a spirit, embodies every law of progress. Whether as a spirit clad in flesh, or as a spirit in the angel realm, he is amenable to the same laws, and by precisely similar methods.

153. Failure of Religious Theories.

It is here that the theories of sects utterly **fail**, and the reflecting mind pauses in doubt. They fail because they do not grasp the wants of the human soul, that rebels against the doctrine of reward and punishment, asking, Why not live on, working out, each for himself, his own individual destiny? It feels a sense of deep injustice, of gigantic, blundering mistake, in any other idea of its future.

154. Does Spiritualism meet this Demand?

We can only determine after a close and careful investigation of its facts and philosophy. This research must not be in the subdued light of a cringing fear of the supernatural and miraculous, but guided by the unimpeachable evidence of positive knowledge.

We are deeply conscious of our pretensions when we set at defiance the high authorities of the schools, and not only affirm the inter-communion of the spheres, but attempt the reduction of the entire domain of ghosts, witches, demons, familiar spirits, prophecy, — in short, the spiritual realm, — to the supremacy of law, and assert over its conflicting elements the most austere positivism. The sciences concentrate here; and all are hewn columns and arches in the spiritual temple, whose foundations rest on the hard, elemental basis of the material world, and whose towers pierce the blue empyrean of heaven.

155. WHAT IS SPIRIT?

Ages before the shepherd kings laid the foundations of the pyramids, or strove to express their innate ideas of the immortal in sphinx and temple, man asked, "What is spirit?" This question has perplexed philosophers in all ages; and, the greater their acumen, the more widely have they deserted the path of truth, and consigned themselves to the bewildering maze of speculation; and, to-day, the churches representing the concrete Spiritualism of the past can give no satisfactory answer.

Spirit, according to the lexicon, is "the intelligent, immaterial, immortal nature of man." Can intelligence exist without materiality? Can nothing think, feel, reflect? You might as well talk of music existing in the air, after the destruction of the instrument which gave it birth, as of a thought standing out disrobed of matter. Matter, according to this definition, is that which is cognizable by form, color, extension, to the senses: spirit, used in contradistinction, is the opposite. It has no extension, and is not cognizable by the senses. Can a better definition be given of nonentity?

If there are spiritual beings, the fact of their existence proves that they are composed of matter; for an effect cannot spring from nothing. If intelligence could exist "detached," that existence could never be made manifest. Through and by matter only can any effect occur.

156. SPIRITUAL BEINGS, — OF WHAT COMPOSED.

The material of which such beings are composed we may not understand. It is different from the matter with which we are acquainted. The fault rests with us; for it is impossible to comprehend that of which we have neither experience nor name. The speculations of a caterpillar on its butterfly state would be as pertinent. Feeding on acrid leaves, and, perhaps, never leaving the branches which yield it support, how can it comprehend the nectar of flowers, and coursing over the plains with the winds? O man! the glory of the immortal as vastly transcends the mortal! Await, groveling worm! wind a cocoon around you, and the sun in the genial spring will resurrect you a winged spirit of the air. Await, O man, the hour that enshrouds your mortal body; and the warmth of angel-love will awake you to spirit-life.

157. What is the Origin of Spirit?

Theologians inform us that it is from God, and, at death, returns to God who gave it. This solution presupposes the eternal existence of spirits, that they exist ready made, awaiting bodies to be developed that they may inhabit them; and that therefore the earth-life is a probationary state. The history of this theory would be extremely interesting, for it is woven through the tissue of received theology; but, in its beginning, we should find it a myth, early taking root in the childish minds of primitive men. From a conjecture, it has become a dogma. It ignores the rule of law, and makes the birth of every individual a direct miracle.

158. Pre-existence.

Where and how does the spirit exist before entering the particular human body from which it ascends to heaven, or descends to hell, granting the foregoing view? A school of philosophers have solved the question by supposing that it passes through successive organisms countless times. This is a very old idea, and is received at present in almost its original form, as advocated by the Pythagorean and Platonic schools, by many Spiritualists. There are those who think they can distinctly recollect passages in their previous existence; who honestly believe that they remember when they animated various animals. It was so in ancient time.

> "Some draught of Lethe doth await,
> As old mythologies relate,
> The slipping through from state to state."

But memory is not always silenced. Sometimes the potent draught is not sufficiently powerful; and then we decipher the mystic lines of some of our previous states:—

> "And ever something is or seems,
> That touches us with mystic gleams,
> Like glimpses of forgotten dreams."

Plato regarded this life as only a recognized moment between two eternities, the past and the future. Innate ideas and the sentiment of pre-existence prove our past. To Plato, representative as he was of the highest attainments of ancient thought, such might be satisfactory evidence; but to us, with the knowledge we possess of physiology and of the brain, they are of no value. The double structure and double action of the brain, by which impressions are simultaneously produced on the mind, fully explain the sentiment of pre-existence. For if these impressions, by any means, are not simultaneously produced, the mind becomes confused, and the weakest impression is referred to the past.*

Beautiful as these dreams appear, we are brought back from their contemplation to the less pleasing, stern, and rugged highlands of science, where, though fewer flowers bloom beneath our feet, the ground is firmer, and our possessions more sure. These dreams are beautiful; but they are only dreams, undefined actions of the mind, whereby it embodies its fancies, and mistakes them for realities. They are as valuable as the vagaries produced by opium or hasheesh, and no more. We vainly ask, "Why do we lose consciousness of our states? Is our earth-life a dream-life? Can we never know the actual?"

The indelibility of ideas and impressions held by mental philosophers is a strong argument against pre-existence, and it really has no scientific support. (§ 182.) It is a pleasing speculation, but necessitates a miracle at the birth of every human being. A detached spirit, though a germ, becomes clad with flesh. There is no fixed order or conceivable law by which such an event could occur. This mortal state is not preferable; for the spirit constantly desires to escape it. Is it forced by God to undergo this metempsychosis? Does it do so from choice? In such event, the growth of man becomes entirely different from that of animals; but we know that he is subject to the same laws as they are.

* See Prof. Draper's "Physiology," where this point is ably discussed; also his "Intellectual Development of Europe."

Or shall we say that they, too, are flesh-clad spirits? Grant this, and we are lost in an ocean of myth. From the animalcule, with its body formed of a single cell, to the barnacle-clad leviathan; from entozoa to the elephant,—all are incarnate spirits. There then is no law of development, no unity of organic forms; or else on this progressive growth and unity a new and extraneous force is exerted, without use or purpose. Creation becomes an ever-present miracle; or, if we refer this scheme to fixed laws in the spiritual realm, we but transpose the causes we see acting in the physical world into the spiritual, when they are at once beyond our recognition.

The individualized man stands before us. He, as a mortal being, had a beginning. We date that by years at his birth. What reason have we for not dating the origin of his spirit at his birth also? If man exists for the purpose of the evolution of an immortal spirit, the contemporary birth and development of body and spirit is a self-evident truth.

159. Man is a Dual Structure of Spirit and Body.

The physical body, by its senses, is brought in contact with the physical world. It is the basis on which the spiritual rests. Though the spiritual body pertain to the spiritual universe, yet the most intimate relations exist between these two natures:

earthly existence depends on their harmony, and death is simply their separation.

Such is the doctrine of the Bible; and it was so interpreted by the holy fathers. Paul, that profound thinker, speaks as follows, in words identical with those of modern Spiritualism:—

"Some men will say, How are the dead raised, and with what bodies do they come? God giveth a body, as pleaseth him. So also is the resurrection of the dead. It is sown in corruption: it is raised in incorruption. It is sown in dishonor: it is raised in glory. It is sown in weakness: it is raised in power. It is sown a natural body: it is raised a spiritual body."

St. Augustine interpreted this doctrine by an anecdote.

"Our brother, Sennardius, well known to us all as an eminent physician, and whom we especially love, who is now at Carthage, after having distinguished himself at Rome, and with whose active piety and benevolence you are well acquainted, could not nevertheless, as he related to us, bring himself to believe in life after death. One night there appeared to him, in a dream, a radiant youth of noble aspect, who bade him follow him; and, as Sennardius obeyed, they came to a city, where, on the right, he heard a chorus of most heavenly voices. As he desired to know whence this heavenly harmony proceeded, the youth told him that what he heard were songs of the blessed; whereupon he awoke, and thought no more of his dream than people usually do. On another night, the youth appears to him again, and asks him if he knows him; and Sennardius told him all the particulars of his dream, which he well remembered. 'Then,' said the youth, 'was it while sleeping or waking you saw these things?'—'I was sleeping,' answered Sennardius. 'You are right,' replied the youth: 'it was in your sleep that you saw these things; and know, O Sennardius, that what you see now is also in your sleep. But, if this be so, tell me then where is your body?'—'In my bed-chamber,' answered Sennardius. 'But know you not,' continued the youth, 'that your eyes, which form a part of your body, are closed and inactive?'—'I know it,' answered he. 'Then,' said the youth, 'with what eyes see you these things?' And Sennardius could not answer him; and, as he hesitated, the youth spoke again, and explained the motive of his question. 'As the eyes of your body,' said he, 'which lies now in bed, and sleeps, are inactive and useless, and yet you have eyes wherewith you see me and those things which I have shown you, so, after death, when these bodily organs fail you, you will have a vital power whereby you will live, and a sensitive faculty whereby you will perceive. Doubt therefore, no longer, that there is life after death.'" *

This episode illustrates a great truth. Man is dual,—a spirit and a body blended into a unit: the body relating to the external world by the senses; the spirit taking cognizance of the spiritual world

* See "Arcana of Nature," vol. ii.

through its spiritual perceptions. The spirit is the companion of the body; and, as long as the two remain united, it perceives the relation of the external world through and by the aid of the corporeal senses. So much is the spirit concealed by the physical body, so intimately are they blended, that it is with difficulty its existence is perceived.*

160. THE SPIRIT RETAINS THE FACULTIES IT POSSESSED WHILE ON EARTH.

Plutarch well observes, in the strict spirit of inductive philosophy, that, if demons and protecting spirits are disembodied souls, we ought not to doubt that those spirits inhabiting the body will possess the same faculties *they* now enjoy, since we have no reason to suppose that any new faculties are conferred at the period of dissolution: such faculties must be considered as inherent, though obscured or latent. The sun does not for the first time shine when it breaks from behind a cloud; so the spirit, when it first throws aside the body, does not then acquire the faculties which are supposed to characterize it, but they are then only freed from the obscurations of the mortal state, as the sun is from the fetters of the cloud.

* The threefold division of body, soul, and spirit, is of very ancient date. Philo represents man as a threefold being, having a rational soul, an animal soul, and a body. As the term "soul" represents nothing but a fancy, it is here discarded.

The physical body evolves the spiritual being. In individualized spirit, creative nature culminates. Individualization of spirit can take place in no other manner. The most exalted angel once was clothed in flesh; and through the flesh only can such existence be obtained.

161. Is there Positive Evidence?

Are there facts to prove these statements that are so dear to the heart? Can it be proved that the spirit exists freed from the physical body? Aside from the facts of spirit-intercourse, the question can be answered by the phenomena presented while the spirit is confined to the body. Spirit-communion is the great and all-conclusive proof; but there is a border-land, over which we can journey to that *ultima thule* of psychological philosophy.

162. The Field almost Unexplored.

In this vast and untrodden domain, we tread the boundaries between materiality and spirituality. We gain glimpses, as it were, of the energy of the refined principles which actuate and vivify the world, and yet remain unseen and unknown. Here we reach the borders of the forces which control materiality, and as yet are not understood.

Science has recorded scarcely a fact to assist the explorer. Scientists scoff and sneer at those who rise above the husks of their technicalities. What can they teach? Nothing. They are content with empiricisms. *They* attempt a solution of spiritual relations! *they* deny their existence! They fail in the solution of much less difficult problems. Why opium or tobacco or alcohol produce their several effects; why certain sounds are agreeable, and others disagreeable; why certain forms are pleasing, and others the reverse,—they know not; and so intent are they with making accurate record of the facts, that they overlook the object for which these facts stand.

163. BETWEEN WAKEFULNESS, AND THE DEEP UNCONSCIOUSNESS PRECEDING DEATH, THERE IS A GRADUAL TRANSITION.

The interval has been divided by authors into stages or degrees; but in an arbitrary manner, and without subserving any end, except to confuse the minds of their readers. There are no lines of demarcation between the various hypothetical divisions; and there is no need of any in pursuing investigation. The magnetic state, as manifested in sleep, becomes somnambulism, or deepens into clairvoyance. The phenomena presented by these states or degrees are resultants of one common law, and are intricately blended.

164. THE MAGNETIC STATE,

In its approach, may perchance be confounded with natural sleep. The spirit is dormant and unconscious.

When it deepens, the mind awakens in a new, spiritual life: its faculties become exalted, and its sensitiveness intensified. A distinguished writer lucidly describes this state.

"Sometimes, however, there is said to supervene a coma; at others, exaltation, depression, or some anomalous modification of sensibility; and occasionally a state somewhat approaching to that of revery, wherein the individual, although conscious, feels incapable of independent exertion, and spell-bound, as it were, to a particular train of thought or feeling. The occurrence of muscular action, and of muscular rigidity, is described as taking place in some instances to a greater or less extent. These results are said to constitute the simpler phenomena of mesmerism. We shall illustrate them by some extracts from accredited writers upon the subject.

"In this peculiar state of sleep, the surface of the body is sometimes acutely sensitive; but more frequently the sense of feeling is absolutely annihilated. The jaws are firmly locked, and resist every effort to wrench them open; the joints are often rigid, and the limbs inflexible; and not only is the sense of feeling, but the senses of smell, hearing, and sight also, are so deadened to all external impressions, that no pungent odor, loud report, or glare of light, can excite them in the least degree. The body may be pinched, pricked, lacerated, or burned; fumes of concentrated liquid ammonia may be passed up the nostrils; the loudest reports suddenly made close to the ear; dazzling and intense light may be thrown upon the pupil of the eye: yet so profound is the physical state of lethargy that the sleeper will remain undisturbed, and insensible to tortures that in the waking state would be intolerable."

165. Testimony of Iamblichus.

Iamblichus, a philosopher of the Alexandrian school, thus describes the state that philosophers, by the practice of theurgy, could arrive at; showing a perfect understanding of what is now called the superior or magnetic state. "The senses were in a sleeping state. The theurgist had no command of his faculties, no consciousness of what he said or did. He was insensible to fire or any bodily injury. Carried by a divine impulse, he went through impassable places without knowing where he was. A divine illumination took full possession of the man; absorbed all his faculties, motions, and senses,— making him speak what he did not understand, or rather seem to speak it; for he was, in fact, merely the minister or instrument of the gods who possessed him." A more correct description of the interior state cannot be found in any work on that subject.

166. Tertullian

Describes one of the inspired sisters of the Montanists, a sect of the second century believing in the direct inspiration of the Holy Spirit.

"There is a sister among us endued with the gift

of revelation by an ecstacy of spirit, which she suffers in church during the time of divine service. She converses with angels, and sometimes also with the Lord. She sees and hears mysteries, knows the hearts of some, and prescribes medicines for those who need them."

167. INSENSIBILITY OF THE MAGNETIC STATE.

The senses in the magnetic state are more profoundly insensible than in sleep. It has, in consequence, often been employed to alleviate pain; and unconsciously it is employed by every nurse and physician. Facts are here introduced, more for the purpose of illustration than proof, though they serve both purposes. Those first produced have a particular significance, as they relate to patients who did not understand the manipulations, — patients severed, by race and speech, from the distinguished physician who relates them.

168. EXPERIMENTS IN INDIA BY ESDAILLE.

His first experiment was made on Madhab Kanra, who was suffering intensely from a severe surgical operation. In three-quarters of an hour, after he began making passes over him, he exclaimed, "I was his father, and his mother had given him life again." "The same process was persevered in; and in about an hour he began to gape, said he must sleep, that his senses were gone, and his replies became incoherent. He opened his eyes when ordered, but said he only saw smoke, and could distinguished no one. His eyes were quite lustreless; and the lids opened heavily. All appearance of pain now disappeared; his hands were crossed on his breast, instead of being pressed on the groins; and his countenance showed the most perfect repose. He now took no notice of our questions; and I called loudly on him by name without attracting any notice.

"I now pinched him without disturbing him; and then, asking for a pin in English, I desired my assistant to watch him narrowly, and drove it into the small of his back. It produced no effect whatever; and my assistant repeated it at intervals in different places as uselessly.

"Fire was then applied to his knee, without his shrinking in the least; and liquid ammonia, that brought tears into our eyes in a moment, was inhaled some minutes without causing an eyelid to quiver. This seemed to have revived him a little, as he moved his head shortly afterward; and I asked him if he wanted to drink. He only gaped in reply; and I took the opportunity to give, slowly, a mixture of ammonia so strong that I could not bear to taste it. This he drank like milk, and gaped for more. As the '*experimentum crucis*,' I lifted his head, and placed his face, which was directed to the ceiling all this time, in front of a full light, opened his eyes, one after the other, but without producing any effect upon the iris. His eyes were exactly like an amaurotic person's; and all noticed their lack-lustre appearance. We were all now convinced that total insensibility of all the senses existed."

This experiment is interesting; for it shows that the magnetic state can be produced without mental sympathy; that the consent of the parties is not necessary; and hence that the result depends on purely physiological causes — a conclusion justified by the influence animals exert over each other, as serpents charming birds, &c.

It furnishes another interesting reflection. The same effects are produced in India as among ourselves: latitude and climate have not the slightest influence.

169. MAGNETIC PRACTICE MAY OR MAY NOT EXHAUST THE OPERATOR.

After operating on patients, the magnetizer may or may not feel exhausted, depending on his magnetic endurance; but the most enduring will, after a continuous exercise in treating disease, become depressed, and temporarily weaken in his power. If the patient be very susceptible, and the operator the reverse, he will be able to induce important results without any effect on himself. If, on the contrary, he be impressible, he will suffer from exhaustion. This will be still greater if he treat a disease under which he is himself suffering. If scrofulous, and he treat a case of that kind, he will surely aggravate his own malady: no degree of positiveness can avail against this danger. Every successive operation renders him more susceptible, and liable to imbibe the disease of his patient: in other words, he loses his resisting power.

To produce the most striking and beneficial results, the operator should be in vigorous health, and in a highly positive state. After operating, the influence should be thrown off, by bathing the hands, and exercise in the open air. Those who are suffering from disease should never attempt to heal others by magnetism.

170. Objects can be Magnetized.

Deleuze first pronounced the fact that objects can be magnetically charged, and that, when sent to distant patients, they will produce the same effect as though the operator were present. This has given rise to repeated charges that it was mere imagination; but it is, rather, a beautiful illustration of the law of magnetic transfer. Some substances absorb and retain this magnetism better than others; and there is a wonderful correspondence between the mental and physical worlds, by which every emotion, passion, and faculty of the mind has its analogue in the material world. This analogy produces the strange and seemingly freakish regard we have for different substances. The precious stones, noble metals, amulets, &c., assume scientific relations; for they represent certain faculties. Silver, gold, diamonds, and flowers are admired because of the fundamental relations they sustain to the sympathies of the brain.

171. Somnambulism.

The mind of the sleep-walker is in a highly sensitive condition, being able to read the thoughts of others, however distant; reading writing or print placed behind his head, and performing the most difficult feats of clairvoyants or magnetized subjects.

In this state, the spirit becomes in a measure independent of its corporeal form, and infinitely expanded. The senses are no longer windows of the soul; but the mind sees and hears by some entirely new method, and becomes *en rapport* with the mental atmosphere of the world.

The following facts are related by the philosopher Fishbough:—

"When a boy, residing in Easton, Pa., we for a time roomed with a young man who was much subject to fits of somnambulism. On one occasion, he was suddenly aroused to a consciousness of his situation, and, as he informed us, for a moment, before he was restored entirely to his natural state, it was as 'light as day,' and he could see minute objects with the utmost distinctness, though a moment afterwards he was obliged to grope his way in darkness to find his bed."

Sunderland, in "Patheism," records a case of a Mr. Collins, of East Bloomfield, N. Y., "who, while asleep, would often arise, and write poetry and long letters in a room perfectly dark. He would make his lines straight, cross his t's, dot his i's, and make it perfectly legible. He seemed to be clairvoyant when in this state, and would often tell what a sister and brother-in-law were doing, and where they were, when several hundred miles off. . . . His statements, though many and often, were always found correct. This was in 1827."

The following case, which has received extensive publicity in the journals of the day, is related on the authority of the archbishop of Bordeaux. A young clergyman was in the habit of rising from his bed, and writing his sermons, while in his sleep. Whenever he finished a page, he would read it aloud, and correct it. Once, in altering the expression, "*ce devin enfant,*" he substituted the word "*adorable*" for "*devin;*" and, observing that the word "*adorable*" (commencing with a vowel) required that "*ce*" before it should be changed into "*cet,*" he accordingly added the "t." While he was writing, "the archbishop held a piece of paste-board under his chin to prevent him from seeing the paper on which he was writing; but he wrote on, not at all incommoded. The paper on which he was writing was then removed, and another piece substituted; but he instantly perceived the change. He also wrote pieces of music in this state, with his eyes closed. The words were under the music, and once were too large, and not placed exactly under the corresponding notes. He soon perceived the error, blotted out the part, and wrote it over again with great exactness."

The case of Jane C. Rider, known as the Springfield somnambulist, created, some years ago, much wonder and speculation among intelligent persons acquainted with the facts. I find the following account preserved in my notebook with a reference to the "Boston Medical and Surgical Journal," Vol. XI., Nos. 4 and 5 (which I have not now on hand), for more particular information. Miss Rider "would walk in her sleep, attend to domestic duties in the dark, and with her eyes bandaged; would read in a dark room, and with cotton filled in her eye-sockets, and a thick black silk handkerchief tied over the whole. These things were witnessed by hundreds of respectable persons. She learned, without difficulty, to play at backgammon while in this state, and would generally beat her antagonist; though, in her normal state, she knew nothing about the game, and remembered nothing whatever which occurred during her fits."

A young lady, while at school, succeeded in her Latin exercises without devoting much time or attention apparently to the subject. At length the secret of her easy progress was discovered. She was observed to leave her room at night; and, taking her class-book, she proceeded to a certain place on the banks of a small stream, where she remained but a short time, and then returned to the house. In the morning, she was invariably unconscious of what had occurred during the night; but a glance at the lesson of the day usually resulted in the discovery that it was already quite as familiar to her mind as household words.

172. Are we more Wise when Asleep than when Awake?

How else account for the wonderful feats and extensive knowledge of the somnambulist? We dwell more exclusively on the sleep-walker than on the magnetized subject, because he is free from the charge, that might be preferred against the latter, of being influenced by the will of an operator. He is free from any such bias; and whatever he accomplishes proceeds from himself, and represents the workings of his own spirit.

X.

SPIRIT — ITS PHENOMENA AND LAWS (CONTINUED).

I AM well convinced, then, that my dear departed friends are so far from having ceased to live that the state they now enjoy can alone with propriety be called life. — CICERO.

The essence of spirit is pure and eternal force.

The ancients supposed the "rational soul" exercised the functions of the senses in its every part, being "all eye, all ear, all taste."

173. MAGNETISM INTENSIFIES THE SPIRITUAL PERCEPTIONS.

WHEN the body is inanimate; when the sluggish flow of the blood is the only indication of life; when the nerves have lost their sensation, and the senses are dead, — the somnambulist, like the clairvoyant, revels in a world of his own, and finds his new senses vastly superior to those that are dormant.

The materialist says, "Look! here is an eye: it is an organ of sight. Images are formed, on the retina, of external objects. Here is an ear: it is adjusted to the waves of sound." Images are formed on the retina after death, and there is no sight: they are formed equally well in a camera. Waves of sound vibrate on the ear, and yield no sound. The eye, on the other hand, may be destroyed, its optic nerves withered, and still sight remain; the ear destroyed, and yet hearing remain, — as illustrated by clairvoyance. There is something behind and beyond all these external organs, which sees, hears, and feels. Millions of vibrations reach it, through the sensitive brain, from the external world, — waves of light, heat, magnetism, electricity, nerve-aura, and sound; but, where the physical avenues are all closed in a somnambulistic or clairvoyant sleep, it rises above them all. In that pure region the mind is most active, and grasps ideas as though robed in light, and becomes *en rapport* with the mental atmosphere of the universe.

174. NOT IMAGINATION.

Dr. Gregory has ably met the theory which accounts for clairvoyance and magnetism by the imagination.

"We have often seen persons in the mesmeric sleep who could see and describe correctly what was done behind them, or otherwise out of the range of their vision had their eyes been open, whereas their eyes were fast closed, and turned up, so that, when forced open, only the whites were visible, and moreover insensible to light. In other words, we have often seen and tested the fact of vision without the use of the external eye. This fact is observed in natural somnambulists, independent of artificial magnetism. When a person with closed and insensible eyes perceives, both in the daylight and in the dark (and sleep-walkers often see better in the dark), the objects which surround him; when his motions and actions are readier and more exact than in his waking state; nay, when he performs feats of climbing, keeping his balance in dangerous positions, writing, and doing various handiwork, which in his ordinary state are beyond his powers, — it is impossible either to ascribe this to imagination, or to doubt that he has a peculiar means of perception of external objects. And this implies some external influence which finds its way to the *sensorium commune.*

"We have seen mesmeric sleepers, without the slightest attempt to use their closed and insensible eyes, discover the contents of sealed packets and closed boxes, either by putting these on the head, or holding them in the hand, and sometimes by laying them on the epigastrium. We have seen the contents, unknown to any one present, described with the utmost accuracy. In Major Buckley's remarkable experiments, upwards of a hundred highly educated persons have read mottoes inclosed in nuts and boxes, the nuts being procured at various shops, by different persons, who were totally ignorant of their contents. Hundreds of mottoes and thousands of words have been thus read; and many of the readers have never been mesmerized at all, but have found themselves enabled to read the contents of the nuts, &c., by the aid of a light, which, when Major Buckley made passes over his own face, and perhaps over the nuts, rendered them transparent to the readers. Can any one suppose that imagination will explain these facts? And is not the natural conclusion from them — namely, the existence of an external influence — greatly fortified by the testimony of Major Buckley's subjects to the luminous emanations?

"We have seen the substance of the contents of a closed letter, unknown to ourselves, and the name of the writer, deciphered in an instant by a sleeper who placed it on her head, and who could not read. The letter had that moment arrived, and was totally unexpected; and, as we were trying some experiments on the sleeper, we asked her, before looking at the letter, whether she could tell me anything about it. She gave me at once the whole substance of it with perfect accuracy. Whatever may have been the means by which she acquired this knowledge of its meaning, imagination at least was not concerned; and the very remarkable nature of the letter no one could by any possibility have guessed. But the patient was always extremely susceptible to the influence of handwriting, and could accurately describe the writer of any letter shown to her.

"We have also frequently seen persons in the mesmeric sleep who described, with perfect accuracy, things and persons at a distance, whether in another room, another house or street, or at greater distances still, to the extent of three or four hundred miles. Some did this with the aid of the writing or hair of the absent person; some obtained the trace of the absent from persons present; some from knowing the absent themselves. But, in all cases, they had a more or less vivid vision of the place, and of the people in it; and, in all those we have studied, there was convincing evidence that they did so, having once obtained the trace or clew, independent of thought-reading. They uniformly stated some facts, afterwards confirmed, which were either unknown to us or to any one present, or even contrary to our belief; and, when they persisted in their own account of a fact, they were always right. No doubt some of these persons possessed the power of thought-reading, even when they did not use it; but granting, for the sake of argument, what is impossible, that they learned all they knew by thought-reading, is that less wonderful than vision at a distance? or is it more explicable by the imagination? Nay, is not thought-reading itself vision at a distance, and through opaque bodies too? Surely our mind, or its organ, the brain, are not in contact with that of the sleeper; and, if in communication with it, this can only be through some external medium, such as is implied in the facts previously adduced. And, admitting such a medium, distance is a matter of small importance, as it is in the case of light, electricity, gravitation. But whatever be the true explanation of the facts, — and they are facts which every patient inquirer can verify, — they cannot be explained by the theory of imagination. For the sleeper evidently perceives for himself, and in spite of suggestion, or of leading questions, or of direct contradiction, adheres to his story, and, as we have often seen, is found to have been right. In the appendix to Mr. Colquhoun's historical work on Magic, Witchcraft, and Animal Magnetism,' will be found a very beautiful case of vision at a distance in a young lady of Edinburgh, the operator being a gentleman of high character and literary standing, who, before he mesmerized this young lady on that one occasion, had never seen a person in the mesmeric sleep. In that case, the sleeper was found right on disputed points. We ourselves have seen, within the last six or seven months, and repeatedly tested, three or four most interesting cases of the same kind, in which the same fact presented itself. And we have also lately seen a sleeper, thoroughly blindfolded, play cards, beating all opponents; dealing more rapidly than they, and reading their hands as easily as her own. We confess ourselves utterly at a loss to perceive how imagination, granting it to have produced, or to have a share in producing, the mesmeric sleep, can explain facts like these, which, we repeat, are well-established facts.

"We have also had frequent opportunities of seeing the interesting facts of medical or physiological and pathological intuition. We have heard uneducated persons, in the mesmeric sleep, describe, in their own language, — which, although not technical, was usually superior to their waking speech, — the structure and functions of their own bodies in a manner truly striking. We have seen them do the same to persons *en rapport* with them, and point out, with singular accuracy, the weak or diseased parts so as to astonish those who best knew the truth. We have seen this repeatedly done, in the absence of the persons whose systems were described, from their hair or handwriting, and, in one remarkable case, without farther aid than the name and residence of the sufferer. We have seen the sleeper go over the whole of his person, and point out, as he did so, the parts in which pain was felt by the other party, whom he had never before seen nor heard of. We have seen two sleepers, unknown to each other, give the same account of the cause, the precise nature of the treatment, and the cure, of an accident occurring at a great distance from either of them; and their statements were in all points confirmed. One of these sleepers was told that an accident had happened, but nothing more. The other discovered it on being simply asked to visit the sufferer, which she was in the habit of doing in her sleep. The imagination theory is quite inadequate to explain these and hundreds of similar facts, which are recorded by trustworthy observers.

"We might go on to adduce many other varieties of mesmeric phenomena, equally beyond the reach of that theory; but this would be tedious, and is quite unnecessary. Those already given are sufficient to establish our proposition, which is, that, granting that the imagination suffices to account for the phenomena of electro-biology, or, more correctly, those in which suggestion is employed, there are yet many facts which cannot be brought into that category. Those physiologists, therefore, who, after having long denied the suggestive phenomena, when observed and described by the cultivators of animal magnetism, as occurring in the magnetic sleep, now admire them under a new name, as occurring in the waking state, are mistaken in supposing that the same explanation applies, or can apply, to all mesmeric phenomena.

"This mistake has arisen from their very imperfect acquaintance with the phenomena to be explained. Had they studied the phenomena of the mesmeric sleep, as they did those of suggestion in the waking state, — and this, as we know for certain, they have not yet done, — they would have been less confident in their theory, or at least in the extent of its application; and we cannot doubt, that, when they have done so, they will find themselves competent to acknowledge facts which that theory is utterly inadequate to explain.

"It is of no avail for them to deny the facts here adduced, because they regard them as impossible, or because they cannot bring them under their favorite hypothesis. Such conclusions, *a priori*, and more especially when the alleged facts have not been investigated by those who reject them, have no logical value whatever. They denied also, until a very recent period, the very facts they now admit; and yet these very facts are true, — nay, they were as true when described by the Mesmerists as occurring in the sleep as they are now. We know, in addition, that these particular phenomena may easily be produced in the waking state; but the phenomena are identical. And surely those whose account of these truly wonderful and long-rejected phenomena are now found to have been accurate and faithful may expect that their statements concerning other equally wonderful phenomena will also, when examined, prove to have been equally faithful and true to nature.

"We have seen several lucid subjects, possessed of the power of vision at a distance, yet who could not read a closed letter, which latter feat would seem to require, if not a higher, yet a different state."

175. CLAIRVOYANCE.

Clairvoyance is independent of the physical body for its existence, but not for its manifestations. It is not a product of disease, as has been supposed. Disease, by weakening the physical powers, may, at times, furnish the conditions essential for clairvoyance. The spirit, overburdened and concealed by the rubbish of worldly life, shines through the darkness of the flesh.

Clairvoyance is simply the clear seeing of the spirit; and to say that it is caused by the disease which allows it to be manifested is confounding cause with effect. It is a positive condition of spirit-life, occurring both during sleep and wakefulness; appearing in different individuals with varying degrees of lucidity.

176. APPLIED TO THE REALM OF SPIRIT.

When applied to the realm of spirit, clairvoyance is decisive. The revelations of different clairvoyants vary; but, in their main features, they coincide as perfectly as can be expected when the ever-changing and extremely subtle conditions of this state are considered. The Seeress of Prevorst was very reliable; and her revelations have a greater significance from the extreme purity and beauty of her spiritual life.

177. TESTIMONY OF THE SEERESS OF PREVORST.

"Unfortunately, my life is now so constituted that my soul, as well as well as my spirit, sees into the spiritual world, — which is, however, indeed upon the earth; and I see them not only singly, but frequently in multitudes and of different kinds, and many departed souls.

"I see many with whom I come into approximation, and others who come to me; with whom I converse, and who remain near me for months. I see them at various times by day and night, whether I am alone or in company. I am perfectly awake at the time, and am not sensible of any circumstance or sensation that calls them up. I see them alike, whether I am strong or weak, plethoric or in a state of inanition, glad or sorrowful, amused or otherwise; and I cannot dismiss them. Not that they are always with me; but they come at their own pleasure, like mortal visitors, and equally whether I am in a spiritual or corporeal state at the time. When I am in my calmest and most healthy sleep, they awaken me: I know not how; but I feel that I am awakened by them, and that I should have slept on had they not come to my bedside. I observe frequently, that, when a ghost visits me by night, those who sleep in the same room with me, are, by their dreams, made aware of its presence. They speak afterwards of the apparition they saw in their dream, though I have not breathed a syllable on the subject to them. Whilst the ghosts are with me, I see and hear everything around me as usual, and can think of other subjects; and, though I can avert my eyes from them, it is difficult for me to do it. I feel in a sort of magnetic *rapport* with them. They appear to me like a thin cloud, that one could see through, which, however, I cannot do. I never observed that they threw any shadow. I see them more clearly by sunlight or moonlight than in the dark; but, whether I could see them in absolute darkness, I do not know. If any object comes between me and them, they are hidden from me. I cannot see them with closed eyes, nor when I turn my face from them: but I am so sensible of their presence, that I could designate the exact spot they are standing upon; and I can hear them speak, although I stop my ears. . . . The forms of the good spirits appear bright; those of the evil, dusky.

"Their gait is like the gait of the living, only that the better spirits seem to float, and the evil ones tread heavier, so that their footsteps may sometimes be heard, not by me alone, but by those who are with me. They have various ways of attracting attention by other sounds besides speech; and this faculty they exercise frequently on those who can neither see them nor hear their voices. These sounds consist in sighing, knocking, noises as of the throwing of sand or gravel, rustling of a paper, rolling of a ball, shuffling as in slippers, &c. They are also able to move heavy articles, and to open and shut doors, although they can pass through them unopened or through the walls. I observe, that, the darker a spectre is, the stronger is his voice, and the more ghostly powers of making noises, &c., he seems to have. The sounds they produce are by means of the air, and the nerve-spirit, which is still in them. I never saw a ghost when he was in the act of producing any sound except speech, so that I conclude they cannot do it visibly; neither have I ever seen them in the act of opening or shutting a door, only directly afterwards. They move their mouths in speaking; and their voices are various as those of the living. They cannot answer me all that I desire. Wicked spirits are more willing or able to do this; but I avoid conversing with them."

178. Testimony of Swedenborg.

Swedenborg also relates similar facts.

"I have conversed with many, after their decease, with whom I was acquainted during their life in the body; and such conversation has been of long continuance, — sometimes for months, sometimes for a whole year, — and with as clear and distinct a voice, but internal, as with friends in the world. The subject of our discourse has sometimes turned on the state of man after death; and they have greatly wondered that no one in the life of the body knows, or believes, that he is to live in such a manner after the life of the body, when, nevertheless, it is a continuation of life, and that of such a nature, that the deceased passes from an obscure life into a clear and distinct one, and they who are in faith towards the Lord into a life more and more distinct. They have desired me to acquaint their friends on earth that they were alive, and to write to them an account of their states, as I have often told them many things respecting their friends: but my reply was, that if I should speak to them, or write to them, they would not believe, but would call my information mere fancy, and would ridicule it, asking for signs or miracles before they should believe; and thus I should be exposed to their derision. And that the things here declared are true, few, perhaps, will believe; for men deny, in their hearts, the existence of spirits, and they who do not deny such existence are yet very unwilling to hear that any one can converse with spirits. Such a faith respecting spirits did not at all prevail in ancient times, but does at this day, when men wish, by reasonings of the brain, to explore what spirits are, whom, by definitions and suppositions, they deprive of every sense; and, the more learned they wish to be, the more they do this."

179. SPIRITS RETAIN, AND APPEAR IN, THEIR EARTHLY FORM.

That spirits appear in their earthly form, and in possession of the senses, is almost the universal testimony of clairvoyants.

180. DO THE SENSES OF THE SPIRIT RECOGNIZE PHYSICAL OBJECTS?

I have made it a subject of investigation; and, aside from the direct affirmation of spirits, I drew, from facts, the conclusion that they can do so. I will mention but one seance; as the chances of error were, in this, perfectly wanting, and the result extremely accurate. Mrs. T—— sat at a small table near which was the light. I sat at the opposite side of the room by another table, on which were some nuts and a pitcher. We were conversing, by means of the tipping table, with a near and dear friend. I asked, "Can you see us with your own eyes?" "Yes."—"Do you see objects in the same manner?"—"Yes."—"To prove to me that you can do so, if I turn all these nuts into the pitcher, and then turn out a part, can you rap once for each nut that remains?"—"Yes." I then transferred the nuts— above a quart—to the pitcher, and turned out a portion. It must be borne in mind that it was quite dark at this table, and by no possibility could I have even unconsciously known the number. Having thus prepared the pitcher, I said, "Please rap." Eleven and a half raps,—the last a feeble or tiny rap. I turned the nuts out,— eleven, and a broken half! It had not occurred to me that it was possible for one of the nuts to be broken. I repeated this experiment several times, and at each trial the number was accurately given. The inference is unavoidable. That spirit must have seen by means strictly its own, and independent of earth. And, as spirits are not organically unlike, all spiritual beings must see likewise.

181. Does the Spirit of the Clairvoyant leave its Body?

It does in proportion as it enters the highest spiritual state, even to complete separation, which is death. The facts cited relative to double presence may be introduced here also.

An interesting magnetic treatment is detailed by Cahagnet in his "Celestial Telegraph," wherein he sets one clairvoyant to watch another.

"I perceive that Adele purposes entering into the ecstatic state: I make up my mind to try a decisive experiment, and I leave her to her will. I forthwith send Bruno to sleep, put him *en rapport* with her, and beg him to follow her as far as possible, recommending him not to be alarmed, and to warn me only if he should see danger. I wished to be assured by myself of the pretended dangers of ecstacy. Frequently had Adele told me that she had been on the point of not coming back to re-enter her body; and, as I thought that she only wanted to alarm me,

I wished to know what opinion to come to. At the lapse of a quarter of an hour, Bruno exclaims, in great alarm, "I have lost sight of her!" I had relied on him, and paid little attention to Adele, whose body in the mean while had grown icy cold; there was no longer any pulse or respiration; her face was of a sallow green, her lips blue, her heart no longer gave any signs of life. I placed before her lips a mirror, but it was by no means tarnished by them. I magnetized her powerfully, in order to bring back her soul into her body, but for five minutes my labor was in vain. Bruno, alarmed at my want of success, as well as the persons present at this sitting, tended greatly to disturb me. I thought for a moment that the work was consummated, and that I had an indubitable proof that the soul had departed from her body. I was obliged to request the persons present to pass into another room, in order that I might recover by myself a little energy. At the lapse of a few moments, I entertained the hope that I should not have such a misfortune to deplore; but, physically speaking, I was utterly powerless."

182. Double Presence.

There is another class of phenomena of unique character, — the double presence, when the spirit is seen and recognized at a distance from the body. The peculiar state which enables a second person in that locality to perceive the spirit on its arrival is simply one of delicate impressibility. The freedom of the spirit from the body is clairvoyance, and any clairvoyant is capable of executing this "double presence," so mysterious to old-school psychological writers.

This "double presence," the body being in one place while the spirit is at another, has been long recognized by the Germans.

"One of the most remarkable cases of this kind is that recorded by Jung Stilling, of a man, who, about the year 1740, resided in the neighborhood of Philadelphia, in the United States. His habits were retired, and he spoke little. He was grave, benevolent, and pious; and nothing was known against his character, except that he had the reputation of possessing secrets that were not altogether lawful. Many extraordinary stories were told of him, and, among the rest, the following: The wife of a ship captain, whose husband was on a visit to Europe and Africa, and from whom she had been long without tidings, overwhelmed with anxiety for his safety, was induced to address herself to this person. Having listened to her story, he begged her to excuse him for a while, when he would bring her the intelligence required. He then passed into an inner room, and she sat herself down to wait: but, his absence continuing longer than she expected, she became impatient, thinking he had forgotten her; and so, softly approaching the door, she peeped through some aperture, and, to her surprise, beheld him lying on a sofa, as motionless as if he were dead. She, of course, did not think it advisable to disturb him, but waited his return, when he told her that her husband had not been able to write to her for such and such reasons; but that he was in a coffee-house in London, and would very shortly be at home again. Accordingly he arrived; and, as the lady heard from him that the causes of his unusual silence had been precisely those alleged by the man, she felt extremely desirous of ascertaining the truth of the rest of the information: and in this she was gratified; for he no sooner set his eyes on the magician, than he said he had seen him before, on a certain day, in a coffee-house in London; and that he had told him that his wife was extremely uneasy about him; and that he, the captain, had thereon mentioned how he had been prevented writing; adding that he was on the eve of embarking for America. He had then lost sight of the stranger amongst the throng, and knew nothing more about him."

A partner of my grandfather, having gone to the West Indies on business, and staying much longer than was expected, he consulted a fortune-teller, who enjoyed a local fame, more from curiosity than any faith in his pretensions.

He was left sitting in a room, while the fortune-teller, excusing himself, went out. After waiting an hour, my grandfather walked out into the orchard. There he saw the fortune-teller lying under a tree as if he were dead. He returned to the house; and in a short time the man came in, and told him that his partner was then taking dinner at such an hotel in Jamaica, and was on his way home. As soon as possible his partner returned, and almost the first words he said was to inquire for the fortune-teller. He said, that, while taking dinner at such a hotel, he saw him pass through the room, but so quickly that he could not speak to him.

183. Impressions made on the Mind never Effaced.

Locke supposed perfect sleep to be dreamless, while the Cartesian doctrine teaches that the spirit never sleeps. The former theory rests on negative evidence, and is opposed to facts. An impression once received is never lost. Even in torpidity, resulting from injury of the brain, when its functions appear completely suspended, it is found that indelible impressions are made.

A case is given, by Dr. Abercrombie, of a boy who had his skull fractured and trepanned. He was quite insensible during the operation, and had not the least memory, after his recovery, even of the accident. Fourteen years afterwards, he was attacked by a fever; and, during the delirium, he astonished his mother by a minute account of the operation, even to the dress worn by the surgeon. After the fever had passed, he again lost the memory of the event.

This is farther shown by the experience of persons when drowning.

"One of the most singular features in psychology is the fact, which is perfectly notorious, that the faculty of memory acquires an activity and tenacity in the case of persons about being drowned which it never exhibits under ordinary circumstances. An accident occurred some weeks since at New York, which threw a number of persons into the North River. Among others were Mr. —— and his sister; the first named, editor of a weekly paper in Philadelphia. They were both finally saved. Mr. —— describes the sensation while under the water, and in a drowning condition, to be pleasant, but peculiar. It seemed to him that every event of his life crowded into his mind at once. He was sensible of what was occurring, and expected to drown, but seemed only to regret that such an interesting 'item' as his sensations should be lost."

In noticing this statement in an exchange, I am reminded of an incident, which, dissimilar as it is to the one just narrated in its general features, had the same remarkable awakening of the memory which such cases sometimes exhibit. I can vouch for the truth of what follows, as well as testify to vivid recollections in my own case, when exposed to the hazards of drowning, which reproduced in a few moments the events of my past life.

"Some years since, A held a bond of B for several hundred dollars, haivng some time to run. At its maturity, he found he had put it away so carefully that he was unable to find it. Every search was fruitless. He only knew it had not been paid nor traded away. In this dilemma he called on B, related the circumstance of its disappearance, and proposed giving him a receipt as an offset to the bond, or an indemnifying bond against its collection, if ever found. To his great surprise, B not only refused to accept the terms of meeting the difficulty, but positively denied owing him anything, and strongly intimated the presence of a fraudulent design on the part of A. Without legal proof, and therefore without redress, he had to endure both the loss of his money, and the suspicion of a dishonorable intention in urging the claim. Several years passed away without any change in the nature of the case, or its facts as above given, when one afternoon, while bathing in the James River, A, either from inability to swim, or cramp, or some other cause, was discovered to be drowning. He had sunk and risen several times, and was floating under the water, when he was seized, and drawn to the shore. The usual remedies were applied to resuscitate him; and, though there were signs of life, there was no appearance of consciousness. He was taken home in a state of complete exhaustion, and remained so for some days. On the first return of strength to walk, he left his bed, went to his bookcase, took a book, opened it, and handed his long-lost bond to a friend who was present. He then informed him, that, when drowning, and sinking as he supposed to rise no more, in a moment, there stood out distinctly before his mind, as a picture, every act of his life, from the hour of childhood to the hour of sinking beneath the water, and among them the circumstance of his putting the bond in a book, the book itself, and the place in which he had put it in the book-case. It is needless to say he recovered his own with interest.

"There is no doubt that this remarkable quickening of memory results from the process which in such cases is going on, — the extinguishment of life. It is somewhat analogous to the breaking-in of the light of another world, which, in so many well-attested death-bed scenes, enables the departing spirit, even before it has absolutely left its clay tenement, to behold and exult in the glories of the future state. Is it not a fair inference, that, when the soul shakes off the clogs and incumbrances of the body, it will possess capacities for enjoyment, of which, on earth, it was unsusceptible?

"As regards the memory, it will be observed by most persons how readily in life we forget that which we do not desire to remember, and in this way get rid of much unhappiness. Can we do this after death? This is an important practical question."

Most important! Death quickens the memory. The past is retained forever. The quick, intense thought of the drowning person is a foretaste of that eternal spirit-life.

184. PROPHECY.

Only by impressions descending from the spirit-world can prophecy be explained. Certain spirits understand and combine causes and effects, and can tell more readily what will be the result. Prof. Gregory remarks, —

"By some obscure means, certain persons in a peculiar state may have visions of events yet future. And, indeed, it is only by admitting some such influence that we can at all account for the fulfillment of prophetic dreams, which, it cannot be doubted, have frequently taken place. Coincidence, as I have before remarked, is insufficient to explain even one case, so enormously great are the chances against it; but, when several cases occur, it is absolutely out of the question to explain them by coincidence."

Volumes might readily be filled with the facts of prevision and prophecy. We do not expect to do more, confined as we are to narrow limits, than to give illustrative facts.

"Major Buckley, twenty-three years ago, before he had heard of animal magnetism, was on the voyage between England and India, when, one day, a lady remarked that they had not seen a sail for many days. He replied that they would see one next day at noon on the starboard bow. Being asked by the officers in the ship how he knew, he could only say that he saw it, and that it would happen. When the time came, the captain jested him on his prediction, when at that moment a man who had been sent aloft half an hour before, in consequence of the prophecy, sung out, 'A sail!'—'Where?' —'On the starboard bow.' I consider this case interesting because it tends to show a relation between magnetic power, which Major Buckley possesses in an eminent degree, and susceptibility to the magnetic or other influences concerned."

"A soldier in a Highland regiment, then in America, named Evan Campbell, was summoned before his officer for having spread among the men a prediction that a certain officer would be killed next day. He could only explain that he had seen a vision of it, and that he saw the officer killed, in the first onset, by a ball in the forehead. Next day an engagement took place; and, in the first attack, the officer was killed by a ball in the forehead. I am told that this instance of second sight may be entirely depended on."

Governor Tallmadge records an experience worthy of repetition, from the high moral and intellectual character of that distinguished man. He was one of the party on board the U. S. war-ship "Princeton," on the memorable occasion when the "Peace-maker" exploded. During the first three discharges, his position had been at the breech of the gun. After dinner, he returned to the deck, when he observed that the great gun was about being discharged for the fourth and last time, and he assumed his former position. There was some delay of the party coming on deck, and, while waiting, he was seized with sudden dread; and, under an irresistible impulse, he retired to the ladies' cabin. Immediately he heard the report, and, the next moment, the intelligence of the terrible disaster. Five distinguished men, two of whom were members of the Cabinet, had been instantly killed. The gun had burst at the very spot where he had stood; and, if he had remained, he would have been demolished.

The day previous to the burning of the "Henry Clay," on the Hudson, Mrs. Porter, being entranced, in the presence of several persons announced the event.

On the authority of Mrs. Swisshelm, it is stated that the Rev. Dr. Wilson, of Alleghany City, prophesied "the great fire of 1845, in Pittsburg; the Mexican war, and its results; the war between Russia and the Western powers; and the speedy limitation of the temporal power of the Pope."

While Napoleon Bonaparte was an exile on the Island of St. Helena, he made the following remarkable declaration respecting the future of the United States: "Ere the close of the nineteenth century, America will be convulsed with one of the greatest revolutions the world ever witnessed. Should it succeed, her power and prestige are lost; but, should the government maintain her supremacy; she will be on a firmer basis than ever. The theory of a republican form of government will be established, and she can defy the world."

History furnishes many examples of the hero's mind becoming ecstatic with the vast labor it was called to perform. Hannibal had his star of destiny, as well as Napoleon. While pausing at Etovissa, he is said to have seen in his sleep a youth of divine figure, who told him that he was sent by Jupiter to guide him into Italy; and bade him follow without turning his eyes on either side. He followed, though he trembled with terror: but, his curiosity becoming too strong for his resolution, he looked back, and saw an immense serpent moving along, felling the bushes and trees in its way; and after it followed a dark cloud, with loud thunder. When he inquired what this commotion meant, he was told that it portended the desolation of Italy; to go on, and ask no more.

The claim that there is an independent organ or faculty of prophecy or prescience is an unsupported hypothesis. As the foreseeing of an event cannot change the cause of the occurrence, the intelligence that foresees must judge from cause to effect. The mortal prophet may not reason, but receive as inspiration; but the source of the inspiration must be ascertained from a thorough knowledge of causes. Prophecy presupposes fixed and unalterable relations between causes and effects. The mind, capable of grasping the chain of causes leading to a given effect, can foreknow that effect.

The prediction of an astronomical event, as an eclipse, although founded on the absolute relations of numbers, is as truly a prophecy as the prediction of an event in history. If the astronomer inform a companion when an eclipse will take place, without giving the data of his calculations, that companion is in the position of the prophet inspired by celestial intelligence. He can hear and understand the prediction; although he cannot arrive at it unaided, nor know the process by which others have gained their knowledge.

The truth of science, of all knowledge, is proved by the facilities it affords to predict the unknown.

XI.

SPIRIT — ITS PHENOMENA AND LAWS (CONTINUED).

ALL the immense space by which we are surrounded is peopled with angels, whose eyes are continually turned towards us. The most hardened in wickedness still shrinks from observation. The thought that he is watched checks the criminal in the fury of his passion. Can the Christian, then, who knows that celestial spirits not only behold his every action, but also read his most secret thoughts, — can he ever, in mere levity and thoughtlessness, deliver himself up to evil?

HILARY OF POICTIERS.

185. CAUSE OF FAILURE.

THE problem of man's immortality has been vexed from immemorial time; yet the theologian and metaphysician, after all their gigantic efforts, have accomplished nothing by way of demonstration. They have never met the question fairly, and scanned it by the light of natural law. Forced to admit certainty into the domain of the physical world, — a term by which we mean what they understand by the world of matter, — they have ever regarded with holy horror the introduction of cause and effect into the realm of spirit. On the threshold of this realm, the inductive philosophy, that magnificent system which traces effects to their causes, which discerns a cause beneath every effect, has been dismissed as a profane and erring guide, and in its place a will-o'-the-wisp has led them through the reeking miasm of metaphysical controversy, and along the slippery paths intersecting the night-enveloped swamp-lands of bigoted and insane theological disputation.

186. VALUE OF CLAIRVOYANCE.

One fact of clairvoyance — one manifestation of spirit presence — outweighs all the logical argumentations the world has ever heard. We said, that, if spirit existed, it must have form. It must retain, whatever others it may acquire, the five senses. It must be organized. Let us investigate this proposition. The clairvoyant has entered the deepest trance. His body lies oblivious; as near the portals of death as it is possible for it to be without entering within the gates. All avenues to the senses are closed; the blood flows slowly and turgidly along its channels; the nerves have lost their irritability; and the brain cannot feel. The blinding lightnings affect not the eye; the crash of thunders are not heard by the ear. Limb after limb can be severed unfelt. Such is the state of the body. What is that of the spirit which has thus temporarily deserted it?

187. CONDITION OF THE FREED SPIRIT.

Not unconscious, not senseless, not inactive, but like a freed eagle it soars in the light of a new existence. The channels through which it obtained a knowledge of the world are closed, it is true: but it has no necessity for them now.; for spiritual light acts on the spirit eye, waves in the spirit atmosphere vibrate on the spirit ear, and feeling becomes as a refined consciousness, which is far more delicate and exquisite by all conception than it ever possessed in the body. It sees, it hears, it feels, while the body can be burned to ashes without pain, or even automatic irritability.

188. CAN THE SPIRIT POSSESS SENSES INDEPENDENT OF THE PHYSICAL BODY?

The materialist, mistaking the instrument of manifestation for the cause, asserts that the spirit originates in certain combinations of matter, and must perish with the combinations which gave it birth. This dependence of mind on the physical body is only apparent, and its independence is shown by clairvoyance as well as by facts drawn from other sciences.

189. LAURA BRIDGEMAN.

The mental development of Laura Bridgeman proves that intellect of a high order may exist independent of the senses. Completely deprived of sight and hearing at an early period of childhood, she was a blind and deaf mute. Dr. Howe, her kind and angelic teacher, says: "As soon as she could walk, she began to explore the rooms and the house: she became familiar with the forms, density, weight, and heat of every article she could lay her hands upon. I found her of a well-formed figure, a strongly marked nervous-sanguine temperament, a large and beautifully shaped head, and the whole system in healthy action." She returned to his institution in 1837.

He continues: "After waiting about two weeks, the attempt was made to give her knowledge of arbitrary signs, by which she could interchange thoughts with others. There was one of two ways to be adopted: either to go on to build up a language of signs which she had already commenced herself, or to teach her the purely arbitrary language in common use; that is, to give her a sign for every individual thing, or to give her a knowledge of letters, by combination of which she might express her idea of the existence, and the mode and condition of existence, of anything. The former would have been easy, but very ineffectual; the latter seemed difficult, but, if accomplished, very effectual. I determined, therefore, to try the latter."

After describing the interesting process by which he taught her to associate names with things, he goes on to say, " Hitherto the process had been mechanical, and the success about as great as in teaching a knowing dog a variety of tricks. The poor child had sat in mute amazement, and patiently imitated everything her teacher did: but now the truth began to flash upon her; her intellect began to work; she perceived that here was a way by which she could herself make up a sign of anything that was in her own mind, and show it to another mind, and at once her countenance lighted up with a human expression. It was no longer a dog or a parrot: it was an immortal spirit, eagerly seizing upon a link of union with other spirits! I could almost fix upon the moment when the truth first dawned upon her mind, and spread its light to her countenance. I saw that the great obstacle was overcome, and that henceforth nothing but patient and persevering, but plain and straightforward, efforts were to be used."

At the end of the year, a report of the case was made, of which the following is an extract: "It has been ascertained, beyond the possibility of a doubt, that she cannot see a ray of light, cannot hear the least sound, and never exercises her sense of smell, if she has any. Thus her mind dwells in darkness and stillness, as profound as that of a closed tomb at midnight. Of beautiful sights, and sweet sounds, and pleasant odors, she has no conception: nevertheless she is as happy and playful as a bird or a lamb; and the enjoyment of her intellectual faculties, or the acquirement of a new idea, gives her a vivid pleasure, which is plainly marked in her expressive features."

Describing the interesting process by which he taught her to associate names with things, he goes on to say, "If she have no occupation, she evidently amuses herself by imaginary dialogues, or by recalling past impressions: she counts with her fingers, or spells out names of things which she has recently learned, in the manual alphabet of the deaf mutes. In this lonely self-communion, she seems to reason, reflect, and argue. But, wonderful as is the rapidity with which she writes her thoughts upon the air, still more so is the ease and rapidity with which she reads the words thus written, — grasping their hands in hers, and following every movement of their fingers, as letter after letter conveys their meaning to her mind. It is in this way she converses with her blind playmates; and nothing can more forcibly show the power of mind over matter than a meeting between them. For, if it requires great skill for two pantomimists to paint their thoughts and feelings by the movements of the body, and the expressions of the countenance, how much greater the difficulty when darkness enshrouds them both, and one can hear no sound! When Laura is walking through a passage-way, with her hands spread before her, she knows instantly every one she meets, and passes them with a sign of recognition; but, if it be a girl of her own age, and especially if it be one of her own favorites, there is instantly a bright smile of recognition, and twining of arms, a grasping of hands, and a swift telegraph upon the tiny fingers.

"When left alone, she occupies and apparently amuses herself, and seems quite contented; and so strong seems to be the natural tendency of thought to put on the garb of language, that she often soliloquizes in the finger-language, slow and tedious as it is. But it is only when alone that she is quiet; for, if she becomes sensible of the presence of any one near her, she is restless until she can sit close beside them, hold their hand, and converse with them by signs. In her intellectual character, it is pleasing to observe an insatiable thirst for knowledge, and a quick perception of the relations of things. In her moral character, it is beautiful to behold her continued goodness, her keen enjoyment of existence, her expansive love, her unhesitating confidence, her sympathy with suffering, her conscientiousness, truthfulness, and hopefulness."

Her spirit was locked within her body, without the least contact with the world through the most useful of the senses; yet she not only thought, but thought in the same manner as those who possess the perfection of the senses. If thought depend on the senses, then the quality of thought should change when the senses are useless. That thought is the same in kind, under all circumstances of expression, is conclusive that it is superior to the organs of the senses. Mind in man is the resultant of the spiritual organism modified by the physical body. After the dissolution of the latter, such modification does not exist, and the mind is animated from the spiritual organism.

190. THE SPIRITUAL ORGANISM.

If the spirit exist in the immortal land as an entity, of what material is its body composed? We say body; for again we meet the division of mind and body, applying with the same force to the spirit as to the man.

Admitting the existence of spirit, we are forced either to believe that it exists as a detached intelligence or as an entity. The first position we have endeavored to show untenable. If the latter be accepted, it follows, as sequence, that that entity is derived from the mortal body, or enters a body prepared for it. The latter position presupposes miracle, the direct interposition of Divinity; presupposes an interference we never see in this life, and have no reason to suppose exists in the hereafter. Mind cannot change from one body to another without a miracle; and as it is possible to account for all connected phenomena by referring them to an entity derived from the physical body, and in a strictly scientific manner, this conclusion must at last be accepted.

191. THE SPIRIT ORGANISM THE MOST SUBTILE FORM OF MATTER.

As the senses cannot recognize the matter of which the spirit-organism is composed, and as all idea of matter is derived from them, we cannot form a just conception of all its qualities. We know that it must be the most subtile form of matter. Electricity, supposed to be the most refined, has often been assumed, and that, too, by intelligent Spiritualists, to be the constituent of the spirit-forms. Somehow it is supposed that spirits are intimately connected with electricity and magnetism.

192. AN ERRONEOUS HYPOTHESIS.

Prof. Hare truthfully observes, "It appeared to me a great error, on the part of spirits as well as mortals, that they should make efforts to explain the phenomena of the spirit-world by the ponderable or imponderable of the temporal. The fact that the rays of our sun do not affect the spirit-world, and that there is for that region an appropriate luminary, (luminosity?) whose rays we do not perceive, must demonstrate that the imponderable elements, to which they owe their peculiar light, differ from the ethereal fluid, which, according to the undulatory theory, is the means of producing light in the terrestrial creation. Thus, although in manifestations our electricity takes no part, their electricity may be the means by which their wills are transmitted effectually to the phenomena which it controls."

193. ELECTRICITY AND MAGNETISM NOT EMPLOYED.

But it is not possible to build an individual out of electricity or magnetism, even if it be considered an element and not a force. If material, its atoms have almost infinite repulsion, on which its phenomena depend; and how, out of such material, can start a form which can never perish? But neither of these are elements: they are forces, and cannot act outside of matter.

194. WHAT, THEN, IS THE CHARACTER OF THE MATTER WHICH FORMS THE SPIRIT ORGANISM?

Refined, ultimated matter is derived from the progress of the physical elements. Eternal progress is written in the constitution of matter. There is a constant flux and reflux through the domain of living beings. By every absorption and elimination the elements advance. This is not recognized by the gross tests of chemistry, but there are other and more conclusive tests.

The rootlets of plants make a delicate analysis, and prove this proposition. In New England, the soil composed of disintegrated granite, and hence rich in potash, is sterile until enriched by ashes. Chemistry pronounces potash from the soil, and potash from ashes, identical; but the delicate spongioles of plants perceive a difference. Lichens and moss, the lower forms of vegetable life, will readily grow in the granite soil, but the higher vegetation require the elements to pass through these lower orders before they can absorb and assimilate them.

Another illustration from the same source is furnished by the results of phosphorus from bones, and phosphorus from limestone deposited in the early ages of the earth. While the former is highly beneficial to growing plants, the latter is useless. While one has been assimilated by living beings a countless number of times, the other has remained fixed in the rock, and has not departed from its primal form. Chemistry declares the two identical, but plants do not acquiesce in its decision.

195. Progress of the Elements.

Such facts, which can be greatly multiplied, prove what may be termed the progress of the elements. This progress is slow, but we cannot doubt its existence. Only in those cases where the elements have been, as it were, fossilized, can we compare their present with their past over a sufficiently long interval of time; but, whenever we can do so, a difference is discernible. However small such progress may appear, infinite time will yield any desired modification.

Every cycle of change through which matter passes eliminates some parts to a higher state. It is from such illustrations that the spiritual elements are derived. They are the aroma of the material world, the fragrance of its perfect bloom.

196. Spiritual Elements Realities.

The spiritual elements, such as the earth emanates, which go to form the spiritual spheres, and enter into the organization of spirits, are realities. They possess all the properties of earthy matter, together with new ones which they acquire by their refinement. Carbon is represented by a spiritual carbon, oxygen by a spiritual oxygen, etc., through the long catalogue.

197. Spirits of Animals.

Another explanation concerning the unindividualized beings whose spiritual essence ascends into the vast ether, and gravitates like an evaporating cloud to its appropriate position, is here afforded. True, they are not individualized, they do not retain their identity; but they again enter into somewhat similar forms. If of sufficient refinement, the aroma passes at once to the spirit-sphere; if not, they re-unite with gross matter, and again enter the cycle of living beings, to be again and again eliminated, perhaps to travel up to the human form divine, and, becoming embodied, stand forth as eternal as the everlasting planets: nay, more,— when these shall fade like the baseless fabric of a vision, they will rise above the wreck of worlds, rejoicing in increasing wisdom.

198. Spiritual Attraction and Repulsion.

The poison wolfsbane, twining its roots around and among those of the fruitful corn, extracts from the same dew, the same rain, the same soil, the most deadly poison; while the corn elaborates the life-giving grain. Particles seek like particles. They are repelled from dissimilar ones, and thus the intricate and mysterious web of nature is woven.

199. In the Spiritual World, the same Laws hold Supreme.

The force which builds up the wolfsbane and the corn, side by side, builds up, from the ascending atoms, the orange and the vine which decorate the landscapes of the spirit-spheres.

200. WHY, IF MATERIAL, CANNOT SPIRITS BE SEEN?

We are here met with an objection which is urged as conclusive. Why can we not see spirits if they are material? We cannot see the atmosphere, and, if we trusted our eyes alone, should never know that it exists; yet it is composed of matter as tangible as iron or adamant. Its name, "gas," came from "ghost," because it was long considered to be the spirit of matter. We learn, by deeper investigation, that vision is a very untrustworthy guide in determining materiality.

Whether a body is visible or invisible depends on the relations the body bears to the light. Experiments instituted by Sir John Herschel and M. Stokes prove that the same rays of light falling on one body remain invisible, while they become luminous on others. If the solar spectrum be received on a screen, and then all the visible light to the extreme violet be cut off, perfect darkness is the result. There is to appearance no more light; but if a piece of glass tinged with oxide of uranium or a bottle of sulphate of quinine, or a paper moistened with the latter, is placed in the space beyond the violet, they become visible. In respect to this extraordinary fact, Grove, in his admirable and profound, yet incomplete, "Correlation of Physical Forces," a work that has attracted the attention of the scientists of the old world and the new, makes these observations, which I quote in full, for they are too choice to be presented otherwise: —

"Other substances exhibit this effect in different degrees; and, among the substances which have been considered perfectly analogous as to their appearances when illumined, notable differences are discovered. Thus it appears, that emanations, which give no impressions to the eye when impinged on certain bodies, become luminous when impinged on others. We might imagine a room, so constructed that such emanations alone were permitted to enter it, which would be dark or light according to the substances with which the walls are coated, though in full daylight the respective coatings of the wall would be apparently white; or, without altering the coating of the wall, the room, exposed to one class of rays, might be rendered dark by windows which would be transferred to another class of rays.

"If, instead of solar light, the electrical light be employed for similar experiments, an equally striking effect can be produced. A design, drawn on paper with sulphate of quinine and tartaric acid, is invisible in ordinary light, but appears with beautiful distinctness when illumined by the electrical light. Thus, in pronouncing on a luminous effect, regard must be had to the recipient as well as emittent body. That which is or becomes light, when it falls on one body, is not light when it falls on another. Probably the retinas of the eyes of different persons differ, to some extent, in a similar manner; and the same substances, illuminated by the same spectrum, may present different appearances to different persons, the spectrum appearing more elongated to one than another, so that what is light to one is darkness to another.

"The force emitted from the sun may take a different character at the surface of every different planet, and require different organisms or senses for its appreciation.

"Myriads of organized beings may exist, imperceptible to our visions, even if we were among them; and we might also be imperceptible to them."

The visual organs of nocturnal animals and birds, such as the felines, bats, owls, etc., can plainly recognize objects in what to other animals is darkness. This is partially accounted for by the enlargement of the pupils of their eyes: but not fully; for the pupil of the eye of a bat, that sees with remarkable quickness, is not as large as that of man, who could not see at all in an equal darkness. Are we sure that these nocturnal animals are not sensible to rays of light to which the animals of daylight are strangers?

Of insects, it has been suggested, by an eminent naturalist, that they see by means of light unknown to man. To them, light may sparkle in colors which we know nothing of, and to each of these tiny beings nature may array herself in hues which even the rainbow does not equal. Their eyes are constructed on an entirely different plan from those of animals, although conforming to the requisites of the known laws of light. This departure must have its origin in adaptation to a different luminosity from that which meets our own vision. Some insects can see well at night; a fact certainly not referable with them to enlargement of the pupils of their eyes, for the thousands of facets composing those organs are not expansive. When the world is wrapped in darkness to other insects, they wing through the air, perceiving objects by a glowing luminosity of too low intensity for the vision of the former.

201. Why seek Immortal Existence outside of Physical Matter?

Why seek immortality among the refined elements rather than in those of the physical world? Why should it be found there more than here? These questions lead to an investigation of what constitutes immortality.

In the healthy organism, the forces of renovation balance those of decay. As soon as a fibre or nerve tissue or bone particle is worn out, new material is ready to supply the waste. So rapid is this wonderful process of decay and renovation, that, according to the latest and most correct researches, all the softer tissues of the body, all, except the bones and teeth, are renewed, in health, every thirty days. Thus the body is restored twelve times every year, and an individual at sixty years of age has had seven hundred and twenty different organisms. This change proceeds during sleep, as well as in the hours of wakefulness: in fact, respiration is most rapid during sleep; but in age is retarded, becoming more and more sluggish, until it ceases altogether, and death closes the earthly life.

We have here, seemingly, as perfect an arrangement as it is possible to obtain; and, we ask, why cannot such an organization be perpetual? Mark the decline of such structures, and the answer is received.

Could such conditions remain forever, could renovation always balance decay, animal and vegeeble living forms would never perish; an immortal lion, oak, or pine would be as possible as immortal man. But they cannot obtain with the material of the physical world.

See how physical forms perish. They reach maturity strong and vigorous; nothing appears to disturb the harmony of their being. But insidiously the power of decay claims mastery. The senses harden; the absorbents become obstructed with bone-forming material, and, deposition going on in the bones, they become hard, almost mineral. In old age, they become too deficient of life to heal when broken. Through the important organs, as the heart, in its very valves on which life depends, bony atoms are deposited. The minute arteries thus obstructed, the muscles waste, contract, and harden at their points of attachment. The entire mechanism of complicated fibres, channels, cells, and fluids, becomes impaired, and, at length, fails altogether.

It is not want of vitality: it is a necessity, growing out of the elements of which they are formed.

The being sets out to be immortal, but fails because it builds with imperfect material. We are thus compelled to look higher, to more elevated and progressed matter.

202. Origin of the Spiritual Body.

With a proper understanding of words, we may employ the terms "matter" and "spirit," the latter meaning the ultimated elements which pervade and arise from and underlie the physical world.

From the former, the physical body is created; from the latter, the spiritual. This dual development commences with the dawn of being, and continues until death. The physical form appropriates the physical portion of the food; the spiritual, the remaining portion.

The two forms mature together; one pervading, and being the exact copy of, the other. Such being the close relation between them, every impression made on one must affect the other. Food which nourishes, stimulants which excite, all exercise a powerful influence,—an influence felt for infinite time. The spirit, when it takes its departure, must bear the stain or beauty of its physical organism.

203. How far the Body affects the Spirit.

Does the mortal affect the immortal? Does the grossness of this life exert an influence on the welfare of the spirit? Reason can make but one answer, and that in the affirmative. The Parable of the Sower is a beautiful illustration of the effect of external conditions on the spirit. The same grains, falling on different ground, produce widely varying results. If an acorn be planted in a rocky soil, it will grow into a distorted shrub. You may transplant that shrub into fertile ground, and bestow on it the best of care, — it will become quite different from what it would have been had it remained; but it will never mature into the noble tree, the forest's pride, as it would had it been planted first in a mellow soil.

The winged seed of the rock-maple, matured by sap drawn from the crevices of stony hills, is blown far away by the winds. Perhaps it alights on a barren rock, just made green by a patch of moss. The moss is moistened by dews, and the seed swells with life, thrusts forth its roots into the moss so full of promise, sends upwards its tiny leaflets, and makes fair augury of a tree like its noble parent. But its food soon fails. There are nights without dew, — it almost famishes; there are frosts telling on its unprotected roots. So a century goes by, when a traveler, chancing to ascend the hillside, sees a scraggy, scarred bush, so different from what he has seen before that he considers it a new species of maple. Perhaps a seed from the same bough was wafted at the same time to some fertile dell, and now stands, straight and tall as monumental shaft, the pride of a century.

As the spirit and the physical body are matured

together; as, while connected, they are mutually related, — it is clearly self-evident that one cannot be injured without at least a sympathetic effect on the other. A wrong done to the immortal is retained forever. If a man lose a limb, he has a scar telling of the wound. Although he live a century, it is not outgrown. The least mark is indelible. If the physical body so tenaciously retain the witnesses of former transgressions, how can any one expect to proceed for a life in a systematic course of wrong to his immortal nature, and escape with impunity?

It is a fearful mistake. The spirit is the REAL, of which the body is the fleeting shadow; and impressions on that real, compared with those of the body, are as lasting as the signature of the storm and whirlwind, scarred with fire on granite mountains, contrasted with the fitful shadows of a phantasmagoria. Write a wrong on the spirit, — only the eternal ages can erase it. Do a deed of sin, and never can it be repealed. The words of the passions, their deeds of error, are written on the adamantine book of the individual's life; and the furnace blast cannot burn their record out, the ocean cannot wash it away.

XII.

PHILOSOPHY OF DEATH. — A REVIEW OF SOME OLD THEORIES.

> THERE'S no such thing as death:
>   'Tis but the blossom spray,
> Sinking before the coming fruit,
>   That seeks the summer's ray;
> 'Tis but the bud displaced,
>   As comes the perfect flower;
> 'Tis faith exchanged for sight,
>   And weariness for power.
>
> Nothing of him that doth fade,
> But does suffer a sea-change
> Into something rich and strange.

The soul, the marvel of this great celestial departure which we call death, is here. Those who depart still remain near us: they are in a world of light; but they, as tender witnesses, hover about our world of darkness. . . . The dead are invisible, but they are not absent.
VICTOR HUGO.

204. WHAT IS LIFE?

RICHMOND defines life as "a collection of phenomena which succeed each other during a definite time in an organized body." This definition applies equally well to death as to life, for in the dead body changes go on in succession as well as in the living. De Blainville defines it as " the twofold internal movement of composition and decomposition, at once general and continuous;" a definition which includes the entire mineral world, and makes a galvanic battery a living being. "Life," says Lewes, "is a series of definite and successive changes, both of structure and composition, which take place within an individual without destroying his identity." Spencer gives this in another form: "Life is a definite combination of heterogeneous changes, both simultaneous and successive."

How completely these definitions fail will be seen if we suppose a philosopher, unacquainted with the phenomena of life, to apply any of them, and draw a conclusion as to what life really is. They all exclude its more refined mental and spiritual phenomena, and apply to mineral changes and mechanical contrivances as well as to the complex manifestations of living beings. Conscious of its weakness, the latter author adds to his definition, making it stand thus: "Life is a definite combination of heterogeneous changes, both simultaneous and successive, corresponding with external co-existences and sequences." Thus completed, what idea does it convey of life, with its wonderful manifestations of intelligence, and subtle workings of spirit? Cut out of the most concrete abstractions, it fails in distinguishing movements in a plant from those in a crystal. His illustration of the growth of a plant towards instead of away from the light is against him; for solutions throw out crystals on the side where the light falls, rather than in an opposite direction.

205. What is Death?

If it be difficult to define life, equally difficult is it to define death. The rule which would apply to everything below man does not hold good with him. As his life stands in the way of all general expressions, so his death prevents a generalization in the definition of death. Ascending through all the lower forms of life, in his being the arch is complete; the structure stands firm, erect, beautiful, after the scaffolding of the body falls off. Death is change, is re-organization: with man, it is immortal life.

206. Christian Idea of Death Terrible, but that of the Ancient Greeks Beautiful.

Christians have connected everything revolting and terrible with Death. They have painted him as a ghastly skeleton upon a white horse, grasping a spear in his fleshless hand, or as a devouring monster.

They have the honor of originating these myths: there is nothing like them in the pagan world. The Greeks painted Death as a beautiful sleeping child or youth. In Eastern countries, it is believed that death results from the love of some god, who snatches the spirit to heaven. The Lacedemonians represented Death as asleep on a bed of down, watched by Morpheus and the Dreams. Death from drowning was imputed to love of the nymphs, by whom the spirit was conducted under water to a beautiful place adorned with evergreens and flowers. All these myths shadow the truth. The pagan was as near it as the Christian. If Spiritualism render any service, it will be in sweeping away all these myths, and giving in their place a positive statement of spirit-existence.

207. Terrors of Death.

Death has long been looked upon as a dreadful gulf, which divides the mortal life perhaps from oblivion,— the vale of tears and sorrows where man's noble faculties would perish in the darkness of eternity. Those who pretended to have full faith in the belief of the church had little else but what has been described, — a deep, everlasting sleep of mind in the cold earth, to comfort them.

A heavy veil of mist has hung over the rudimental sphere, in regard to the great change all must meet when the body becomes worn and wasted, and many depart for the second sphere with these dreadful conceptions in their minds, and with dear friends and relations near by whose minds are full of terror at the approaching scene, while the departing spirit approaches that gulf which, when passed over, it had been told could not be repassed, and from the other side of which no traveler could return. With these dark clouds encompassing the departing spirit, death was feared as the fell destroyer of the race; and the safe and easy journey was rendered tedious, and a real gulf of anguish.

208. MYTHS OF THE RESURRECTION OF THE BODY.

The doctrine of the final resurrection of the body has prevented a true conception of death. No matter to what dogmas the devotees clung, in the finale all agreed in this. This belief is not dependent on Christianity: it extended throughout the ancient world. In Egypt, it was the death of Osiris by the malignant Typhon, and restoration to life by the lovely Isis, which was represented in religious festivals. In Syria, it was Adonis, cut down in the bud of his age. Every year, his death and resurrection were celebrated, at Bylus, with magnificence. It lasted two days. The first was given to sorrow for his death; the second, to universal rejoicing at his resurrection. In India, the same story is related, except that Adonis is Sita, the last consort of Mahadeva, whom he finds, and bears with lamentations around the world. In Phrygia, Atys and Cybele were the personages of the myth. Atys, a beautiful shepherd-boy, beloved of the mother of gods, suddenly dies; and she, frantic with grief, wanders over the world, scattering the blessings of agriculture. He is at last restored to her. Every year the assembled nations performed the drama with sobs and tears, succeeded with frantic demonstrations of joy. The Northmen constructed the same drama; but Atys became Baldur, their god of gentleness and beauty.

In the Druidic Mysteries, the initiate was led through the most terrible scenes, shadowing forth their belief in the transmigration of souls. He died, was buried, was resurrected. The priests inclosed him in a little boat, and set him adrift on the black, stormy waves, pointing him to a distant rock as the harbor of life.

Among the Incas of Peru and the Aztecs of Mexico, the Mysteries were enacted with the horrible accompaniment of human sacrifice. The walls and floor of the obscurely lighted temple were washed with human blood. The initiate descended into the dark caverns under the temple, along a path called the "path of the dead." Shadows flitted before him, and shrieked and wailed around him, sacrificial knives threatened him, and dreadful pitfalls and snares yawned before him. At last he reached a narrow fissure, through which he was thrust into the open air, and received by awaiting thousands with indescribable acclamations.

There existed, among the most prominent North-American Indian tribes, a dim and shadowy resemblance to these systems.

209. Christianity takes a Deep Draught from Paganism.

Christianity at its rise presented the aspect of a new Jewish sect; and, through the apostolic age, it was only the more liberal growth of the Jewish tree. In consequence, it imbibed the myths and dogmas of the Hebrew world in a great degree. Among these dogmas was that of the resurrection of the body. Vague allusions are made to this doctrine in the New Testament. The phrase "resurrection of the body" does not occur in the Scriptures, and is not referred to in any public creed until the fourth century. This was not because the doctrine was not believed, but because it was so generally received that it was not mentioned. As soon as it was disputed, it was at once almost unanimously affirmed, and its disbelief was stigmatized as heresy. The uniform belief of all Christendom, from the time of the Apostles to the present, has been that the identical body of flesh which we now possess shall be resurrected, and again serve the spirit for habiliment. St. Augustine says, " Every man's body, however disposed here, shall be restored perfect in the resurrection ;" and his words have never been disputed by orthodox Christians.

Young, who is commonly classed with the poets, thus dolefully sings : —

> "Now charnels rattle ; scattered limbs, and all
> The various bones, obsequious to the call,
> Self-moved advance, — the neck, perhaps, to meet
> The distant head ; the distant head, the feet.
> Dreadful to view ! See, through the dusky sky,
> Fragments of bodies in confusion fly,
> To distant regions journeying, there to claim
> Deserted members, and complete the frame."

How refreshing to turn from this disgusting scene of horrors, and listen to a song of truth ! —

> " If lightning were the gross, corporeal frame
> Of some angelic essence, whose bright thoughts

> As far surpassed in keen rapidity
> The lagging action of his limbs as doth
> Man's mind his clay, with like excess of speed
> To animated thought of lightnings flies
> That spirit body o'er life's deeps divine,
> Far past the golden isles of memory."

Through the middle ages, this doctrine prevailed, with only an occasional dissenting voice. It was supported by scholasticism, with subtlest logic and metaphysical hair-splitting. Science has shattered it to dust; but most conservative theologians still cling to it, and hold up its disgusting details as boldly and nauseatingly as ever. They contend that the example of Christ's resurrection proves the resurrection of all. A distinguished divine, Dr. Spring, writes:—

"Whether buried in the earth, or floating in the sea, or consumed by the flames, or enriching a battle-field, or evaporating in the atmosphere, all, from Adam to the latest-born, shall wend their way to the great arena of the judgment. Every perished bone and every secret particle of dust shall obey the summons, and come forth. If one could then look upon the earth, he would see it as one mighty excavated globe, and wonder how such countless generations could have found a dwelling beneath its surface."

When this doctrine is held up in its ugly deformity, its utter untenableness shown, and the keen edge of ridicule pointed against it, the Christian will spiritualize the whole scheme. He has no right to do so. The recognized authorities in theology receive the words literally, and it is heterodox to believe otherwise.

Mohammed engrafted this dogma into his theological system, and it is taken now in its literal sense by orthodox Moslems, though a powerful sect represents the heterodox idea of spiritualization.

210. The Resurrection of Christ.

"The resurrection of Christ proves the resurrection of all human bodies," says a distinguished theologian: "Christ rose into heaven with his body of flesh and blood, and wears it there now, and will forever. Had he been there in body before, it would have been no such wonder that he should have returned with it; but that the flesh of our flesh, and bone of our bone, should be seated at the right hand of God, is worthy of the greatest admiration."

The Christian dogma of the resurrection of the body has its source in the wild speculations of Zoroaster, the Persian law-giver and prophet; and in the dogmas of the Egyptian priesthood. It was adopted by the Jews, who, in their close relations to that ancient people, were deeply impressed with the melodramatic outlines of this doctrine as taught at its source. The scheme ran thus: The good Ormuzd created man pure and happy, and to pass to a heavenly immortality; but the baleful Ahriman insinuated his hateful presence, and destroyed the plans of the Creator by introducing corruptions among mankind, to be expiated by disease and death of the body, and the consignment of the unclothed spirit to the terrible sufferings of hell.

But the great battle between the god of evil and the god of good goes on unceasingly; and, in the end, the good shall triumph, and the evil one sink into discomfiture. All evil deeds will then be canceled, and the original order of things restored. Then all souls shall have their shattered bodies restored intact, and the grand march of creation commence anew.

If we substitute Satan for Ahriman, we have the Jewish doctrine complete. Satan corrupts mankind; for which they suffer death, and the punishment of hell. The resurrection of the body restored man to his original condition of purity. In other words, God, the infinite and eternal spirit, came to earth, took on a human body, and ascended with it to heaven, and eternally retains the garments of flesh and blood, in order to teach man that in like manner his spirit will ascend. But Paul says, "Flesh and blood cannot inherit the kingdom of God."

211. Teachings of the Bible.

The church has misunderstood the teachings of the gospel. You will not accuse me of desiring to uphold the infallibility of the Bible. I wish to do it justice as a record of spiritual impressions and phenomena. Its teachings are filled with Spiritualism. Paul writes, "But some one will say, How are the dead raised up, and with what bodies do they come?"

"Thou fool! that which thou sowest, thou sowest not that body that shall be, but naked grain ; and God giveth it a body as it has pleased him." "There are celestial bodies and terrestrial bodies." "There is a natural body, and there is a spiritual body." "The first man is of the earth, earthy: the second man is the Lord from heaven." "Flesh and blood cannot inherit the kingdom of God." "We shall all be changed ; and bear the image of the heavenly, as we have borne the image of the earthy."

212. OBJECTIONS OF SCIENCE.

Let us look at the objections against the resurrection of the flesh, and the assigned reasons which render it a necessary part of the orthodox scheme of salvation. The dogma of a literal hell of fire being received, that of the resurrection is unavoidable ; for fire and physical torture cannot apply to a disembodied spirit. The old body must be drawn from the tomb, and united with the spirit, that both together may suffer for sins that both together have committed. A living Presbyterian divine, in the fervor of his zeal for the welfare of sinners, exclaims, "The bodies of the damned in the resurrection shall be fit dwellings for their vile minds. With all those fearful and horrid expressions which every base and malignant passion wakes up in the human countenance stamped upon it for eternity, and burned in by the flaming fury of their terrific wickedness, they will be compelled to look upon their own deformity, and to feel their fitting doom."

When the reasoner starts from wrong data, he runs as wild a course as the mathematician when he begins with wrong figures to work a problem. The admission of the dogma of hell brought with it this one, still more absurd. If the body be resurrected, what body shall arise, — the body that died, or that which is possessed while in health? Physiologists affirm that the fleshy portions of the body change in from seven to thirty days: at the end of a year, not a particle of the former body remains. If the body changes every month, we have twelve new bodies a year, and at threescore years and ten we have possessed eight hundred and forty bodies. At the final day, which shall be the honored seat of the soul? One has as good claim as the other. Perhaps all will be claimed, — a theory which seems necessary if it be necessary for the flesh and spirit to suffer together for the sins committed together, — and the miserable soul will possess a body as large as the writhing Titan, Tityrus, whose fabled body covered nine acres! If the last body be the honored one, and resurrected just as the spirit left it, as a major portion of mankind die of disease, what a loathsome assemblage must the last day present! In this case the saint will be obliged to drag his deformed body through eternity! The "living skeleton" must forever remain a skeleton; Daniel Lambert, the mammoth man, will weigh half a ton, either in one place or the other. The pale, sickly, cadaverous, deformed, remain pale, sickly, cadaverous, deformed, for ever and ever. But Dr. Hitchcock evades the otherwise inexplicable difficulty, by saying, "It is not necessary that the resurrected body should contain a single particle of the body laid in the grave, if it only contain particles of the same kind, united in the same proportion, and the compound be made to assume the same structure, as the natural body." What, then, becomes of the cardinal idea which renders resurrection necessary, the punishment of the sinful body? Such a resurrection would not at all meet the requirements and necessities of the hypothesis. The explanation is a denial and desertion of the dogma, and more unreal than that stupendous myth. It illustrates how entangled the philosopher becomes when he attempts the impossible task of harmonizing science and theology. The device is a willful subterfuge to escape the difficulty; a forlorn hope of an expiring cause.

XIII.

THE CHANGE CALLED DEATH.

For my own part, I feel myself transported with the most ardent impatience to join the society of my two departed friends. I ardently wish also to visit those celebrated worthies of whose honorable conduct I have heard and read much, or whose virtues I have myself commemorated in some of my writings. To this glorious assembly I am speedily advancing; and I would not be turned back in my journey, even on assured conditions that my youth, like that of Pelius, should again be restored. . . . And, after all, should this my firm persuasion of the soul's immortality prove to be a mere delusion, it is at least a pleasing delusion, and I will cherish it to my latest breath. — CICERO.

O my sons, do not imagine, when death shall have separated me from you, that I shall cease to exist. . . . If the souls of departed worthies did not watch over and guard their surviving fame, the renown of their illustrious actions would soon be worn out from the memory of men.
CYRUS, AS REPORTED BY XENOPHON.

Dying, she shall be welcomed by her father, her mother, and her brother, in that other world. — SOPHOCLES.

Do not say, SOCRATES is buried: say that you buried my BODY.
SOCRATES.

213. ULTIMATE OF NATURE'S PLAN.

NATURE, by one plan ever pursued, seeks one grand and glorious aim, — the elimination of an immortal intelligence. From the chaotic beginning, through the monsters of the primeval slime, through all the evanescent forms of being, up to man, that plan has been undeviatingly followed, and that aim held in view. Without this attainment, creation is a gigantic failure, and the results are objectless combinations of causes. The great tree of life strikes its roots deep into the soil of the elemental world, and stretches up its branches into the present. Its perfect fruit is man, immortal in his spiritual life. Such is a necessity of his constitution. Through no other being can that result be reached. The laws that perfect a tiger, a lion, an ox, or a horse, each after its type, making them more and more perfect of their kind, apply to him physically. With them, however, the end in that manner is reached. After a perfect tiger or deer or ox is attained, what then? Nothing. Causation in that direction is satisfied. After a perfect physical man is created, what then? Everything. Only a small fragment is gained. He walks on the boundaries of a vast and illimitable ocean of capabilities, only the means of attaining which have been acquired. Does nature satisfy herself with the bud of promise, the flower even, or with the mature fruit?

Man, as man, cannot fulfill his destiny. There is want of time, there is want of opportunity. A being, capable of infinite growth, must have infinite duration in which to expand. The opportunity, the duration, is bestowed by death.

214. DEATH IS NOT CHANGE OF BEING: IT IS CHANGE OF SPHERE.

The spirit, whether in the body or out of it, is the same; so the man, who goes out of the door of his house, is the same individual that he was within.

215. THE SPIRIT AND THE BODY.

The spiritual being is severed from the physical body, perhaps forcibly, perhaps slowly, by the maturity of age. However severe the forces that rend and obliterate the mental form, they have no permanent effect on the spirit, for that is unaffected by physical forces or elements. If the body be crushed to atoms by the falling avalanche, the spirit is unaffected, because the mineral mass is a void, through which it passes swiftly and unharmed. So, of all the terrible forms in which death presents itself, the spirit passes the storm, leaving the body wrecked and shattered. The kernel is left; and, although the chaff is blown away, existence remains.

216. MAN SHOULD MATURE, LIKE THE FRUIT OF AUTUMN, BEFORE DEATH.

Yet the plan of nature teaches that man should mature in age, and the separation take place as gradually and beautifully as the fruit drops in autumn from its parent limb. It is not desirable to enter the spirit-world before a ripe experience in this. There is a great loss by so doing. The instinct of life is a barrier against the temptation to enter the spirit-world. Death is fearful, and justly so, to those who regard it as a leap into profound darkness, and it is idle to talk to a heart lacerated by the iron hand which tears from it the dearly loved.

217. DEATH NO OCCASION FOR REJOICING.

As every extreme induces an opposite extreme, — from the grim picture of the fleshless skeleton with his remorseless scythe, from the lament and low moan of utter desolation, — the Spiritualist paints death with rapture, and entitles apotheosis "gone to the summer-land," "passed on," "re-born," and speaks of the shroud as a marriage-robe. Let us not be hasty. As flesh-clad spirits, we walk the courts of immortality as much now as we shall in the infinite future. We, as spirits, are now in the spirit-world; and, unless we pass from this sphere with all its duties completed, we have nothing for which to rejoice. Enter the chamber of the dead. The senses reign supreme. They stifle our intuition. They have the logic of appearance. Call to the dear one; and over that narrow chasm no answer will return. Dark, terribly still, fearfully sullen, the oblivion! — Oblivion?

Wait, lacerated heart, and throbbing brain; wait, until the senses are less active, and the interior soul asserts itself. Then, perhaps, you will feel more reconciled with fate.

218. THE SPIRIT AFTER DEATH — HOW RECEIVED.

Not alone passes the spirit to its new domain. Those it has loved, those gone before, are there to welcome it. The outcast and prodigal are met on the threshold by benevolent spirits, who lead them into the new and delightful pastures, and endeavor to awaken their understanding to the new and supreme life they have entered. Death comes as a liberator. The body can no longer subserve the purposes of the spirit. It can only inflict pain. Worn out by age, destroyed by disease, or lacerated by casualty, it fails in its uses, and is cast off. The steps, by which the doorway is reached, are painful; but, once there, all is rest. The quivering limbs, the contracting muscles, do not indicate pain, but simply the disturbed equilibrium of forces. The spirit enters the clairvoyant state deeper and deeper — that is, more and more separated from the body — until the final parting. Often, while yet connected with the body, it recognizes dear friends on the heavenly coast; and, as the setting sun gilds the landscape, so the spirit reflects on the countenance the glories it beholds, and the pale lips smile sweetly, as though they would speak of infinite beatitudes.

From the threshold it is led by welcoming friends, and introduced to its new life. It has lost nothing: it has gained nothing. It is the same individual, with no faculty diminished or increased, before whom extends the same vast and interminable ocean of progress, to be navigated only by the culture of its own inherent powers.

219. Mourn not the Dead.

The believer in this beautiful apotheosis should not shadow the joys of the departed by putting on the weeds of woe. To those who regard death as the "King of Terrors," it may be well; but, for him, it is contradictory to the belief expressed. We know the feelings of the lacerated heart, and deeply sympathize with its agonized throbs when robbed of its idols. Over the grave the mourner gazes sadly and wearily, the senses crushed and torn, and the spirit dimmed by the pelting rain, insensible to the impressions of the invisible world. The dark clouds of the physical senses obscure the spiritual sun; and we cry out, from our rack of torture, to those who are gone, and over the chill void even echo refuses her answer. If we loved the living, we worship the dead. We would pay them respect. We would change for them the order of our lives, and constantly give outward expression to our grief. We give such expression in our garments. The sackcloth and ashes of the heathen devotee become with us crape and black satin. If the dead are truly dead; if they go down to the grave as a final goal; if they pass to an infinitely removed hell, or, almost equally deplorable, to a heaven where they forget us in the new scenes with which they are surrounded; if death destroy all human emotions and feelings, and if we meet on the shining shore our departed ones as cold, intellectual passivities, — oh, then, let us put on, not only mourning garments, but the hair-cloth of the ancients, that its irritation may constantly remind us of our irreparable loss! Let us wear it, not for a year, but for our mortal lives, till it cuts through nerve and sinew, and the bones to their marrow.

If, on the contrary, we receive the Spiritual philosophy, and believe that death is only the gateway to another, better, and brighter state of existence; that the spirits of the departed are constantly around us, and that all that is required is a channel for us to receive words of love from them, — why should we put on the meaningless weeds of woe?

If our grief repeat itself on the minds of the departed, it is selfish in us to repine, and, by our sorrow, give pain to those for whom we suffer. Mourning garments perpetuate and keep alive this unwarranted grief. They are fitting for a barbarian, or a believer in the doctrines descended from an age of barbarism, but not for those who know that death is the usher to a higher plane of existence.

Respect for the dead! — not to be paid with crape and solemn faces, sighs and tears, but by a well-ordered life, that shall reflect the purity of those loved ones, who look down on us from the vernal heights of immortality.

XIV.

MEDIUMSHIP.

> They are the mystic lyres,
> Attuned by hands above,
> That waft from heaven's celestial choirs
> The songs of angel-love.

I believe there is a supernatural and spiritual world, in which human spirits, both bad and good, live in a state of consciousness. I believe that any of these spirits may, according to the order of God, in the laws of their place of residence, have intercourse with this world, and become visible to mortals. — Dr. Adam Clarke.

No man was ever truly great without divine inspiration. — Cicero.

220. Mediumship and Spirit Influences among Savages.

THE rude and childish methods of savage tribes to divine the future depend on the supposed interferences of spiritual beings, with which they people the regions of the air.

I have gathered up the various views entertained, by different nations and tribes, of the influence of spirits. Childish and conflicting as many of them appear to be, it will be seen that one cardinal idea underlies them all.

221. The Australians.

When the Australians desire success in the chase, they make a grass image of the kangaroo, and dance around it, believing that the image gives them power over the real kangaroo. The same custom is found with the Algonquin Indians; and they believe that an arrow touched with the magical medawin, fired into the track of an animal, arrests it in its course until the hunter can overtake it. Among other tribes, images of persons over whom injurious influences are wished to be exerted are made, and the destruction of the images is supposed to affect the persons represented. The same custom is found with the Peruvians, in Borneo, and in India.

222. THE MAORI.

Among the Maori, the magicians set sticks in the ground, to represent each warrior who is to start on an expedition, and they whose sticks are blown down are to die. The Feejeans divine by shaking a branch of dry cocoanuts: if all fall off, the sick person will recover; if, not he will die. They divine by observing their limbs: if the right trembles first, it is well; if the left, it is bad: by the taste of a leaf, or whether they can bite it through, or whether a drop of water will run down their arm, or drop off.

223. THE AFRICAN AND NEW ZEALANDER.

Even the spirit of the dead can be affected, by charms, incantations, and prayer, or directly through its body. The African fastens the jaw-bone of his enemy to a drum, that the constant jar may torment him. The Indian wears the paws of the bear, or the tusks and teeth of savage brutes, to give him courage. The New Zealander forces small pebbles down the throat of an infant to harden its heart. If the properties of amulets pass to the wearer, much more would the food influence the character. The flesh of timid animals makes the courageous man weak, while that of ferocious animals gives him strength and courage.

224. CONNECTION BETWEEN THE PERSON AND HIS NAME.

The supposed connection between the person and his name led to a diversified series of superstitions. The Indians of British America have the greatest aversion to repeating their names, as have the aboriginals of the United States, of South America, and Van Dieman's Land. A Hindoo wife never under any circumstances mentions the name of her husband, a custom also observed in East Africa. The Kafirs extend this custom beyond the husband to his relatives. Savages avoid speaking the names of the dead with mysterious horror, speaking only by allusion. They avoid speaking the names of fatal diseases. . . . The Yezides never mention the name of Satan. The Laplanders dislike calling the bear by name, and in Asia the same dislike is found for mentioning the name of the tiger. Brahma is a sacred name in India, as Jehovah is to the Jews, or the great name of Allah to the Mohammedans. To speak the name is to connect one's self, or get *en rapport*, with the object named. Among savage peoples, the belief in the existence and presence of spiritual beings is almost universal; and, though the means employed to hold converse with them may appear undignified and juvenile, the communications thus received are adapted to the wants of the receiver. The shaking of the bunch of cocoanuts gives as divine a revelation to the Feejean as the pen of the inspired medium to another race.

225. THE HERMIT OF THE GANGES

Retires to the eternal solitudes of the mountain caverns or the impenetrable wilds, and, by fasting and prayer, reduces the physical body, thereby becoming susceptible to the influence of immortal intelligences.

226. THE RED INDIAN,

When arriving at the age of manhood, retires to the forest, and fasts until he receives a revelation. So do their "medicine men," by reducing the flesh, bring themselves in contact with the spirit.

227. THE PYTHONESS AND ORACLES.

The prophecies of the Delphian oracle, which, perhaps, were the most truthful the world has ever possessed, were delivered by susceptible women, under the narcotizing influence of a subtle vapor, issuing from a crevice of the rocks; and the other

Grecian oracles, though not as famous, were, at times, of a remarkable character. The Pythons, or mediums, in all instances purified themselves by fasting and ablution. The unclean could not enter the presence of the divine spirits.

228. POSITION OF THE MEDIUM.

The medium occupies a fearful position. He is the channel through which the thoughts of angels flow, and the purity of their expression depends on the purity of his life. . . . The most crystal water, when made to flow over bogs and marshes, becomes foul with slime, and the most heavenly thoughts and emotions become turbid and fermented to error, when forced through the channel furnished by an impure mind.

229. WHY DISREPUTABLE MEDIA ARE USED.

"But," it is asked, "why do spirits descend to employ such persons as mediums? Do they not know that this very thing is a stumbling-block to the believer, and a weak point for the attack of the skeptic?"

All this is well considered; but are you sure they do so from choice? The number of persons organized for mediums of necessity is small. There are thousands of spirits wishing to communicate, for one medium. So anxious are they, that every opportunity, offering the least chance for intercourse with their friends, is eagerly seized.

230. Sensitiveness does not Exonerate Mediums for their Waywardness.

The sensitive condition, the cause of mediumship and its necessary accompaniment, renders the medium easily affected by surrounding circumstances. Hence, the waywardness of character they too often exhibit, and for which they are unqualifiedly censured. They should seek the best gifts, and order their lives after the highest ideal. The fact of their mediumistic susceptibility does not remove in the least their responsibility; nor can their shortcomings be excused by saying that they are instruments in the hands of controlling intelligences. No good and pure spirit will ever lead astray; and if intelligences, whatever may be their claims, attempt to lead from the path of rectitude and honor, they should be at once discarded. True and noble spirits will ever urge onward in the way of right; encourage the faltering, and heal the wounds of the fallen.

231. Mediumship Constitutional.

Mediumship, both for physical manifestations and of a psychological character, is purely constitutional. It cannot be bought or sold. It does not depend on moral or intellectual development. We have seen wonderful physical manifestations through individuals of most questionable morals, and received communications in writing of a very satisfactory character from dear departed friends, through ignorant and inferior persons.

232. INFLUENCE OF THE MEDIUM.

As every medium has a personality more or less positive, every one colors his communications in a more or less decided manner. Each has a peculiarity of his own. Subtile differences in organization allow certain manifestations more readily than others; and, by a permutation of innumerable conditions on the part of the medium and spirit, a wonderful variety of phenomena results.

233. WHAT IS THE STATE OF MEDIUMSHIP?

What is this peculiarity of organization, and how acquired? It would be difficult to tell what it is. It is often, and usually is, possessed at birth; or may be slowly or suddenly acquired. The spirit seems to have less hold of the body, and to be more sensitive for that reason. By sitting in circles, the condition may be acquired, after the manner that a musical string will, by repeated vibrations, become harmonious with another, if that be fixed.

334. ILLUSTRATION FROM MUSICAL INSTRUMENTS.

If two strings are stretched with unequal tension, — one having the points of tension fixed, while those of the other are movable, — the latter will not respond in unison with the former. But every vibration of the first will tend to move the points of tension of the latter, and will, after a time, bring them into such position that the two strings will be in unison. The time required to produce this result will depend on the violence of the vibrations, and the facility with which the points of support yield. This may result by a single vibration, or it may require days, months, or years.

"When a tuning-fork receives a blow, and is made to rest on a piano-forte during its vibrations, every string, which, either by its natural length or by its spontaneous subdivisions, is capable of executing corresponding vibrations, responds in a sympathetic note." The strings not thus in harmony remain silent. "Some one or other of the notes of an organ are generally in unison with the panes or the whole sash of a window, which consequently resound when those notes are sounded." The same effect may be often observed in thunder; the sound rolling away, growing gradually lower, until a note is touched which makes the windows and the whole house jar. The long-continued vibrations of neighboring bodies, when not in unison, affect each other, every vibration striving to reduce the other to concord. Adjacent organ pipes, not in unison, will often after a time force each other into harmony; and "two clocks whose beats differed considerably, when separate, have been known to beat together when fixed to the same wall, and one clock had forced the pendulum of another into motion, when merely standing on the same stone pavement." These illustrations may not appear at first pertinent; but, on mature reflection, they will be acknowledged as the rough exponents, in the physical world, of the science, adaptations, and harmonic relations of the spiritual.

235. INFLUENCE OF THE CONTROLLING SPIRIT.

A spirit, determined to develop a friend as a medium, may, by constant magnetic effort, induce a state of harmonious vibration between himself and his friend, just as the fixed string, by throwing the other into vibration, at length, by slow approximations, draws it into harmony, or, in other words, makes it echo its own notes. It then becomes a medium for the utterance of the other.

236. SPIRITS NOT EVIL BECAUSE THEY FAIL IN THEIR COMMUNICATIONS.

Here we have unfolded much that passes as the work of "evil, undeveloped spirits." Suppose, while the above-mentioned strings are out of harmony, we strike one, and the other vibrates: it only yields discord. Its tone has no resemblance to that which awoke it. It has spoken, but it has not spoken a word of what it was told to speak. Is it false? No. It has made an effort, and done the best it can. That effort will enable it to respond more truthfully at the next trial. It may fail again and again, but sooner or later it will give forth harmonious responses.

While holding a *séance* of peculiar interest with Dr. D. and family, his wife's sister became subject to strange muscular vibrations. Some laughed, others wisely said it was fancy, while others would have said an evil spirit had taken possession.

A few evenings after this, the family held a *séance* alone; and a beloved brother, who was accidentally killed a year previous, wrote wonderful communications through her now firm hand. The eagerness of the spirit rapidly broke down the opposing obstacles; but had the friends cried, "An evil spirit!" at the commencement, the nervous vibration would have corresponded with this opposition, until a diabolic influence would have readily suggested itself. There are spirits far from good, but the greatest prudence should be employed when judging of phenomena from the material plane.

While the medium is passing through this transitional state, he is often violently controlled; and the paper on which he essays to write is covered with hieroglyphical marks. With perfection of control, contortions and unintelligible writing will cease, and a beautiful sense of harmony yield exquisite thoughts, set to musical words.

237. Impressibility — How Induced.

Impressibility may be natural or induced. Fasting, the use of narcotics, stimulants, sickness, or loss of sleep, are favorable to the manifestation of the spirit-power. Whatever weakens the body increases impressibility, and thus allows the nearer approach of the spirit-world.

Various substances from the vegetable and mineral kingdoms have been employed, more especially by savage peoples, to induce a state of excitement or intoxication, whereby sensitiveness might be produced. Tobacco, the maguey, coco, and chucuaco, were used by the Californians; the coaxihuitle, or snake-plant, by the Aztecs; the cassine yupon, or ilex, and the *iris versicolor*, or blue-flag, by the Northern Indians.

It was the custom of the ancients to purify themselves, and fast, going out into the deserts, amid solitude and gloom, to obtain what they mistook as divine inspiration. Christ went out into the wilderness, and fasted forty days. Narcotizing drugs and vapors were also used by the priestesses at the oracles; and hasheesh, and other substances which excite the brain, are now employed in the East to induce a delirious trance.

The state produced by any of these methods is unreliable, and may be compared with the natural or true trance, as muscular motion, produced in the dead body by galvanism, may be compared with the movements of life.

238. A HIGH DEGREE OF MENTAL EXCITEMENT, BY PROSTRATING THE BODY, AWAKENS SPIRITUAL IMPRESSIBILITY.

P. B. Randolph has related some facts of his early experience, among which we regard the following as specially remarkable: He said, that, some eight or ten years ago, he followed the sea, in the capacity of cabin-boy. The captain and mate were severe men, and he was subjected to much abuse from them. On one occasion they had beaten him cruelly, and driven him to utter desperation, when he felt an interior impulse to cast himself into the sea, and so end his troubles. He ran for that purpose towards the side of the vessel; but, just as he was about to take the fatal leap, he saw the apparition of an arm and hand rising above the water, and motioning to him to go back. He suddenly stopped, and nearly fell backward; but, after persuading himself that this figure was a mere phantom of the imagination, he rallied, for a still more desperate effort, resolving not to be diverted from his purpose that time. As he approached the side of the vessel, however, he saw the whole form of his deceased mother floating above the waves, and this time she addressed him, speaking to his internal hearing, and commanded him to desist from his purpose, saying that the time for him to leave the world had not yet arrived, and that there was an important work for him to do in the future. He was thus saved from the suicide's death, and strengthened to endure the insults of his persecutors. In several other instances, he had been saved from danger, and strengthened under adversity, by the interposition of his spirit-mother.

239. THE EXALTATION PRODUCED BY SICKNESS

Is illustrated in the case of Prof. Hitchcock, detailed by himself in "The New-Englander," and it is one of the most striking on record. He had, "during a fit of sickness, day after day, visions of strange landscapes spread out before him, — mountain and lake and forest; vast rocks, strata upon strata, piled to the clouds; the panorama of a world, shattered and upheaved, disclosing the grand secrets of creation, the unshapely and monstrous rudiments of organic being." He became sensitive, by sickness, to the atmosphere of the strata. It is recorded by his son, that, during a recent illness, he saw spread out before him the beds of sandstone of the Connecticut Valley covered with tracks, and by them was enabled to determine points on which he had during health studied in vain.

240. MEDIUMSHIP INDUCED BY FASTING.

The sensitive state induced by fasting is often seen in the case of religious enthusiasts. The practice was valued by all the nations of antiquity, and is yet held in high veneration by savages. The young Indian must go out into the wilderness, and fast until the Great Spirit manifested himself, before he could become a brave. Trance and ecstasy were usually attained by fasting. The ideal prophet never tasted food, and held constant intercourse with the Deity. Frequently the fasting was carried to such an extent as to develop the most fearful form of madness.

241. SPIRITUAL PERCEPTIONS AT DEATH.

Death, by annulling the physical powers, seems to produce a state of clairvoyance; and, under favorable circumstances, the spiritual faculties are awakened in a remarkable degree.

A gentleman says, that, during partial drowning, "he saw, as if in a wide field, the acts of his being, from the first dawn of memory to the moment of entering the water. They were all grouped and arranged in the order of succession in which they happened, and he read the whole volume of existence at a glance; nay, its incidents and entities were photographed on his mind, limned in light, and the panorama of the battle of life lay before him."

"Miss Nancy Bailey, of Merrimac, formerly employed in the factories here, visited Nashua last week, for the purchase of a wedding-dress, bonnet, bridal-cake, etc., preparatory to her marriage on Wednesday next. She had completed her purchases, and was on her way to the depot, on Saturday evening, when the cars left. She therefore returned to the house of a friend, Mrs. Mitchell, on Canal Street, near the Jackson Corporation. About half-past three on Sunday afternoon, as she sat at the window, she threw up both hands, exclaiming, 'Why, there is Mr. Drew!' (the name of the gentleman to whom she was to be married, and who is a resident of Concord, Vt.) Mrs. Mitchell went to another window, but no one was in sight. At this moment a crash of glass called her attention to Miss Bailey, who had fallen forward against the window. Help was instantly called. She was placed upon a bed, and soon expired.

"Miss Bailey was about twenty-six years old, and latterly had not been in perfect health."

242. ORGANIC IMPRESSIBILITY PREFERABLE TO THAT WHICH IS INDUCED.

There is always incompleteness and imperfection in sensitiveness produced by the methods previously stated. The state may be induced by various means, but the most reliable is the normal organization which bestows sensitiveness and health at the same time. Sensitiveness is common to all individuals: it only varies in degree. It appears in intuition, discrimination of character, and many other forms. It depends on the delicacy of the nervous system,—the more delicately this is toned, the greater its liability to disease; and hence the majority of sensitives suffer more or less from pain. Perfect health is essential to the highest order of impressibility. Abstaining for a time from food or contact with the world conduces to sensitiveness of the nervous system, but, carried beyond narrow limits, introverts the mind on itself, and destroys the essential conditions. This state is often seen in the insane, who are usually highly and painfully impressible; but impressions of their own minds are received as foreign, and strange hallucinations result.

The body must be pure. When inflamed with an improper diet, or saturated with stimulants and narcotics, the mind, reciprocating the physical condition thus created, is a seething mass of passions, a magazine which a spark may explode, and not willingly do the pure spirits approach to it. The prophets of old fasted and dieted, that they might gain immortal inspiration: they ordered their lives in purity, that they might allow the invisible world the closer to approach them. Be assured, that, although, for want of better, all mediums are employed, sooner or later those who are not lifted out of the moral sloughs into which they have fallen will be discarded, and only those who possess an upright character will be reserved for the noble office.

243. Desire for Mediumship.

Such is a general view of the conditions favorable to mediumship. It is not a gift to a few, but is possible to all. Obedience to its essential requirements, an honest purpose, a pure heart, are demanded of those who would attain its highest walks.

244. How to become a Medium.

You may have natural powers as yet unawakened, or you may be capable of becoming mediumistic after sufficient trial. There is only one course. If you understand animal magnetism, you know that the subject must become passive, and have no care for the result. As the law of magnetic control is the same, whether mortal or spirit be the operator, the same passivity must be observed by the medium. Sitting in circles is the best of all means, especially if a medium already developed be present. Retiring alone at a certain hour is also a good discipline. Anxiety to receive communications is among the greatest obstacles to success. Pray for the best gifts, and according to your possibilities your prayer will be answered; for remember that the dear departed of the realms of light are equally desirous with yourself to converse, and will avail themselves of every opportunity to do so. Remember, that, though they avail themselves of every channel, the noble angels of light love best to approach the pure in heart and pure in body.

245. INFLUENCE OF INDIVIDUALS ON THE COMMUNICATIONS.

The presence of some persons wholly prevents communications. Often in circles have we seen a single word, or the nearer approach of a particular person, wholly interrupt the spirit-control. This has occurred even when the offending person was a near and dear friend of the spirit purporting to communicate. Some persons have remarked, and very naturally too, that, if the spirit were the one it claimed to be, it would certainly continue its communications. They did not understand the delicacy of tone existing between the medium and spirit, or the wonderful fragility of the conditions necessary for communications. It is not that the medium or the spirit is offended, but it becomes impossible to proceed. To draw an illustration from the physical world, take the effects of certain vapors on the processes of photography. Prof. Draper says that the artist often fails in taking daguerreotypes most inexplicably. All conditions apparently are perfect, yet no distinct impression is made. This will always result if the minutest quantity of the vapor of iodine, bromine, chlorine, or other negative substance, is present. So sensitive is the plate to their vapors, that he recommends never to leave those substances in the same room with the camera.

The brain of the medium and the auric chain by which communication is held are far more sensitive than the daguerrean plate to the presence of negative bodies. The harsh word, the suggestion of trickery and fraud, disturb the medium in the circle far more than when in a normal condition; for he is, by his mediumship, thrown into the most susceptible state his organism will allow, and the least inharmony affects his nerves with greater force.

246. A Physical State Negative to Mediumship.

Incredulity, or a reasoning skepticism, produces no ill result; but bigotry, sneering unbelief, and a rude curiosity, can never be gratified with satisfactory communications. Persons with such characteristics, if they are able to communicate at all, must do so with spirits of their own grade,— spirits who are not to be repelled by their insolence, and who are of unreliable character; and, thereby, such inquirers may be led to repudiate the whole matter.

There is a physical state negative to mediumship; and, in a circle, it acts directly against "control." This may be independent of mentality, and is of a purely constitutional character; and mediums may fall into it by exhaustion. For this reason, there are times when the spirit-world is able to approach much nearer than at other seasons. Besides a flood-tide, there is an ebb-tide of inspiration. It results, not from the fault of the departed, but from the deficiency of the medium.

The investigator, for the same reason, who expects least, usually receives most; and it is observable that the most astounding tests are received when least expected. Strong desire and an exacting expectation defeat themselves by re-acting on the conditions of passivity, which are absolutely essential.

247. WHY COMMUNICATIONS ARE CONTRADICTORY.

There are many causes beside the ready one usually assigned,—namely, that of evil spirits. By education, we regard spiritual beings as infallible and omniscient. They do understand more than we; their views are broader, and their judgment more penetrating: but they are otherwise as fallible. We ask questions a deity only can answer; and because they make an attempt, and fail, or do not make an attempt, we are too ready to refer the deficiency to intentional fraud. There is as much diversity among spirits as among mortals, and the method of communication with them is not perfect.

First, of the imperfection of the method. If a chemist wish to test an experiment in which delicate and refined manipulations are necessary, how carefully he studies all the involved conditions, and how accurately he attempts to fulfill them! Even then, employing substances he can see and feel, he often fails. But, of the spiritual elements, little or nothing is positively known, and it is impossible for a circle to fulfill every requirement. The members of it deal with emanations too subtle for the senses, yet inconceivably susceptible. Can it be thought strange that circles meet with disappointments?

The second consideration is explained by a correct view of spirit-life. A thousand million people toil and strive on earth: the rich, by depressing the poor, strive to grow richer; the poor take vengeance on their oppressors. On one hand are the savages of civilization, the law-breakers; on the other, the merciless artificial law gibbets the offender. On every side is war, deception, falsehood, jealousy, passion, rage, hypocrisy, bigotry; and the dark parent of all this foul brood, ignorance.

The spirit-world is the extension of earthly life. When spirits from such earthly conditions gain access to a medium, they present their personality; and nothing less than intentional falsehood and deception, or error through ignorance, can be expected.

"Can an evil tree bring forth good fruit?" "Do men think to gather grapes of thorns, or figs of thistles?" "A tree is known by its fruit." Then how can any rational mind expect to gather truth from an untruthful mind? How arrive at the truth, when these thriftless minds distort and confuse the little truth which may be uttered through them even by low spirits? How can they trust the spirits of those whom they would not trust while on earth?

Is it rational to throw away all communications, and declare none to be spiritual, because there is disagreement? Would it be in accordance with reason to say there was no human race, because there exists disagreement among the minds which compose the human family? In all the spiritual communications yet given, there is not the thousandth part of the contradiction that exists among authors on earth.

The truth must be forced upon the human mind, that, after death, the spirit is as much an *individual* as before the change. Death effects no alteration in the form, or organization of the mind, but leaves the spirit the identical individual it was in this life, with its own peculiar thoughts and ideas. As every spirit is a separate being, every one thinks and acts for himself, at his *own cost*.

248. CONTRADICTIONS REFERABLE TO THE CIRCLE.

Do not men enjoy heaven on earth? Are there not many who enjoy heaven forever? Are there not those who carry a hell in their minds continually? But these "live, move, and have their being," on the same earth! So it is in the spirit-world, as has often been declared by clairvoyant mediums.

A circle is formed. Its members are all of a strongly positive character. There are spirits who wish to communicate. The members of the circle are not unfolded, and hence a spirit of narrow development is attracted. The circle ask questions on various topics, and, at length, touch on doctrinal themes. If the circle be of Universalists, the spirit will appear to be a Universalist, and will declare that there is no hell or devil, and that God is a being of love and benevolence. If the circle be of Presbyterians, the spirit will appear to adopt that creed, and declare there is a hell, a triune God, etc. If the circle be of Atheists, and ask if there be a God, the spirit will answer in accordance with their minds. If of Unitarians, then God will be a unity, and the spirit will agree with the circle. And, let the circle be composed of what sect or society it may, the spirit will appear to be of corresponding belief. Not that every spirit will thus change, but there are many who will. On earth, such minds may be seen in every community, — minds that ever agree with those present, let them be who they may, or whatsoever be their belief. They die, and, as their spirits change not, when they would converse with a circle, their opinions are entirely ruled by the positiveness of that circle. Here is one of the greatest sources of disagreement; for the different circles who receive such communications compare them, and discover contradictions. Suppose, that, in the Atheistic circle, there be one person who believes that there is a God. He asks whether it is so. The spirit never has seen such a being; but, seeing the mind of the questioner so positive that such a being exists, it answers affirmatively. Now, if the Atheist ask the same question, the spirit looks into all their minds, and sees but one dissenting opinion. He says he has never seen one, and he does not believe that such a being exists! In all probability, if a circle should receive several contradictions like this, its members would become disgusted, and cry, "Delusion!" Ignorant of the principles of this communication, and of the philosophy of the spirit-world, they are blind led by the blind. "And, if the blind lead the blind, both will fall into the ditch."

Again, a circle is formed of low and vile characters, who commence by swearing, and intend nothing but sport. They wish for no instruction how to be better, or how to become developed. Who is so irrational as to suppose that developed angels will converse with this assembly? None, certainly. But spirits *lower* than themselves — those who love to lie, to cheat, and to steal, who disregard all right — are attracted to such a circle, and answer all questions by lies, except so far as they may secure to themselves the confidence of their questioners. Test questions they may answer correctly. Meantime, they will send those persons who repose confidence in what they say in a vain and wild chase after wealth. The members of such a circle will report what they have seen and heard, and how well they have enjoyed themselves. Those who know their character will say, in heart, that with such they want nothing in common. There are also spirits who delight in torture. If these can find a medium suitable for their purpose, they will do with him as they choose, making him act and speak in a most reprehensible manner. The position of such a medium is not enviable.

Another circle is formed of honest investigators. Their motives are pure and worthy: their minds are elevated and refined. To this circle no lying tongue utters sentiments derogatory to the high character of the circle; but the most elevated and exalted minds will be attracted towards the place, and there deliver their sublime truths. Here is a circle formed upon the right principles; and its members can hold perfect, good, and worthy intercourse with the invisibles.

249. How a Circle should be Formed.

When a circle is to be formed, the spirits, if possible, should determine who should compose it; but, if this cannot be done, candor, purity, and harmony should be made necessary pre-requisites to entering it. The number of members is immaterial, but it is seldom possible for more than ten or twelve to be brought together in sufficient harmony. The regular meetings should not be oftener than twice, nor less than once, a week. When the circle meet oftener than this, the conditions, by which communications are held, become weakened; and, if longer intervals occur, the influence of the previous circle is lost. Music is promotive of harmony; a fact recognized in all ages. Having thus formed the circle, the mind should cast aside all care and anxiety, and become passive; asking nothing, but ready to receive whatever manifestation may occur, be it small or great. Remember that satisfactory results cannot be commanded: they must flow of their own accord.

250. Responsibility of Mediumship.

The position of the medium is one of greatest responsibility. As the clearest mountain-stream is contaminated by passing through fens and sloughs on its way to the sea, so the purest spiritual truths are distorted in their transmission through an impure or imperfect medium. It is a terrible force with which he deals. He should not venture to play with the lightning unless he understand its laws. If he be not conscientious, and honestly desirous of knowledge, it is better for him to stand aloof. Reflection, thought, is the gateway of intuition. The gods love the worker.

"Pray for the best gifts," and improve such as are given you, in the gentle spirit of humility, and with earnest striving for improvement. It is not well to scorn mundane means; for, so far as their knowledge extends, men are more practical teachers than are spirits, and it is not to supply a royal road to knowledge for indolence that communication is held. If mediumship does not ennoble you, you are the worse for it.

Do not suppose that the spiritual agency is to furnish an easy road to learning, or that it will elevate you without effort on your own part. The mortal author is of equal authority with the spirits, and in some paths may be even more valuable. Written language has preserved the thoughts of ages, and none can avoid the labor of their acquisition. If you enter this great field, determined to make the truth your own, and to excel in your search, your impressibility will be of greatest service; and, with the care and wisdom of a father or a teacher, your spirit-friends will guide and direct you. The higher the mental culture you attain to, the more impressible you become to unrecognized truths; and, receiving them, you can gain a better understanding of them, and give them clearer expression. The medium can be an automaton, a machine for communication, without receiving more benefit to himself than does the planchette when it writes: he can enter the sphere of ideas only by the culture of his intellect.

XV.

MEDIUMSHIP DURING SLEEP.

ALL good thoughts, words, or actions, are the productions of the celestial world. — ZOROASTER.

Nothing so nearly resembles death as sleep; and nothing so strongly intimates the divinity of the soul as what passes in the mind on that occasion: for the intellectual principle in man, during this state of relaxation and freedom from external impressions, frequently looks forward into futurity, and discerns events before time has yet brought them forth; a plain indication of what the powers of the soul will hereafter be, when she shall be delivered from the restraints of her present bondage. — XENOPHON.

251. SLEEP.

THE rarest occurrences are by no means the most extraordinary. On the contrary, the most wonderful cease to attract attention, because they are daily presented. Every night man falls into a state resembling death, from which he awakes a resurrected spirit. Activity and repose are alternate states of the body. During sleep, the waste is reduced to a minimum, and the recuperating processes go forward with increased activity. This is the external aspect of sleep; but, on attentive study, it exhibits a class of phenomena equally astonishing and mysterious with those attending the waking hours. It is not a simple, but a very complex, state;

in which ecstasy, trance, clairvoyance, and mediumship can be recognized.

252. DREAMS.

We shall discuss the occult problem of the origin of dreams, showing to what extent they are referable to impressibility, and in what degree to other sources. They are not susceptible of explanation by one common cause. The dreams of the dyspeptic are entirely different from those of the prophetic cast. There are dreams originating from the disturbed body, and from the restless mind; and there are other dreams wherein mesmeric and psychometric influences are discernible; and yet others, with high states of clairvoyance; and still others, resulting from purely spirit impressions.

It is not presumable that the mind is more wise, or has greater capacity, while asleep than while it is awake; yet, in the class of dreams now under discussion, it is enabled to do what it could not do during its waking moments, and, what is more, it obtains knowledge wholly independent of the senses, as is proved by the following facts: —

It is related that a lady, blind from birth, was enabled in dreams to see objects distinctly, and describe them accurately; yet, on *post-mortem* examination, it was found that the optic nerves were completely destroyed.

Harriet Martineau relates a story of an old lady, blind from her birth, who yet saw in her sleep; and, in her waking state, correctly described the clothing of individuals. This fact has many bearings. If dreams are only *renewed* cerebral impressions, and we do not dream of anything of which we do not already know the elements, as the Spencerian materialists teach, how account for dreams revealing objects when the eye has never received a ray of light? It can be done successfully only by admitting that the mind, during sleep, passes into a superior state, and acquires new capabilities; and does not such an admission strike at the basis of the vaunted system? If mind can thus arise above, and pass beyond, its material or physical existence, can it be presumed that it is simply the result of the elements of its physical existence? If the mind can appreciate color and form, without ever having received knowledge of such qualities through the eye, then it is independent of the sense of vision for its knowledge.

This independence of the mind is farther shown by the strange phenomena dreams present in their annihilation of time and space, thus trenching on the domain of spirit-existence. Every one will have remarked this in his own experience.

Dr. Abercrombie speaks of a friend, who, in a dream, crossed the Atlantic, and spent two weeks in America. On re-embarking, he thought he fell overboard, and awoke to find that he had been asleep but ten minutes.

Macnish says, that he dreamed he made a voyage to India, spending several days in Calcutta, continued his journey to Egypt, visited the cataracts and pyramids, and held confidential interviews with Mohammed Ali, Cleopatra, and Saladin, the whole journey apparently occupying several months; but he slept only an hour.

Addison says: "There is not a more painful action of the mind than invention; yet in dreams it works with such ease and activity, that we are not sensible when the faculty is employed. For instance, I believe every one, some time or other, dreams that he is reading books, papers, or letters; in which case, invention prompts so readily that the mind is imposed on, and mistakes its own suggestions for the composition of another."

Coleridge composed "Christabel" and "Kubla Khan" in sleep; and Tartini dreamed that the Devil came, and played what he afterwards wrote out as the "Devil's Sonata." Dr. Franklin solved difficult political problems, and Dr. Gregory obtained important scientific ideas, in dreams.

Animals frequently dream, especially the dog, to whom man imparts a strong magnetic influence. The dog is also sometimes somnambulic, as the following anecdote shows:—

"I was attracted by a very curious sound from the dog, and a strange, fixed look from his eyes, which were set, as though glazed in death, and neither changed nor quivered in the slightest degree, though the blaze of a cheerful wood fire shone brightly upon them. After stretching his limbs several times, and whining, he gradually arose to his feet, and assumed the attitude of pointing, in every particular just as I had seen him a hundred times in the field. When my surprise had a little abated, I spoke to the dog: but he manifested no consciousness, nor took the slightest notice of my voice, though several times repeated; and it was only when I touched him that the spell was broken, when, running several times around the room, he quietly resumed his place before the fire." *

253. SOMNAMBULISM

Is to sleep what the magnetic state is to wakefulness, and presents a parallel series of phenomena.

Many instances are recorded, and have been brought within the observation of many, that some persons will answer questions correctly when they are soundly asleep. Such can be made to dream anything desired by whispering in their ears. They, in other words, naturally fall into a magnetic slumber, differing only from that artificially induced by the superior vividness of the impressions of the latter. As an illustration, take the following fact from Macacio: — †

"In his work on sleep, he relates a striking example as having occurred in his presence. It was in the case of a certain patient of a friend of his, Dr. Gromier, — a married lady, subject to hysterical

---

* Quoted by S. B. Brittan.

† *Reports et Discussions.* Paris, 1833. Quoted in "Footfalls on the Boundaries of another World."

affections. Finding her one day a prey to settled melancholy, he imagined the following to dissipate it. Having cast her into a magnetic sleep, he said to her, *mentally*, "Why do you lose hope? You are pious: the Holy Virgin will come to your assistance. Be sure of it." Then he called up in his mind a vision, in which he pictured the ceiling of the chamber removed, groups of cherubim at the corners, and the Virgin, in a blaze of glory, descending in the midst. Suddenly the somnambule was affected with ecstacy, sank on her knees, and exclaimed, in a transport of joy, "Ah, my God! So long — so very long — I have prayed to the Holy Virgin; and now, for the first time, she comes to my aid!"

254. SPIRITUAL COMMUNICATIONS GIVEN IN DREAMS.

The following facts are presented as illustrations and proofs of spirit-intercourse during sleep. No philosophy but that accepting direct spiritual influence can explain them.

"A farmer in one of the western counties of England was met by a man whom he had formerly employed, and who again asked for work. The farmer, rather with a view to be relieved from his importunity than with any intention of assisting him, told him he would think of it, and send word to the place where the man told him he should be found. Time passed on, and the farmer entirely forgot his promise. One night, however, he suddenly started from his sleep, and, awaking his wife, said he felt a strong impulse to set off immediately to the county-town, some thirty or forty miles distant; but why, he had not the least idea. He endeavored to shake off the impression, and went to sleep again; but awoke a second time with such a strong conviction that he must start that instant, that he directly rose, saddled his horse, and set off. On his road he had to cross a ferry, which he could only do at one hour of the night, when the mail was carried over. He was almost certain that he should be too late, but nevertheless rode on, and, when he came to the ferry, found, greatly to his surprise, that, though the mail had passed over a short time previously, the ferryman was still waiting. On his expressing his astonishment, the boatman replied, 'Oh, when I was on the other side, I heard you shouting, and so came back again.' The farmer said he had not shouted; but the other repeated his assertion that he had distinctly heard him call. Having crossed over, the farmer pursued his journey, and arrived at the county-town the next morning. But, now that he had come there, he had not the slightest notion of any business to be transacted, and so amused himself by sauntering about the place, and at length entered the court where the assizes were being held. The prisoner at the bar had just been, to all appearance, proved clearly guilty, by circumstantial evidence, of murder; and he was then asked if he had any witnesses to call in his behalf. He replied, that he had no friends there; but, looking around the court amongst the spectators, he recognized the farmer, who almost immediately recognized in him the man who applied to him for work. The farmer was instantly summoned to the witness-box; and his evidence proved, beyond the possibility of a doubt, that, at the very hour the prisoner was accused of committing murder in one part of the county, he was applying for work in another. The prisoner was of course acquitted, and the farmer found, that, urged on by an uncontrollable impulse, which he could neither explain nor account for, he had indeed taken his midnight journey to some purpose, notwithstanding it had appeared so unreasonable and causeless. 'This is the Lord's doing, and it is marvelous in our eyes.'"

255. PRESENTIMENTS.

There are many cases recorded of persons hurrying home impelled by some presentiment. "Mr. M. Calderhood was once, when absent from home, seized with such an anxiety about his family, that, without being able in any way to account for it, he felt himself impelled to fly to them, and remove them from the house they were inhabiting; one wing of which fell down immediately afterwards. No notion of such a misfortune had ever occurred to him, nor was there any reason whatever to expect it; the accident originating from some defect in the foundation."

A circumstance exactly similar to this is related,

by Stilling, of Prof. Bohm, teacher of mathematics at Marburg; who, being one evening in company, was suddenly seized with a conviction that he ought to go home. As, however, he was very comfortably taking tea, and had nothing to do at home, he resisted the admonition; but it returned with such force that at length he was obliged to yield. On reaching his house, he found everything as he had left it: but he now felt himself urged to remove his bed from the corner in which it stood to another; but, as it had always stood there, he resisted this impression also. However, the resistance was vain; absurd as it seemed, he felt he must do it: so he summoned the maid, and, with her aid, drew the bed to the other side of the room; after which, he felt quite at ease, and returned to spend the rest of the evening with his friends. At ten o'clock, the party broke up; and he retired home, and went to bed and to sleep. In the middle of the night, he was wakened by a loud crash; and, on looking out, he saw that a large beam had fallen, bringing part of the ceiling with it, and was lying exactly on the spot his bed had occupied.*

A gentleman residing some miles from Edinburgh had occasion to pass the night in that city. In the middle of the night, he dreamed that his house was on fire, and that one of his children was in the midst of the flames. He woke, and so strong was the impression upon his mind, that he instantly got out of his bed, saddled his horse, and galloped home. In

* " Univercœlum."

accordance with his dream, he found his house in flames, and, arriving in time, saved his little girl, about ten months old, who had been forgotten, and left in a room which the devouring element had just reached.

A clergyman of distinguished ability and truthfulness relates the following. It shows how vividly the mind may be impressed with the perception of foreign intelligences, or that it is capable of leaving the body, or of acquiring or perceiving through spiritual senses, in either case confirming spiritual existence.

"I was engaged at that time in pursuing theological studies with the Rev. Mr. G., in a village in the vicinity of Boston. During the night, I seemed to enter a place which I had never before seen. I walked up the main street, which was shaded with large trees, noticing the prominent buildings as I passed them. It seemed to be Sunday evening: the shops were closed, and all business suspended. The street led me to a large building containing a hall. I saw horses and carriages in great numbers standing near. Entering the hall, I found a large audience gathered. It was a meeting for religious purposes. At last the preacher rose up, and his features impressed themselves upon me, and his very words, although he seemed an utter stranger. The vision made a deep impression upon my mind. It seemed not a dream, but a reality.

"On the Sunday evening ensuing, I walked with a friend to attend a religious meeting in a neighboring village where I had never been. On entering the street, it seemed familiar to me, and I remembered it to be the place I had seen in a vision a few days preceding. Anxious to see if my dream would correspond with the reality throughout, I pursued the path which I seemed to have taken before, till it led me to the building, which I at once recognized. Entering it, the hall was familiar; and, when the preacher arose, I knew him at once. The street, building, and preacher corresponded, in every particular, with those impressed on my consciousness during the previous vision."

I have heard my mother relate an episode of parallel character in her life. She was always highly impressible, and was called "our family seer." She dreamed that she was traveling over a very mountainous country in a wagon. Being fatigued with riding, she alighted, and walked up a hill, from the summit of which she obtained a charming prospect of a beautiful river and its valley.

Three years afterward, she was traveling through Alleghany County, N.Y., became fatigued, alighted, and walked. When she came to the summit of the hill, she thought the prospect familiar; and, all at once, she remembered her dream. She had been there before in spirit, although not in body.

If all we know is derived by and through the senses, of course knowledge of a scene we are to see three years hence must be denied. Ah, materialist! with your sensatory scheme, how do you meet these facts of prescience? Is a mind asleep more active than a mind awake? We do not want to hear about "unknown laws of mind;" but, if these facts can be explained, let us have the explanation.

"Mr. Robert Curtis, a citizen of Newport, Ind., who bears the reputation of being a very honest man, related to us the following wonderful statement of facts and circumstances: About twenty-eight years ago, he was very sick, and it was thought by his friends and physicians he could not live. Although they each and all endeavored to conceal their opinions from him, yet he well knew what their views were from conversations he overheard. This caused him to feel wretchedly. During this state of feeling, he dreamed that a man came to Richmond who cured him by the use of his hands. This made him feel better, and he commenced regaining his health, and in the course of a few months was able to go to work. About four years after, he became quite sick again, and from that time the state of his health was very poor until cured as hereinafter stated. About three weeks before Dr. A. J. Higgins came to this city, he dreamed again that a man came to this city, and that he was cured by him in the manner above stated. This time he saw the man distinctly in a dream, and retained in his memory his personal appearance, and knew him to be the same man he had dreamed about twenty-eight years ago. When Dr. Higgins arrived, he was impressed that he was the man who had come to cure him. He at once repaired to this city, and, on seeing Dr. Higgins, recognized him as the man whom he had seen in his vision three weeks before. He applied to him for treatment, and, sure enough, was cured in the manner suggested in his dreams." *

The following are related by William Fishbough, and are of almost parallel character : —

"Mrs. W., a lady of unquestionable veracity, residing in Taunton, Mass., informed me, that, several years ago, a family, intimately related to her, removed to the State of Ohio. Some time subsequent to their removal, the family, by some untoward occurrence which I do not remember, was thrown into deep affliction, which rendered the presence and sympathy of Mrs. W. very desirable. About this time, Mrs. W. had an impressive dream, in which were represented to her mind the general condition of the family, the appearance and architectural structure of the house in which they resided, the species of the trees, and the relative positions and appearance of these and all other objects near the house. The whole scene, with all its minutiæ, was, as it were, at one glance vividly daguerreotyped upon her mind, although she had never had the slightest description of the place. On subsequently relating her dream to her friend who had returned from Ohio, he confirmed it as *true in every particular.*"

"Many of our readers will remember the blowing-up of the steamboat 'Medora,' at Baltimore, several years ago, attended with the loss of many valuable lives. An authentic account (which I must

* Correspondent " Religio-Philosophical Journal."

now relate from memory) subsequently appeared in the papers, of a sailor, belonging to a small vessel which plied up and down the Chesapeake Bay, foreseeing the occurrence, with all its essential particulars, in a dream, a night or two before it took place. He related his vision to his shipmates, who of course deemed it unworthy of attention until after they heard of the fate of the steamer. The vessel to which the man belonged sailed up the bay on the day of the catastrophe; and, as she approached the city of Baltimore, a vessel was seen lying at anchor in the harbor, with flag at half-mast. On seeing this, the man who had had the dream immediately exclaimed, 'That's for the "Medora"!' Strange to say, they found that the 'Medora' had been blown up, and lives had been destroyed, precisely, in all essential particulars, as had been foreshadowed in the dream."

"The reader will remember the tragedy of the murder of Mr. Adams by John C. Colt, which took place in New York several years ago. Two days before the murder of Mr. Adams, his wife dreamed twice that he was murdered; and that she saw his body cut to pieces, and packed away in a box. The dreams made a deep impression upon her mind; and on the disappearance of her husband, and before he was found, she was inconsolable. The facts were precisely in accordance with the dream."

The following is a condensed account of a case recorded in Sunderland's "Pathetism."

"On the night of May 11, 1812, Mr. Williams of

Scorrier House, near Redruth, in Cornwall, dreamed *thrice* that he saw a man shoot, with a pistol, the Chancellor of the Exchequer, in the lobby of the House of Commons. The dreams made a deep impression upon his mind; and, the next day, he related them to many of his friends whom he met, describing minutely the man whom he had seen assassinated. A friend, to whom Mr. Williams related his dream, recognized his description of the person assassinated as answering precisely to Mr. Perceval, Chancellor of the Exchequer, whom Mr. Williams had never seen. Shortly afterward, the news came, that, on the evening of the 11th of May, a man of the name of Bellingham had shot Mr. Perceval in the lobby of the House of Commons, precisely as Mr. Williams had dreamed, and on the same night. After the astonishment had a little subsided, Mr. Williams described most particularly the appearance and dress of the man whom he saw in his dream fire the pistol, as he had before done of Mr. Perceval. About six weeks after, Mr. Williams, having business in town, went, accompanied by a friend, to the House of Commons, where he had never before been. Immediately that he came to the steps at the entrance of the lobby, he said, 'This place is as distinctly within my recollection, in my dream, as any room in my house;' and he made the same observation when he entered the lobby. He then pointed out the exact spot where Bellingham stood when he fired, and which Mr. Perceval had reached when he was struck by the ball, and where and how he fell.

The dress, both of Mr. Perceval and Bellingham, agreed with the description given by Mr. Williams, even to the most minute particular."

"A mother, who was uneasy about the health of a child who was out at nurse, dreamed that it had been buried alive. The horrid thought woke her; and she determined to set off for the place without a moment's delay. On her arrival, she learned, that, after a sudden and short illness, the child had died, and had just then been buried. Half frantic from this intelligence, she insisted upon the grave being opened; and, the moment the coffin-lid was raised, she carried off the child in her arms. He still breathed, and maternal care restored him to life. The truth of this anecdote has been warranted. We have seen the child so wonderfully rescued: he is now, in 1843, a man in the prime of life, and filling an important post."

"The Jesuit Malvenda, the author of a Commentary on the Bible, saw one night, in his sleep, a man laying his hand upon his chest, who announced to him that he would soon die. He was then in perfect health, but soon after, being seized with a pulmonary disorder, was carried off. This is told by the skeptic Bayle, who relates it as a fact too well authenticated even for the apostle of Pyrrhonism to doubt."

"Sir Humphrey Davy dreamed one night that he was in Italy, where he had fallen ill. The room in which he seemed to lie struck him in a very peculiar manner; and he particularly noticed all the details of the furniture, etc., remarking, in his dream, how unlike anything English they were. In his dream, he appeared to be carefully nursed by a young girl, whose fair and delicate features were imprinted on his memory. After some years, Davy travelled in Italy, and, being taken ill there, actually found himself in the very room of which he had dreamed, attended upon by the very same young woman whose features had made such a deep impression upon his mind. The reader need not be reminded of the authenticity of a statement resting upon such authority, eminent alike for truth that would not deceive, and intelligence that could not be deceived."

Brittan thus relates a case of spiritual impressions given in a dream : —

"I made the acquaintance of a Mr. S., who has, in several instances, been the recipient of spiritual impressions, communicated generally during the hours of sleep. In the course of our interview, he related the following, which is worthy of record. For some time he had visited a young lady, whom he had selected as his companion for life. They had pledged their fidelity to each other, and the day on which it was proposed to legalize their union was at hand. . . .

"We were standing on the bank of a stream, whose waters, like the current of human life and love, were divided, broken, and interrupted by many obstacles, when he related its vision and its fulfillment, in substance, as follows : He slept, and dreamed of walking on the bank of that stream. Suddenly the object of his love appeared walking by his side. She was arrayed in a white flowing dress. A white handkerchief was folded under the chin, and tied on top of the head. Her countenance was pale as marble. She walked by his side for some distance, and finally, extending her hand, she said, 'Reuben, I must leave you, —*farewell!*' — and anon disappeared.

"Several days had elapsed, when a messenger came in great haste to request his immediate presence at the residence of his loved one. He obeyed the summons, and found her the victim of incurable disease. Her stricken form was invested with white apparel, and her whole appearance corresponded to his vision. He seated himself by her bedside, to watch the irregular and feeble pulsations which marked the last efforts of expiring nature. At length she held out her hand, which he received in his own; and, as the spirit went out of its fallen temple, there was a faint utterance from the lips of mortality, and the attentive ear caught the last words, — 'Reuben, I must leave you: *farewell!*'"

256. Prophetic Dreams.

If the preceding facts point to the communion of spiritual intelligences, the following more conclusively establish the proof of this intercourse.

"About three years ago, a seafaring man by the name of Toombs returned to his family, who resided in this place. His widow resides here still.

One night, not long after his return, he awoke his wife, telling her to look at the coffin standing by the side of the bed ; but she replied that she could not see it, nor anything in the room, as it was totally dark. He insisted on getting up, and looking into it ; as he said he saw a coffin there as truly as he was alive. He arose, and, on looking into it, immediately exclaimed, 'It is myself! it is me!' She tried to convince him the next morning that it was a dream ; but he said he was certain that it foreshadowed his death. The second day afterward, as he was walking on the edge of the wharf, his foot slipped, he was precipitated into the river, and, before assistance could be rendered, he was dead. His body was taken home, and his coffin at last stood in the identical place to which his attention had been directed in the vision." *

" The next example I shall cite came, in part, within my own personal knowledge," says Moore, in his work on " Body and Mind." " A colleague of the diplomatic corps, an intimate friend of mine, M. de S., had engaged, for himself and his lady, passage to South America in a steamer, to sail on the ninth day of May, 1856. A few days after their passage was taken, a friend of theirs and mine had a dream, which caused her serious uneasiness. She saw, in her dream, a ship, in a violent storm, founder at sea ; and an internal intimation made her aware that it was the vessel on board which the S.'s proposed to embark. So lively was the impression,

* " Univercœlum." 1848.

that, on awakening, she could scarcely persuade herself that the vision was not a reality. Dropping again to sleep, the same dream recurred a second time. This increased her anxiety; and the next day she asked my advice as to whether she ought not to state the circumstances to her friends. Having at that time no faith whatever in such intimations, I recommended her not to do so, since it would not probably cause them to change their plans, yet might make them uncomfortable to no purpose. So she suffered them to depart unadvised of the fact. It so happened however, as I learned a few weeks later, that fortuitous circumstances induced my friends to alter their first intention, and, having given up their places, to take passage in another vessel.

"These particulars had nearly passed from my memory, when long afterward, being at the Russian Minister's, his lady said to me, 'How fortunate that our friends, the S.'s, did not go in the vessel they had first selected!'—'Why so?' I asked. 'Have you not heard,' she replied,' 'that the vessel is lost? It must have perished at sea; for, though more than six months have elapsed since it left port, it has never since been heard of.'

"In this case, it will be remarked the dream was communicated to myself some weeks or months before its warning was fulfilled. It is to be conceded, however, that the chances against its fulfillment were not so great as in some of the preceding examples. The chances against a vessel, about to cross the Atlantic, being lost on that particular voyage are much less than are the chances against a man, say of middle age and in good health, dying on any one particular day.

"In the next example we shall find a new element introduced. Mrs. S. related to me, that, residing in Rome, in June, 1856, she dreamed, on the thirtieth day of that month, that her mother, who had been several years dead, appeared to her, gave her a lock of hair, and said, 'Be especially careful of this lock of hair, my child; for it is your father's, and the angels will call him away from you to-morrow.' The effect of this dream on Mrs. S.'s spirits was such, that, when she awoke, she experienced the greatest alarm, and caused a telegraphic notice to be instantly despatched to England, where her father was, to inquire after his health. No immediate reply was received; but, when it did come, it was to the effect that her father had died that morning at nine o'clock. She afterwards learned that two days before his death he had caused to be cut off a lock of his hair, and handed it to one of his daughters, who was attending on him, telling her it was for her sister in Rome. He had been ill of a chronic disease; but the last account she received of his health had been favorable, and had given reason to hope that he might yet survive for some years.

"I proceed to furnish, from among the narrratives of this character which have thus recently come to my knowledge, a few specimens, for the authenticity of which I can vouch.

"In the year 1818, Signor Alessandro Romano, the head of an old and highly respected Neapolitan family, was at Patu, in the province of Terra d'Otranto, in the kingdom of Naples. He dreamed one night that the wife of the Cavaliere Libetta, Counselor of the Supreme Court, and his friend and legal adviser, who was then in the city of Naples, was dead. Although Signor Romano had not heard of the Signor Libetta being ill, or even indisposed, yet the extreme vividness of the dream produced a great impression on his mind and spirits; and the next morning he repeated it to his family, adding that it had disturbed him greatly, not only on account of his friendship for the family, but also because the Cavaliere had then in charge for him a lawsuit of importance, which he feared this domestic affliction might cause him to neglect.

"Patu is two hundred and eighty miles from Naples; and it was several days before any confirmation or refutation of Signor Romano's fears could be obtained. At last he received a letter from the Cavaliere Libetta, informing him that he had lost his wife by death; and, on comparing dates, it was found that she died on the very night of Signor Romano's dream.

"This fact was communicated to me by my friend Don Guiseppe Romano, son of the gentleman above referred to, who was living in his father's house when the incident took place, and heard him relate the dream the morning after it occurred.

"Here is another, which was narrated to me, I

remember, while walking, one beautiful day in June, in the Villa Reale (the fashionable park of Naples, having a magnificent view over the bay), by a member of the A—— legation, one of the most intelligent and agreeable acquaintances I made in that city.

"On the 16th of October, 1850, being then in the city of Naples, this gentleman dreamed that he was by the bedside of his father, who appeared to be in the agonies of death, and that, after a time, he saw him expire. He awoke in a state of great excitement, bathed in cold perspiration; and the impression on his mind was so strong, that he immediately rose, though it was still night, dressed himself, and wrote to his father, inquiring after his health. His father was then at Trieste, distant from Naples, by the nearest route, five days' journey; and the son had no cause whatever, except the above dream, to be uneasy about him, seeing that his age did not exceed fifty, and that no intelligence of his illness, or even indisposition, had been received. He waited for a reply with some anxiety for three weeks, at the end of which time came an official communication to the *chef* of the mission, requesting him to inform the son that it behooved him to take some legal measures in regard to the property of his father, who had died at Trieste, after a brief illness, *on the sixteenth day of October.*

"It will be observed, that, in this instance, the agitation of mind in the dreamer was much greater than commonly occurs in the case of an ordinary dream. The gentleman rose, dressed himself in the middle of the night, and immediately wrote to his father, so great was his anxiety in regard to that parent's fate. The same may usually be noticed in the record of cases in which the dream is fulfilled, even if the person to whom it occurs is a skeptic in all such presentiments.

"Such a skeptic is Macnish, author of the 'Philosophy of Sleep;' yet he admits the effect which such a dream, occurring to himself in the month of August, 1861, produced upon his spirits. I quote the narrative in his own words : —

"'I was then in Caithness, when I dreamed that a near relation of my own, residing three hundred miles off, had suddenly died, and, immediately thereafter, awoke in a state of inconceivable terror, similar to that produced by a paroxysm of nightmare. The same day, happening to be writing home, I mentioned the circumstance in a half-jesting, half-earnest way. To tell the truth, I was afraid to be serious, lest I should be laughed at for putting any faith in dreams. However, in the interval between writing and receiving an answer, I remained in a state of most unpleasant suspense. I felt a presentiment that something dreadful had happened or would happen; and, though I could not help blaming myself for a childish weakness in so feeling, I was unable to get rid of the painful idea which had taken such rooted possession of my mind. Three days after sending away the letter, what was my astonishment when I received one written the day subsequent to mine, and stating that the relative of whom I had dreamed had been struck with a fatal shock of palsy the day before,— that is, the very day on the morning of which I had beheld the appearance in my dream! I may state that my relative was in perfect health before the fatal event took place. It came upon him like a thunderbolt, at a period when no one could have the slightest anticipation of danger.'

"Here is a witness disinterested beyond all possible doubt; for he is supplying evidence against his own opinions. But are the effects he narrates such as are usually produced, by a mere dream, on the mind of a person not affected by superstition? Inconceivable terror, though there was no nightmare; a presentiment lasting for days, taking rooted possession of the feelings, and which he strove in vain to shake off, that something dreadful had happened, or would happen! Yet, with all this alarm, unnatural under ordinary circumstances, how does the narrator regard the case? He sets down his terrors as a childish weakness, and declares, as to the coincidence which so excited his astonishment, that there is nothing in it to justify us in referring it to any other origin than chance."

Major Andre, the circumstances of whose lamented death are too well known to make it necessary for me to detail them here, was a friend of Miss Seward's, and, previously to his embarkation for America, he made a journey into Derbyshire to pay her a visit; and it was arranged that they should ride over to see the wonders of the Peak, and introduce Andre to Newton, her minstrel, as she called him, and to Mr. Cunningham, the curate, who was also a poet.

"While these two gentlemen were awaiting the arrival of their guests, of whose intention they had been apprised, Mr. Cunningham mentioned to Newton that on the preceding night he had had a very extraordinary dream, which he could not get out of his head. He had fancied himself in a forest; the place was strange to him; and, while looking about, he perceived a horseman approaching at great speed, who had scarcely reached the spot where the dreamer stood, when three men rushed out of the thicket, and, seizing his bridle, hurried him away, after closely searching his person. The countenance of the stranger being very interesting, the sympathy felt by the sleeper for his apparent misfortune awoke him; but he presently fell asleep again, and dreamed that he was standing near a great city, among thousands of people, and that he saw the same person whom he had seen seized in the wood brought out, and suspended to a gallows. When Andre and Miss Seward arrived, he was horror-struck to perceive that his new acquaintance was the antetype and reality of the man whom he had seen in the dream.

"One fact, however, may still be related, as a specimen of many others which occurred in Stilling's experience. Having at one time occasion to write on business to his friend Hess, Stilling, while engaged in writing, suddenly felt a deep internal impression, as though a voice had spoken with him, that his friend Lavater 'would die a bloody death,— the death of a martyr.' He was impressed to write this to Hess, which he accordingly did. In ten weeks after Stilling had this impression, Lavater received a mortal wound from the hand of a Swiss grenadier, incited, as it was supposed, by some political jealousy.

"Dr. George De Benneville, a physician and Anabaptist preacher, who resided at Germantown, Pa., before and during the American Revolution, was also subject to interior impressions. Being an exceedingly benevolent man, he spent much of his time in bestowing gratuitous medical attention upon the poor.

"One morning he told his family that he felt impressed to ride into Philadelphia, nine miles distant, by a consciousness that a vessel had just arrived in port, having on board a poor sick sailor who needed his assistance. He accordingly went to Philadelphia, and found the sick sailor just as he had described.

"During the Revolution, while Philadelphia was occupied by the British, Dr. De Benneville resided a portion of the time at Reading, Pa. One day while there, he ordered his horse and chaise, saying that the British had on that day evacuated Philadelphia, and that matters there required his immediate attention. His family at first thought him wandering in his mind; but they suffered him to depart. A day or two afterward, intelligence arrived that the

British had actually evacuated Philadelphia on that very day." *

The following is, if anything, of a still more positive character, and is vouched for by high authority: —

"In the winter of 1835-6, a schooner was frozen up in the upper part of the Bay of Fundy, close to Dorchester, which is nine miles from the River Pedeudiac. During the time of her detention, she was intrusted to the care of a gentleman of the name of Clarke, who is at this time captain of the schooner 'Julia Hallock,' trading between New York and St. Jago de Cuba.

"Capt. Clarke's paternal grandmother, Mrs. Ann Dawe Clarke, to whom he was much attached, was at that time living, and, so far as he knew, well. She was residing at Lyme-Regis, in the County of Dorset, England.

"On the night of the seventeenth day of February, 1836, Capt. Clarke, then on board the schooner referred to, had a dream of so vivid a character that it produced a great impression upon him. He dreamed, that, being at Lyme-Regis, he saw pass before him the funeral of his grandmother. He took note of the chief persons who composed the procession; observed who were the pall-bearers, who were the mourners, and who was the officiating pastor. He joined the procession as it approached the church-yard gate, and proceeded with it to the grave. He thought, in his dream, that the weather was

* "Univercœlum."

stormy, and the ground was wet, as after a heavy rain; and he noticed that the wind, being high, blew the pall partly off the coffin. The graveyard which they entered, the old Protestant one, in the centre of the town, was the same in which, as Capt. Clarke knew, their family burying-place was. He perfectly remembered its situation; but, to his surprise, the funeral procession did not proceed thither, but to another part of the churchyard, at some distance. There, still in his dream, he saw the open grave, partially filled with water, as from the rain; and, looking into it, he particularly noticed, floating in the water, two drowned field-mice. Afterward, as he thought, he conversed with his mother; and she told him that the morning had been so tempestuous that the funeral, originally appointed for ten o'clock, had been deferred till four. He remarked, in reply, that it was a fortunate circumstance; for, as he had just arrived in time to join the procession, had the funeral taken place in the forenoon he could not have attended it at all.

"This dream made so deep an impression on Capt. Clarke, that in the morning he noted the date of it. Some time afterward, there came the news of his grandmother's death, with the additional particular that she was buried on the same day on which he, being in North America, had dreamed of her funeral.

"When, four years afterward, Capt. Clarke visited Lyme-Regis, he found that every particular of his dream minutely corresponded with the reality. The pastor, the pall-bearers, the mourners, were the same persons he had seen. Yet this, we may suppose, he might naturally have anticipated. But the funeral *had* been appointed for ten o'clock in the morning; and in consequence of the tempestuous weather, and the heavy rain that was falling, it *had* been delayed until four in the afternoon. His mother, who attended the funeral, distinctly recollected that the high wind blew the pall partially off the coffin. In consequence of a wish expressed by the old lady shortly before her death, she was buried, not in the burying-place of the family, but at another spot, selected by herself; and, to this spot, Capt. Clarke, without any indication from the family or otherwise, proceeded at once, as directly as if he had been present at the burial. Finally, on comparing notes with the old sexton, it appeared that the heavy rain of the morning had partially filled the grave; and that there were actually found in it two field-mice, drowned.

"This last incident, even if there were no other, might suffice to preclude all idea of accidental coincidence.

"The above was narrated to me by Capt. Clarke himself," says Moore, in his work on "Body and Mind," "with permission to use his name in attestation of its truth."

257. PRESENTIMENTS OF DEATH.

Presentiments of the person's death are by no means rare: volumes might be filled with them.

During the late war, I have noticed many such recorded. No philosophy but spirit-impression can explain the origin of such presentiments; for knowledge is conveyed, which, to say the least, is supermundane, and outside of and above the capacity of man. To prophecy the hour of a person's departure has never been achieved by the reason of man.

"Mrs. Dorothea Foos, aged ninety-nine years, died at her residence in Ensor Street, Baltimore, on Saturday evening, having lived to see five generations. Mrs. Foos dreamed, some nine years ago, that she would die on the 5th of April, 1845, and her acquaintances have often heard her state her presentiment. About ten years ago, she accidentally fell out of bed, and broke her hip, and otherwise injured herself, so that all hopes of her recovery were given up; but she steadily insisted that she should get about again, and not die until the 5th of April, 1845; and singular though it be, yet such is the fact. She did live until Saturday, the 5th of April, 1845, and *died* on that day.

"A young lady of this city, highly esteemed and respected, who had been sick for some length of time, but was supposed to be convalescent, had a dream a few nights since, in which it appeared to her that she would die at eight o'clock the same evening. On awaking, she informed her family of her dream, and remained firmly impressed with the idea that she should die at the hour designated, and, under that belief, called her brothers and sisters around her, giving them good advice with reference to the future. Strange to say, and remarkable as it may seem, on the approach of eight o'clock she manifested a calm resignation, and, almost as the clock tolled the hour, her spirit took its flight. Thus she foretold, by a singular presentiment, the day and hour of her own death."*

"One of the most remarkable cases of presentiment I know, is that which occurred not very long since on board one of Her Majesty's ships, when lying off Portsmouth. The officers being one day at the mess-table, a young Lieutenant P. suddenly laid down his knife and fork, pushed away his plate, and turned extremely pale. He then rose from the table, covering his face with his hands, and retired from the room. The president of the mess, supposing him to be ill, sent one of the young men to inquire what was the matter. At first, Mr. P. was unwilling to speak; but, on being pressed, he confessed that he had been seized by a sudden and irresistible impression that a brother he had, then in India, was dead. 'He died,' said he, 'on the 12th of August, at six o'clock: I am perfectly certain of it.' No argument could overthrow this conviction, which, in due course of post, was verified to the letter. The young man had died at Cawnpore, at the precise period mentioned." †

"Barrow, in his interesting book entitled 'The Bible in Spain,' gives a singular instance of presentiment,—the coming event casting its shadow before. A sailor, on coming on deck in the morning,

* "Rochester American." † Fishbough.

informed him, with deep solemnity, that, during the night, he had been impressed, that, in a few hours, he should meet his death by drowning. The sailor was the most active and intelligent of the crew. No reasoning or ridicule could efface the impression that he had received: it seemed written upon his very soul. During the evening, the wind arose, and freshened to a gale. The sailor in question went aloft to take in sail. While engaged in that duty, he lost his hold and footing, and fell overboard. A boat was immediately lowered, and every effort made to save him, but in vain. The narrator saw his face shining out like a thing of light as he sank fathoms deep beneath the waves." *

Last year, on bidding my aunt adieu after a short visit, and hoping to see her soon, she told me in tears that she had a presentiment that she should not live until the summer had passed. When attacked at length with mortal sickness, in midsummer, she said that medicine would be unavailing, and prophesied the exact hour of her departure.

There is a class of presentiments received in regard to those who are near and dear to us for which animal magnetism gives a partial explanation, and probably does account for many facts; but spiritual impression must be called to fully account for others. The same law by which one person obtains an impression from another enables him to obtain an impression from a spirit.

"A lady of my acquaintance correctly saw, in a

* "Univercœlum."

dream, all the main particulars of the burning of the steamboat 'Lexington,' on Long-Island Sound, a few years ago, on the night of the occurrence; and, on awaking, she related the account to her husband in general terms just as it subsequently appeared in the newspapers."*

It is a singular fact, that, notwithstanding their educational fears, children are never frightened at the appearance of spectres.

"A lady with her child embarked on board a vessel at Jamaica, for the purpose of visiting her friends in England, leaving her husband quite well. It was a sailing packet; and they had been some time at sea, when one evening, while the child was kneeling before her, saying his prayers previous to going to rest, he suddenly said, looking eagerly to a particular spot in the cabin, 'Mamma, pa!'—'Nonsense, my dear!' the mother answered: 'you know your papa is not here!'—'He is indeed, mamma,' returned the child: 'he is looking at us now.' Nor could she convince him to the contrary. When she went on deck, she mentioned the circumstance to the captain, who thought it so strange that he said he would note down the date of the occurrence. The lady begged him not do so, saying it was attaching a significance to it which would make her miserable. He did it, however; and, shortly after her arrival in England, she learned that her husband had died exactly at that period.

"A gentleman of this city, in whose veracity I

* Fishbough.

have every confidence, recently related to me a fact which came under his personal knowledge, as follows: A lady, residing with her son in one of the Eastern States, recently dreamed that her daughter, living in New York, was taken suddenly and dangerously ill. *Her son dreamed the same dream on the same night.* Though neither of them had previously had any faith in dreams, in this instance their dreams made a deep impression on their minds, and they mutually related and compared them on the next morning. Shortly afterward, a telegraphic despatch arrived, announcing that the daughter was severely and dangerously ill. The mother set off for New York with the first conveyance, and found her daughter in a condition precisely as represented in the dream of herself and son."

258. Conclusions.

It thus appears, that, during sleep, many individuals become susceptible to spirit-influence who are not so in the waking state. During the positive conditions of day, they are incapable of receiving impressions; but the negative influence of night, and the passive state of sleep, open the gateway for the entrance of spiritual impressions. Sometimes, as is proved by preceding facts, the sleeper passes into a truly clairvoyant state. It is from these that we conclude normal sleep to be its first stage, deepening into it by imperceptible gradations.

There is one other consideration, — that of the

allegorical form in which dreams that we refer to impression often appear. This is susceptible of easy explanation. Persons usually have signs, well determined in their own minds, by which they recognize the coming of events. Thus one believes, that, if he dream of fire, he is sure to have a quarrel; or, of dark and turbulent water, that sickness is in store. If, it is said, a spirit can impress these signs, why not impress the plain truth? We say, because the sign is more easily impressed. If the spirits attempted to impress the details of sickness or of disputation, they would be obliged to call into activity the organs of fear, combativeness, etc., which might at once destroy the passiveness of the person, and abruptly terminate their communication. By using a sign that the sleeper, *during sleep*, does not recognize as significant, they obviate this difficulty.

But they do not employ signs except in those cases where from experience they have found them necessary. The passivity of individuals varies; and often the unvarnished facts can be presented, even when revolting, without disturbing the essential conditions, or not until presented, when the sleeper generally passes at once to wakefulness.

XVI.

HEAVEN AND HELL, THE SUPPOSED ABODES OF THE DEPARTED.

HEAVEN is a place with many doors, and each one may enter in his own way. — HINDOO MAXIM.

259. WHERE LOCATED BY THE ANCIENTS.

THE abode of the departed was placed, by the ancients, in unexplored regions of the globe. The sphericity of the earth is of recent discovery. The world was thought to be a level plain, bounded by the sea; and the Persians thought a chain of inaccessible mountains, two thousand feet high, surrounded it, preventing any one from falling off. When the Roman general, Decius Brutus, with his army, reached the coast of Portugal, and for the first time gazed on the infinite expanse of water, and saw the great red sun go down into the crimson billows, he was seized with horror, and turned back the eagles of his legions.

To the Greek and Roman, only a very small area was known, and their ardent imaginations reveled in creations outside of this geographical knowledge. There was ample space to locate the realms of the dead, and transfer the mystic under-world to the surface.

On the starry heights of Mount Olympus, the synod of the gods met in luxurious bowers, and from its summit Jupiter thundered his mandates over the world. In the remote west extended the golden gardens of the Hesperides. In the east, the tall towers of the divine city of Maru pierced the amber light. Far in the raging desert of Ethiopia gleamed the banquet-hall of the blessed. In the Central Ocean lay the Isles of Immortality; and far to the north, beyond the sunny avalanches of the Caucasus, spread the happy land of the Hyperboreans.

Those were beautiful dreams, and it is with regret we see the iron hand of science encroach on this exciting realm of poesy.

260. The Childhood of the Race Outgrown.

The child grows to manhood. He can no longer detect the face in the moon, which, in childhood, he so plainly saw.

> "How pleasant were the wild beliefs
> That dwelt in legends old!
> Alas! to our posterity
> Will no such tales be told?
> We know too much: scroll after scroll
> Weighs down our weary shelves.
> Our only point of ignorance
> Is centred in ourselves."

It is the mystery, growing out of vague, undefined knowledge, which clothes the distant land with the poetic garb of a paradise.

The dying Hindoo hoped to reach the "white isle," the fragrant dwelling of immortal man. The ancient Briton, at death, found a home in the "noble island," far amid the dashing waves of the Western Ocean.

The Hebrew Scriptures, in similar manner, referred to the lost paradise, the Garden of Eden. As its reception extended among the nations, conjectures were rife as to the locality of the wonderland. It was once thought to be in the bosom of India; then in the fragrant vales of Georgia; then in the inaccessible recesses of Mesopotamia; then to be some oasis in the Arabian desert, where life met death in strange contrast, and the weary pilgrim saw the spirit-like palm, shading the sparkling fountain, in the midst of desolation.

The cosmography of the twelfth century confined paradise to the extreme eastern part of Asia, made inaccessible by a wall of fire, surrounding it, and ascending to heaven.

Still later, the Canaries were named the Fortunate Islands, from a supposition that they were the original Eden. To discover the original site of Eden was one of the strong motives actuating Columbus in his voyage to the west.

261. Located beneath the Earth.

The most popular ancient belief of Jews, Greeks, Romans, Etruscans, Germans, and Christians, was, that beneath the earth there was a vast, gloomy world of the dead. This was held by the Scandinavian nations, and lingered to recent times in the beautiful fictions of elves and fairies. Its name was derived from the grave. The Hebrew word "*sheol*," and the Greek "*hades*," meant the grave. It was a dark, gloomy world of shadows, from which only a few peerless heroes and sages, by the interference of the gods, were transplanted to Elysium. The classical description of this abode is terrible, — a scene of gloom, of passion; suffering, or a lethargic state that only relieves from suffering.

From Hades lead two paths, — one to Elysium, one to Tartarus. If the blessed spirit reached the former, life became a joy. Flowery fields, fragrant breezes, social happiness in friendly reunions, contributed to his peace. Here the hero-gods of pagans, and the saints of the Christians, found repose.

If the doomed spirit walked the other path, it reached Tartarus, where the old earth-giants lay, transfixed with thunderbolts, like mountain masses half concealed by cinders and lava. The furies are seen in the darkness, by the light of the rivers of fire on the banks of which they stand. All around groan the wretched sinners, torn by tortures, the recital of which curdles the blood. Here is the pagan system, worked up by the Romish hierarchy into purgatory, paradise, and hell. Hades is the probationary stage. In quite modern times, excited ecclesiastics have seriously taught that volcanoes were entrances to the awful under-world, and many a legend now told records this early belief.

262. Heaven above the Clouds.

The cloudland has not been left unoccupied. There the Caledonians fixed their realm of shades. The vast atmosphere is the hall of spirit-existence. The departed heroes ride on the wings of the tempest. The shriek of the wind, the bellow of the thunder, are their voices, and the lightning flames their red eyes of wrath.

The Lapland heaven is in the pure regions of the *aurora borealis.* The streamers are the play of the departed.

263. Heaven between the Earth and Moon.

The Platonists located heaven in the space between the earth and moon. The Manichæans thought the departed went to the moon, where their sins were washed away; and then to the sun, to be purified by fire.

The Hebrews thought the sky a solid arch, supporting an inexhaustible supply of water, beyond which dwelt God and his angels in regal splendor. This conjecture of a solid firmament the ignorant mind at once receives as direct evidence of the senses, and is world-wide. Beyond the solid firmament, in which the stars are set, a mysterious region of space exists, which invites the fancy to people with its own creations.

264. Heaven in the Sun.

The Aztecs and Incas regarded the sun as the third and highest state of future existence. While the wicked, comprising the great majority, were confined in everlasting darkness, and a second state of innocent contentment was enjoyed by those more favorable to the gods, the heroes who fell in battle, and sacrificial victims, passed directly to the sun, to follow his shining course through the heavens; and, after years, they became the spirits of the clouds, and singing birds, reveling in the rich fragrance of the gardens of paradise. It is extremely singular, that, with this complexity and variety of being for the future life, these strange races assigned no form of physical torture, which is often the first notion of the after-life to suggest itself to rude minds.

265. Comets the Location of Hell.

The diffusion of astronomical knowledge has broken the heavenly crystalline sphere to fragments: but theologians are not at a loss to avail themselves of the smattering of science they usually acquire; and a comet, appearing in the celebrated Dr. Whiston's time, convinced him that it was the real hell so long sought. He thought it admirably contrived for punishment,—rushing to the sun, and acquiring a temperature thousands of degrees above molten iron, and then traversing regions of space where the cold reaches an intensity inappreciable to us. Truly, this is a fine arrangement for torture. God's wrath has fixed itself in the mechanism of the cosmos! In the cometary hell, the undying soul oscillates between the extremes of heat and cold, suffering from a kind of intermittent fever.

266. HEAVEN THE ACTUAL OF DESIRES.

Heaven, as idealized by the world-weary, is a place of eternal rest. It is not strange that such should be the toiler's dream of felicity. Bowed beneath the excessive labor of this life, without means of escaping its drudgery, or a hope of bettering his condition, to him the most desirable state possible is one of rest.

Heaven is always what the mind most desires. The weary traveler in the desert, famished and dying with thirst, has no higher aspiration than the palm groves of an oasis, with its leaping fountains and luscious dates, where, sheltered from the sun's fierce rays, he can slake his thirst, satisfy his hunger, and repose in undisturbed quietude.

It is thus with those weary of life's incessant struggle. The mass of mankind are born to poverty and labor. Their lives are an unceasing battle with hunger and cold. They have no moments of recreation, wherein the noble aspirations which the lowest human being is capable of feeling can be gratified.

267. WHY ANOTHER STATE IS ASKED FOR.

At death, after fourscore years of struggling, when we look back across the fleeting years, when we retrospect all we have done, how small has been the work accomplished! We have supported the wants of the body as best we could, and have given it bread to appease its hunger, and protected it from cold, but many find it impossible to supply even a crust and a ragged garment. The superior spiritual nature lies an uncultivated waste; briers and brambles, slimy morasses and hideous dismal swamps, everywhere.

When the old man asks himself, "What have I accomplished in all my past life?" too often his answer is, "You have existed; just *existed*." The world never knew it possessed you; and, when you die, it will not miss you. You have *existed*.

The man feels such to be his history, and his unsatisfied spirit prays for another state, where he can retrieve the mistakes of this, and find ideal happiness. The *form* of that happiness varies with each individual. What one considers as most delightful is not so to another; but the main idea promulgated by Christianity is of *rest*. Heaven is where the wicked shall cease from striving, and the weary shall be at rest.

268. THE "NEW JERUSALEM."

The "New Jerusalem" of the church is a celestial city, which, if words mean anything, is believed to be founded for the express accommodation of earthly mortals. Some genius, skilled in theological dogmas, has instituted the following calculations, from data furnished by the Bible, and his results have been published by leading orthodox journals.

"And he measured the city with the reed, twelve thousand furlongs. The length, the breadth, and the height of it are equal. Rev. xxi. 16.

"Twelve thousand furlongs — 7,920,000 feet, cubed, is 496,793,088,000,000,000,000 cubic feet. Half of this we will reserve for the throne of God and court of heaven, and half the balance for streets, leaving a remainder of 124,198,272,000,000,000,000 cubic feet. Divide this by 4066, the cubical feet in a room 16 feet square and 16 feet high, and there will be 30,321,843,750,000,000 rooms.

"We will now suppose that the world always did, and always will, contain 900,000,000 inhabitants, and that a generation lasts 33 years and 4 months, making 2,700,000,000 every century, and that the world will stand 100,000 years, making in all 270,000,000,000,000 inhabitants. Then suppose there were a hundred such worlds equal to this in number of inhabitants and duration of years, making a total of 270,000,000,000,000,000 persons; then there would be a room 16 feet square for each person, and yet there would be room."

Whoever the author of this sublime nonsense of mathematics may be, he has exhibited the folly and ignorance of the day. Is humanity to be thrust into such a dove-cote of a heaven? Are we to be incarcerated for eternity in such a gigantic *bee-comb?* Every rational sense forbids. Such is the church view of the future life. How degrading! how puerile! how unmanly! Let the waters of Lethe close over the soul forever, let oblivion's wing nestle it, rather than endure a spiritual existence in such a place! The streets of gold, and throne of God covered with precious stones! What a show of learning! How little sense! Contemplate the miklyway. Every sweep of the telescope brings thousands and thousands of suns to view, each having its fleet of attendant worlds. If each of the worlds which flash through the crystal vault of night were to send a single delegate to the throne of God, this heaven would overflow, being packed to its utmost capacity.

Such a heaven would be the grand miracle of creation, such as an Oriental despot would build could he possess Aladdin's lamp, and have all his desires gratified by the discovery.

It is not the sage's heaven, nor that of the rational man, any more than is the sensual paradise of Mohammed.

In this nonsense, the mathematician omitted what, in theological discussions, is of most vital importance. He has assumed that all mankind are to be saved, when *any* divine would have assured him that at least nine out of ten are doomed to quite another place. According to his calculations, the "Celestial City" has been created many times too large for the accommodation of earth.

Many will go in through the church, if not otherwise. Men with arithmetics for consciences, and vultures for hearts, are entering through the church doors, and obsequious divines are bowing them through just because their hearts are vultures, and fat with prey. Ah! is there a *police* in the streets of the "Celestial City"?

The soul in the Christian heaven is not quite at rest. One faculty is retained. It can sing. Divines say that this is about the only employment of ransomed souls, — singing praises to God on golden harps! They always sing a tune of praise. What a delightful world, where all emotions are lost in swells of music! Is heaven to be a singing-school?

This ideal is higher, but of the same kind, as that of the Hottentot, who dreams of heaven as an immense cauldron of soup walled in by sausages. Nor is it far from Mohammed's paradise, gratifying to Orientals, peopled with houri, sweeter and more beautiful than visions of beauty, and perfumed with musk.

Such beliefs debase instead of elevate. They are the ideals of individuals, not humanity's desires. They answer not its prayers. On the one hand, they present ignoble and unworthy incentives: on the other, they appeal to the lowest passions of man. The same may be said of the ideal of hell, an imaginary region concocted from the Greek idea of Hades, by the imagination of bigoted sectaries. Superstition, the child of ignorance, united with bigotry, offspring of malice and hate, personified a God possessing these qualities pre-eminently; and this God, in his vindictiveness, forms a hell where he chains the spirit, cursed with immortality, to suffer inconceivable tortures.

269. The Popular, Evangelical Idea of Heaven

Is a narrow place, where the soul, so happy at its narrow escape from torment, thinks of nothing but a song of praise; and hell is a burning pit where their God can wreak out his vengeance.

In human affairs, law never punishes for punishment's sake, but for some benefit intended. But this punishment has no such meaning. It is given after the whole world has been judged, and no more offences can be committed. Then the major portions of humanity are thrust into eternal perdition.

The bigoted church-member, who has held falsehood cheap, and conscience a bad guide, but has made long prayers, and paid his parson, will have the extreme satisfaction of seeing the infidel, who has comforted his fellow-man, and endeavored to aid the needy, and share their burdens with the suffering, go down into the maelstrom of fire. If he has an enemy, that enemy is predestined for wrath. He has no faith in himself. He believes *deeds* of no avail: belief is all in all. And in that he is right.

As a red-faced divine, bloated with a high salary and "faith in godliness," remarked, "If we reject our Saviour, and depend on ourselves, we depend on a poor staff!" He knew very well that he could not depend on himself.

Away with this demoniac doctrine, sanctioning malice, hate, revenge, the foul brood engendered in the dark struggles of man's passionate nature! Away with doctrines representing the Supreme Ruler of the universe as more satanic than Satan; representing Him who dwells in light unapproachable, whose attributes are infinite love, justice, and truth, as gratifying infinite revenge!

How horrid are these doctrines! how repugnant to humanity! how contrary to reason! Confession of sins, prayer, eating a morsel of bread, subscribing a ritual and baptism, ordaining a man for heaven, while the omission of these dooms him to hell!

The Catholic confesses his sins to a priest, and is forgiven: the Protestant sets the priest partially aside, and appeals directly to the Son of God, acting as his own priest, and obtains forgiveness. Belief is all that is required, — faith, faith, faith. Nothing that one can *do* balances a farthing in his favor. Prayer and belief outweigh all the good deeds of a lifetime. My infidel friend, you are stigmatized while living, and the chances are all against you after death. The holy church will not even open its portals for your funeral ceremonies, unless its anointed preacher officiates, and preaches you straight to destruction, and holds you up as an example and warning to all. Perhaps, in unwonted benevolence, a hope for you will be expressed, but so dubiously that it implies more than direct assertion.

And, over childhood's tiny grave, the agonized mother is reminded of infant depravity by the godly preacher. Unregenerated, depraved infants! O humanity! how awful the depths of thy conception where superstition and bigotry control! Emotion, feeling, the noble and generous and angelic thought, is blotted out; and hate, misanthropy, malice, revenge, are mistaken for the love of God. I appeal to the mother for decision. Mother! behold your child nestling in your arms, beautiful as a vision; its sunny curls falling over its high forehead, its eyes joyous as heaven, its smiles an angel's gleam, — do you hold to your heart a depraved being, who, until regenerated, is a demon?

I anticipate your answer, as I anticipate that of Mother Nature, when asked, whether all mankind, whom she holds to her bosom, are depraved. Man's fall, his inherent depravity, his redemption through sacrifice, and his final heaven or hell, are intricately blended, logical sequences of each other, and rivals in absurdity.

The churches are fast being forced to admit that the Adamic creation is a myth; and science demonstrates that man, so far from being created perfect, was ushered into existence a nude savage. His history has been one of progress. He has never retrograded, never fallen; but step by step has he conquered ignorance, tamed the elements, bound the forces of nature, until the present time, wherein he stands superior to any past age.

Man fallen? Then is civilized man below the savage! Progress is retrogression, and noonday is Egyptian night!

It is quite certain, that, had we not what is called revelation, we never should have dreamed of man's fall, and still less of his redemption through the sacrifice of another. They are a part of the theological trappings, outgrowths of ignorance forced on a better age, and only serve to fetter its power.

But, it is said, the church does not believe in a hell now. Why then, because a Beecher chooses to deny its existence, is there such a clang and clatter in church circles? Don't believe in it? It cannot do otherwise. It can do without a heaven, or a God; but it cannot do without a hell, or a devil.

Heaven and hell, as those terms are understood, mean harmony and discord. They are not localities, but conditions of mind.

As God is associated with happiness, or heaven, so is evil personified in a devil, or hell. All goodness is centred in one, all evil in the other.

270. THE ARTISTS AND THEIR INFLUENCE ON THE FEATURES AND CHARACTER.

We are not to suppose heaven or hell all in the future. They are not to be reached by death, but are already with us. We shall reach them continually through all the future eons. They are of yesterday, to-day, and to-morrow. We constantly express, in our physical contour, the motives which actuate us. The indwelling devil or angel cannot and will not be concealed.

As the blossom expresses a prophecy of autumn,

so youth reveals the infinite possibilities of manhood. Man and woman, words standing for the crowning glories of creation; yet how strangely contradictory thereto are the faces one meets in the streets! Men and women, who should meet us radiant as immortal angels, pass us like disturbed demons. Childhood is beautiful; but, as soon as we pass that boundary, how the features distort! how ugly they become! Why is this? Because every faculty of the mind is a sculptor who incessantly works with finest chisel at the features. Sleeping or waking, constantly they mold the plastic clay. They are never satisfied with their model. The passions chisel their wrinkles and lines, deep, terribly deep, and hideous; and the intellect and the morals set their artists to smooth them out, polish them off, and sharpen the outlines. Yield to the former, and the countenance becomes ugly and coarse and brutal, more and more so, from year to year; and, when old, the man is animal and repulsive. But, if the intellect and the morals are allowed to work, the man becomes beautiful, and the aged somewhat divine. Delicate artists are these. They force the plastic body to become an exact semblance of the mind. They pluck the hairs from the head; they polish the scalp; they sprinkle with gray; they stoop the form; they hold it erect; they change the tone of the voice, the laugh, and the glance of the eye. How terrible is the work of some of these artists! The bloated form, the leering eye, the foul blood revealed in purple veins, the thin white locks, the palsied step, the feeble intellect, — such models fill the world. How beautiful the image of noble age, when from the cradle the artists of truthful and living thoughts, of the keen intellect and godlike morality, and the sensitive chisels of spirituality, have constantly labored, toning down, softening, sharpening, and vivifying the features! Such men we sometimes see reposing on the brink of the river of time; and they always electrify our souls, and fill us with emulation. They are like gleams of golden sunlight amid darkness, and quicken our faith in immortality.

271. Election — how Known.

It is a question often asked by Christians, "Am I elected for heaven?"

It is presumable they were, for they set out in the prescribed route, joined a church, and assented to a creed, but they have no *certain* knowledge. There are marks by which a church-member can readily be distinguished from the so-called worldling; but the marks by which a church-member *elect* can be distinguished are more obscure. Hence Christians are often, if not always, in *doubt*.

They need not be; for their lives, their thoughts, and actions, tell them each day, each hour, where they are, and whither they are going.

Can we then doubt the future of that man who gloats over that part of the judgment which thrusts nine-tenths of humanity into utter darkness, and gnashing of teeth? He who desires such a *finale* would be first to share it were it real.

272. FROM WHENCE CAME THESE DOGMAS?

It is difficult to determine except by comparative mythology. They, with many other dogmas, — the resurrection of the body, the fall, &c., — sprang originally from the heated imagination of savage men, who understood little of nature, and less of themselves. The mythology of the ancients, scorned and despised with loathing by the church, reveals a wonderful story. It contains the germ of theology. The Greeks and Romans believed in a state called Hades, or the region of departed spirits. This they divided into Elysium and Tartarus. It was located, both by Jew and Pagan, in the interior of the earth, or, as they understood, supposing the earth to be flat, beneath its foundation. Hence the word came to express darkness and obscurity.

Impressed with the correspondence which · must exist between things spiritual and things physical, the ancients believed that the departed spirit or shade retained all its faculties, thoughts, feelings, desires, and in a phantom world pursued imaginary occupations corresponding to those most pleasing to it while on earth.

This primitive idea, the belief in a future life, gathered around it the wildest and the greatest fancies of poesy.

To the Egyptians, more than to any other people,

theology owes its dogmas. It has derived them from their simple customs. It has transferred history into the future life. In Egypt, when a person died, even if a king, his corpse was carried over the Lake Styx, at night, by a ferryman, Charon, to the judges of the dead. All his good deeds were balanced against his evil. If the latter predominated, the corpse was refused the honor of being embalmed by the inexorable judge. As they believed, that, unless the body was preserved, the spirit could not enter it again, — either perishing, or wandering in darkness, — it was the most fearful of punishments.

The Greek poets translated it beyond this life, and gave the judges power over the departed spirit. Christianity has adopted the myth, with the resurrection of bones and the scattered dust of mummies, and substituted Christ for the judge of the dead, hell for Tartarus, paradise for the Elysian Fields.

Greek imagination then possessed a wide and exhaustless field. It peopled Tartarus with spirits who had, while mortal, offended the gods, and pictured exquisite suffering for each offender, — starvation, with fruits and food suspended only a hair's breadth beyond reach; a burning thirst, with unattainable water gushing past; and similar punishments, — that made immortality a curse, and annihilation a blessing. In the Elysian Fields dwelt good and perfect spirits, enjoying, in the most delicious climate, everything they desired. These myths have been fostered from age to age, always combined with the religious element, always its concrete expression.

They have been nurtured by theological teachers, for they support the entire fabric of Christianity. It will be readily seen that a devil is as necessary to its schemes as is a God, and *much more so.* Hell is a resultant of heaven. If reward for right-doing be offered, there must be punishment for wrong action.

Hell, the "burning pit," the "heated furnace," where "the worm"—man—dieth not, and the fire is unquenched, where even one drop of water is denied the parched tongue, is the place where an all-just God sends the children of men, whom he has created in his own image; created *just as he desired to create them; sends them there because they* ARE *as he made them, and do as he intended them to do!* Such is the teaching of the Christian Church.

273. THE TERRORS OF HELL.

Hell is the place unspeakably awful, where the redeemed will have the holy joy of seeing their friends, their dearest relations, their bosom companions, burning in the sullen waves! It is the place where the pious churchman will have the unspeakable satisfaction of seeing his infidel brother at last brought to realize the truth by experience, and where he will suffer the wrath of a justly indignant Godhead!

In this enlightened day, is there one who believes

a doctrine so monstrous, — so opposed to humanity, and such a libel on God? There are many who *say* they do believe; and whoever has attended a revival well knows that these dogmas are a part of the machinery by which the bewildered convert is urged forward to what has rightly been called the "anxious seat," and into the *church* wherein his manliness and individuality are swallowed up.

The preacher speaks gently of the beauty of heaven; the joy of the redeemed; then of the sinfulness and weakness of that worm of the dust, — man, and his utter inability to save *himself*. He can only expect salvation through *Christ*, resting on his sufferings for us poor sinners. Then, when the partial convert begins dimly to feel his position, the preacher bursts on him in tones of thunder, "Hell is beneath you, and Satan behind you; fly, fly from the wrath to come! fly!" Where? "To the church, — to *our* church. Its doors are open, leading to heaven!" Well, he rushes — not into heaven, but into the church. I think such converts *are* always in doubt whether they are *elected*. *I doubt about them too.*

This is the way of church religion, — belief in hell! Ah, wretched belief!

Father, in that final day, your impious son, your impious daughter, will be seen on the other side; husband and wife will be separated; friends torn from the bosom of friends, and the eyes of the saved will be greeted by the sufferings of the doomed, — father, mother, husband, neighbor, friend. Your children, your wife, your neighbor, your friends, will be cast off. Standing on some eminence, you will see them writhing in flames, whose every pulsation is a throb of their hearts, and whose every swell is a sigh of their anguish! You can see them there for eternal ages, doomed to suffer unending misery while the ages go slowly by. Worlds will dissolve, suns and stars melt away like early frost-work, yet shall their agony be just begun. And God, who created them for his own pleasure, to do as they have done, that they may be damned just as they are damned, will smile as he gathers the righteous, a mere wreck of mankind, — smile at the glorious result of his infinite wisdom, love, and justice!

Go to the savage cannibal of the South Seas, — ask him for his idea of God and hell; go to the wild Indian, dancing around his tortured captive, — and their answer will put to blush the ideal of Christianity!

274. The Joys of the Redeemed.

What can be the joy of the redeemed? It is the joy the holy inquisitor feels when he gloats over the quivering body of the tortured heretic. Emotions, love, affections, the *human*, lost, — all that we prize worth living for is gone. Redeemed or otherwise, such existence is a curse. I should prefer condemnation to such redemption. From my very soul I loathe and despise the God of infinite hate held up for worship by the theological world. He is a heathen idol, and nothing more. Let me follow those I love. Let me share their sufferings, rather than rejoice over them.

A heathen teaches us a lesson of humanity. When missionaries from Rome, more than twelve centuries ago, penetrated the northern wilds to preach to the Saxon savages, it is said that Rothbod, a Frison chief, was converted; "but, at the moment in which he put his foot into the water for the ceremony of baptism, he suddenly asked the priest whither all his Frison companions-in-arms had gone after their death.

"To hell," replied the priest.

"Well, then," said Rothbod, drawing back his foot from the water, "I had rather go to hell with them than to paradise with you and your fellow-foreigners."

Such would be the response of every human being, unless blinded by theological dogmas; for theology is that kind of learning, of which, the *more* one learns, the *less* one knows, and of which erudition is *worse* than ignorance.

The priests who perform very long prayers, and the churchmen, have a religion which may be summed up in praying, quarterage, and remaining in doubt whether they are elected; on the "left" will be the philosophers and sages, all the brave and noble minds of the past ages, and nine-tenths of the rest of the world. There the infidel will meet that long line of freethinkers, greatest and most noble of whom is THOMAS PAINE, — men who fought bravely for human freedom, and with great-hearted benevolence sacrificed their positions and their happiness, and endured contumely and bigoted hate for the sake of principle.

275. THERE WILL BE GOOD COMPANY THERE.

Throwing these dogmas aside, losing the incentives they furnish on the one hand, and the fear of punishment on the other, are we in danger of the immoralities from which they were invented to guard us? I would present the examples of the illustrious men who have cast them aside, and, if they prove it, I answer, Yes; but, if otherwise, No.

We may lose the *inhuman* incentives of fear; but we gain that which is of immeasurably more advantage, — the *human* elements.

Guided by them, by our moral instincts, we shall rarely stumble, and, walking in the sunlight of righteousness, we shall know "if our faith be abiding, and our calling sure."

XVII.

THE SPIRIT'S HOME.

Is there no grand immortal sphere,
  Beyond this realm of broken ties,
To fill the wants that mock us here,
  And dry the tears from weeping eyes;

Where winter fades in endless spring,
  And June stands near with deathless flowers;
Where we can hear the dear ones sing
  Who loved us in this world of ours?
                    JAMES G. CLARKE.

There is another invisible, eternal existence, superior to this visible one, which does not perish when all things perish. — BHAGAVAT GEETA.

Go, give to the waters and the plants thy body, which belongs to them; but there is an immortal portion, O Djaatavedas! transport it to the world of the holy. — RIG VEDA.

276. PREPARATION.

ON entering the spiritual domain, and in our investigation of the spiritual philosophy, we must cast off the trammels of the schools, which have so long fettered the natural action of our minds. The cant of the metaphysician, and the egotism of the theologian, are the chaff which has for centuries buried the truth from the honest thinker. They avail us not. As candid investigators, nothing but positive testimony will avail;

and, in obtaining that testimony, we must walk out into the fields of nature, and question the great principles which speak in sighing winds, babbling brooklets, in the myriad-tongued forest murmuring to the passing zephyr.

277. Law Rules Supreme.

When we question Nature, she tells us law reigns supreme. Not a thistle-down floats on the breeze, not a sand-grain is thrown on the ocean's beach by the rolling billows, not a bubble of foam floats on the hurrying stream, but its every motion is governed by immutable laws. Law bounds the great world, and dashes it on in its orbit. It sends the rushing comet round the central fire, and floats whole solar systems on their courses as a feather is upborne by the passing winds. Not an atom finds its appropriate place in the living organism but is guided by unerring law.

What more uncertain than the wavy motions of the gossamer thread as it dances in the summer winds? Yet every motion is governed by law, — by the same power that chains the moon in its orbit, or rolls the earth around the sun.

278. The Same holds good in the Spiritual Realm.

If we think that we are leaving the province of order and control of established principles when we pass from the material to the so-styled spiritual, we labor under the greatest possible mistake. As the ultimation of the material universe, the spiritual is governed by the same established principles, modified by superior conditions. Gravity, attraction, and repulsion, the properties of atoms, the relations which exist between them, all are preserved; and we enter as real and substantial a world as is the one we leave.

279. No Miracles

Are observed in the phenomena of spiritual life. True, we do not understand many of the manifestations we observe, because the substances with which we deal are impalpable to our senses, and are recognized only by their effects; but this only shows our ignorance, and not the interposition of a miraculous power.

280. An Unknown Universe

Exists beyond the material creation. It is formed from emanations arising from the physical universe, and is a reflection of it. This is the spiritual universe. We have been taught by our learned teachers a system of spiritual philosophy so vague and undefined that it has served rather to blind than to enlighten us. It has inculcated the wildest errors, and by its influence, even now, we are liable to be led astray.

If spirit be identity, if it be organic after its separation from the body, then it must have a home, and that home must be a reality. These are incontrovertible propositions, and are necessarily inferred from the fact of spiritual existence. A single proposition crushes the spiritual fabrication of the theologian, whose definition of spirit is the best one possible of non-entity. According to his system, a spirit is a refined shadow of nothing, — a collection of thoughts. But thought is an *effect*, not a *cause;* and standing in his position, and expecting thought to exist after the decay of the body, is as rational as to look for the hum of a dead bee, or the song of a bird after it has flown.

Nothing cannot originate something. If the spirit exist, it must be an entity; and, if such, must be composed of matter. It must be organized; and, if organized, it must have a dwelling-place. This conclusion brings us back to the first inquiry, —

281. WHAT AND WHERE IS THE SPIRIT-WORLD?

To understand this subject, we must inquire into the secret processes of nature, beneath its external manifestations to the senses. In this, as well as the manner of spiritual life, and kindred subjects connected with spirits, the revelations of the clairvoyant and of departed intelligences must be relied on for our information.

282. THEIR TESTIMONY IS RELIABLE.

When the fact of spiritual communion and identity is proved, then the intelligence they impart is as reliable as the report of a traveler in a distant country. The major portion of our knowledge depends on such reports; and, if the tale of travels in England or Europe be received as true, why not receive the report of a departed spirit, who has made himself familiar with the scenes he describes? This subject does not admit of argument. It is self-evident, that, if spirits exist, their description of their abode is as authentic as is the report of travelers.

283. AND WHAT DO THEY TELL US?

That the universe is undergoing a refining process, and the spirit-world is formed from the ascending sublimated atoms.

Before entering on the discussion of how this is effected, let us inquire philosophically whether this refining process is really going on; whether there really is a progressive movement in creation, from crude and undeveloped conditions to ethereality and perfection.

The present order of nature cannot have had an infinite existence. If we trace backward the geological records, through the rocky tablets of earth, through fossiliferous, transition, and primitive rocks, we arrive at a beginning of the present system.

The earth has the marks of infancy, and has yet attained but its youthful state. In the beginning, geology tells us, it was a vast ocean of gaseous matter; then it cooled down to a liquid globe; then a crust formed over it, and, by slow degrees, it was molded into the beautiful creation of the present.

284. Nature Works in Great Cycles,

Every returning coil being above the preceding. Matter, without a beginning, must have passed through an infinite number of changes, of which the present order is but a single and incompleted coil.

In the infinite duration of the past, universe after universe must have been born, have grown old and decayed, and new ones have been breathed forth from the chaotic elements of the preceding. Still labored the forces of organic nature, and at every mighty return matter became more refined, its capabilities enlarged, and consequently the next system became more perfected. This continued until matter, by its superior refinement, became capable of forming a universe as perfect as the present.

The object of the mutations of the organic world is the individualization of spirit in man; so the ultimation of inorganic mutations is the refining of spiritualized matter for the support of that spirit when identified.

These cycles of revolution are like those of the Hindoo theo-cosmology, which teaches that every three hundred and sixty thousand years all created things flow back into the infinite soul of Brahma, or God, and from thence are evolved as a new creation. But the periods of return are millions of ages, instead of a few thousand years, and, at every return, matter arises above its former level.

In the individualized spirit, the atoms which compose its organism are elaborated by and derived from the physical body. So are the spiritualized atoms, which ascend from animate nature, elaborated.

To the perception of the spirit, or of the clairvoyant, these ascending atoms are as plainly perceptible as is the ascent of vapor from water. It exhales from all substances, as mist rises from a sheet of water.

The mineral mass, by the processes at work among its atoms, and the disintegrating chemical action of electricity and magnetism, throws out ethereal particles into the great ocean of unindividualized spirit.

The plant, taking up crude mineral atoms, subjects them to the refining process in its interior cells, and eliminates the finer particles.

The animal feeds on the vegetable, and subjects it to a refining process, ultimating a proportion of its atoms and exhaling them into the atmosphere. When the animal dies, the spiritual element, which retains not its identity after the dissolution of the body, escapes, as a drop of water evaporates, and mingles with the great ethereal ocean.

The spirit-world is derived from these atoms. Hence it is born from this earth as the spirit is born from the body. It depends on the earth for its existence, and is formed through its refining instrumentality. Without the earth there could not have been corresponding spirit-spheres, and there would not have been a necessity for them; so that the existence of the spirit-sphere presupposes the existence of a central world.

285. WHERE DO THESE PARTICLES GO?

Attenuated as they are, these atoms gravitate, or they are impelled by attractions and repulsions. They are not attracted to earth more than the inflated balloon; and, like it, they arise from the earth's surface until they reach a point where their gravity and repulsion are in equilibrium. There they rest. But atoms will partake of different degrees of refinement, and the most refined will not rest where the grosser find an equilibrium. Hence more than one zone will be formed.

286. THE FORM OF THESE ZONES.

If the earth were at rest, these ascending particles would rise in straight lines from the earth's centre, and a complete sphere would be formed, entirely enveloping the earth. But the earth rotates on its axis every twenty-four hours, or a thousand miles an hour, a velocity sufficient to throw out the equator twenty-six miles further from the centre than is the distance of the poles from the same.

As the understanding of this proposition is essential to the proper conception of the subject, we will illustrate it by the familiar instance of drops of water being thrown from the surface of a grindstone in rapid motion. Two forces produce the phenomena. The centrifugal force tends to throw the water off in straight lines from the surface: the same force tends to throw the world off in a straight line from its orbit. The centripetal force draws the drops of water to the centre of the wheel, and chains the earth to the sun. The motion of the earth in its orbit is a mean between these two forces. The same principles are true in regard to the diurnal motion of the earth on its axis. All its atoms are chained to the centre by gravity, but the rapid motion which they are obliged to perform ever tends to project them in straight lines from the surface into space. This does not occur, but their gravity is lessened, more at the equator than at the poles, as they are obliged to move faster at the former than in the latter position; and hence the poles draw inward, while the equator bulges outward. The tendency is to produce a ring, if the velocity were sufficiently increased.

287. SPIRITUAL ATOMS, BEING AFFECTED BY THE SAME LAWS,

Partake of the earth's rotary motion, and revolve with it. If the spheres completely surrounded the earth, as first supposed, the earth remaining at rest, as soon as it began to move, the superior velocity of the equatorial regions over the poles would draw away the particles from the latter, and concentrate them at the equator, producing a zone, the axis of whose revolution would coincide with the earth's axis, or it would revolve parallel with the equator.

288. The Rings of Saturn

Furnish a fine illustration of the form and appearance of the spirit-zones. They are belts or rings rotating around that planet, and sustained in their position by the equilibrium between the centripetal or tangential force and the gravity which draws them toward the central body.

The spirit-spheres are rather zones than spheres. They are one hundred and twenty degrees wide; that is, they extend sixty degrees each side of the earth's equator. If we take the sixtieth parallel of latitude each side of the equator, and imagine it projected against the blue dome of the sky, we have the boundaries of these zones.

289. How far are they from the Earth's Surface?

The first zone, or the innermost one, is sixty miles from the earth's surface. The next external is removed from the first by about the same distance. The third is just outside of the moon's orbit, or two hundred and sixty-five thousand miles from the earth.

Although atoms may be sufficiently refined when they are first ultimated from earth to pass by the first and enter the second zone, yet the second zone is, speaking in a general sense, the offspring of the first, as the first is the offspring of the earth; and, from the second, the third is elaborated by a similar process to that by which the earth exhales spiritualized matter. From the third sphere rise the most sublimated exhalations, which mingle with the emanations of the other planets, and form a vast zone around the entire solar system, including even the unknown planets beyond the vast orbit of Neptune.

Our sun is a star belonging to the milky-way. The mild radiance of the galactic zone is produced by an immense assemblage of stars, so crowded together that their light blends, and appears as a solid mass to the eye. With the telescope, however, it appears as a dense mass of stars. This system of suns, if it could be viewed from a great distance, would appear on the sky as an extremely flattened sphere, and our sun would be seen as a little star placed in the southern extremity of the starry mass.

As the emanations from the refined planetary spheres form a sphere around the solar system, so the refined emanations from all the solar systems form a still more sublimated series of zones around the milky-way. The same great principles pervade all of these spheres. The impress of the same law is witnessed in the magnificent spheres which surround the almost infinitely extended galaxy, as in the primary zones which surround the earth and planets.

290. There is no Miracle here,

But the supremacy of the same great principles which cause the stone to fall to the ground or the sun to shine.

291. The Thickness of the Spheres Varies.

The first is nearly thirty, while the second is twenty, and the third is but two miles in thickness. The first is the oldest by immeasurable time, as it was the first to begin to form; and, until it supported organizations, it could exhale but a small amount of refined matter to the second, and of course the process was delayed still longer in the creation of the third.

How beautifully harmonious nature has framed, not only the constitution of physical, but of spiritual things! There is observable the nicest adjustment of harmony and adaption. So fast as creations are called for, they are supplied. Nature toiled through illimitable ages to produce an identified intelligence. She looked through all these ages, and with prophet's eye saw that she would succeed, and that her success would necessitate a home for that spirit other than the gross world it had left. Then she began to build its habitation, and that, too, by the same process by which she sought to perfect her masterpiece of creative force, — an identified human spirit. Creative energy is at work now as much as when earth was evoked from chaos. It toils unceasingly; and, as the heat and vapor of its workshop, the refined atoms constantly rise, floating away to their appropriate spheres.

It will be inferred from this that the spheres are gradually increasing, while the earth is slowly diminishing. Yes: this is one of the most beautiful truths which we can contemplate. The tall mountain which proudly rears its granite peak among the clouds, bidding defiance to the sleet and storm, on whose atlas shoulders the sky lovingly rests, on whose brawny back vast forests slumber, from whose sides great rivers well; the earth-engirdling ocean, with its countless isles and bordering continents; the moon and planets which light up the evening sky, — all are undergoing the refining process, and in future ages will be resolved into spiritual elements.

The mountain shall crumble, the ocean shall become dry, and the moon and stars fade from the canopy of night; but they will exist, in a more active and perfected form, carrying out the grand design of creation.

The surface of these zones is diversified with changing scenery.

292. MATTER, WHEN IT AGGREGATES THERE, IS PRONE TO ASSUME THE FORMS IN WHICH IT EXISTED HERE.

Hence there are all the forms of life there as on earth, except those, such as the lowest plants and animals, which cannot exist surrounded by such superior conditions. The scenery of mountain and plain, river, lake, and ocean, of forest and prairie, are daguerreotypes of the same on earth. It is like earth with all its imperfections perfected, and its beauties multiplied a thousand-fold.

293. THE SPIRIT HOLDS THE SAME RELATION TO THIS SPIRITUAL UNIVERSE THAT MAN HOLDS TO PHYSICAL NATURE.

The surface of the spheres is solid earth, in which trees and flowers take root, and the waters of the ocean surge perpetually on the shore. An ethereal sky arches overhead, and the stars shine with increased refulgence. The spirits *breathe* its spiritual atmosphere; they drink its crystal waters; they partake of its luscious fruits; they bedeck themselves with its gorgeous flowers.

It is not a fancy world, nor world of chance or miracle; but a *real* world, — in fact, more real than is earth, as it is its perfection.

The spirit walks on its surface, it sails on the lakes and oceans; in short, follows whatever pursuit or pastime it pleases, and the elements there hold the same relations to it that the elements of earth held to it while in the physical form.

I will not enter at present into a minute description of scenery as it appears to the spirit or the clairvoyant. Words are but feeble auxiliaries in the delineation of a subject so far removed above mortal comprehension. It is a reflection of the earth, and holds a close correspondence to it, but can no more be compared with it in beauty than the finest miniature with the coarsest charcoal sketch.

I pass to the consideration of the next important inquiry.

294. How do Spirits pass from Earth to the Spheres?

Philosophers teach us that an ether pervades all space, on which the pulsations of light and heat are thrown by luminous bodies. This ether, they tell us, pervades all space and all substances, and is the medium for transmission of the influence of the imponderable agents.

By their description of this ether, we can readily understand the spiritual ether, which also pervades all space. It is not, however, like the former, except in its universal diffusion. It is a much more refined and active agent, and is a peculiar emanation from all globes.

Ultimated as it is, the organization of the spirit is still more refined, and hence it floats as a cork immersed in water, or a balloon in the atmosphere, having its gravity with respect to the earth entirely destroyed.

The ultimated particles from the earth rise and rush out of the vast openings at the poles in a spiral direction produced by the rotation of the earth. Then they diffuse themselves through the atmosphere of the first zone, each following its own peculiar attractions.

On these rivers the spirit is wafted from the sublunary scene, and is ushered, in a moment, into the spirit-world.

295. The Philosophy of the Spirit traveling with such Rapidity

Is as simple as is that of the other great principles. As its gravitation is destroyed by immersion in an ether more dense than itself, it rises, or is repelled from all the physical worlds. When it comes to earth, the action of the gravitation of the earth is to repel it from it, and not to attract. But, by an effort of will, the spirit becomes positive to the place where it desires to go. Then there arises an immediate attraction to that place, and it flies through the thin ether.

296. Can they pass to other Globes?

This depends on their degree of refinement. While some are very pure and ethereal, others are gross and unrefined. The sensualist, the depraved debauchee, in many instances are so gross that gravity chains them to the earth's surface as it does man. They are denser than the spirit ether, and hence have weight, and cannot rise from earth. Others, who are more spiritual, can only rise to the first sphere; while others, still more refined, pass at will through the universal ocean of ether, visiting other globes and other solar systems. The degree of purity or spirituality determines whether or no the spirit shall be chained to earth, or allowed freedom to travel the ocean of space.

297. Objections may Arise.

If the spheres spread out above us, why do we not see them?

Why do we not see spirits with the normal vision?

The questions are easily answered. It is from the relation which they bear to light. Air, like almost all other gases, is invisible. No one ever saw atmospheric air, yet no one doubts its existence. It transmits light without intercepting the rays, and hence is invisible; for we cannot see anything unless it reflects light by which we can see it. If so material a substance as air is unseen, though it surges above our heads in a great ocean forty-five miles deep, how can we expect to see the refined ether of which these zones are formed?

Still further. When we look through a clear plate of glass, we cannot see the glass interposed between us and the objects beyond. Perfectly clear water transmits the rays of light so completely that it is invisible unless seen by reflection.

After such instances, can we ask why the spheres are not visible, and why they do not intercept the light of the sun and stars? The objection is fully met here on scientific grounds, and does not depend, for its explanation, on the mere words of the angels.

One question more arises, namely:—

298. WHAT IS THE RELATION OF LIGHT TO THE SPHERES? IS THERE DAY AND NIGHT THERE AS HERE?

The sun's light, as is well known to the chemist, is composed of an indefinite number of rays mingled together. He divides them with his prism, and shows the seven colored rays, the chemical rays, the magnetic rays, &c. We find that light, as it is emanated from the sun, is composed of different kinds of rays, each adapted for peculiar purposes.

Each of the spheres retains the rays useful to it, and transmits the more gross rays which are adapted to earthly conditions. The spiritual portion of light is retained as it passes from the sun to earth, while the coarser portion is transmitted. Hence the sun and stars as certainly appear from the surface of the zones as they appear from the earth, and the superior do not intercept the view from the lower spheres, because they are much more refined than the latter, and these are more ethereal than earth. The rays of light designed for the first sphere pass through the higher without interruption, for they retain only their own element.

The light of the heavenly bodies is much greater when seen from the spheres than when observed from the earth. The splendor of the stars is greatly increased, and the radiance of the sun fills the atmosphere with a flood of silver, gilding the scenery with an ethereal, indescribable light.

If the sun is the source of the light received by the spheres, and these revolve around the earth, it follows, as a necessary deduction, that there, as on earth, day and night must follow each other with the unvarying regularity of the rising and setting sun. That there should be such alternations of light and darkness is a necessity of man's spiritual nature. He wearies of the never-changing scene, and the activity and repose of nature are more agreeable to him than is a monotonous sameness. It is also essentially the result of the plan of creation; for nature allows of no rest. Worlds and zones must revolve around central luminaries; and, as they bring different portions of the surface beneath the central light, day and night — that is, the presence and absence of the luminaries — must result.

Thus have we glanced at some of the prominent principles connected with the spirits' home, and sought to sustain them by the facts of science. They may excite prejudice by their novelty; they may be rejected by credulity; they may be scorned by the pride of external philosophy: yet they depend not on any of these for support, but on their own truthfulness. *

* Prof. Hare, speaking of the spirit-spheres, says, —
"From the information conveyed by communications submitted in the preceding pages, as well as others, it appears

XVIII.

RELIGIOUS ASPECT OF SPIRITUALISM.

Love for all men, but fear of none. — Luther.

But though he has been brave in battle, killed wild beasts, and fought with all manner of external evils, if he has neglected to combat evil within himself, he has reason to fear that Arimanes and his Devs will seize him. — Zoroaster.

299. Spiritualism is not wanting in the Religious Element.

SPIRITUALISM is considered to be wanting in a vital system of ethics, to be wanting in vivifying religious tendencies, and, as a philosophy, to be thoroughly infidel. As a divine remarked, "It is the teachings of the demon allies of the infidel world."

that there are seven spheres recognized in the spirit-world. The terrestrial abode forms the first or rudimental sphere. At the distance of about sixty miles from the terrestrial surface, the spirit-world commences. It consists of six bands or zones, designated as spheres, surrounding the earth, so as to have one common centre with it and with each other. An idea of these rings may be formed from that of the planet Saturn, excepting that they are comparatively much nearer to their planet, and at right-angles to his equator, instead of being, like Saturn's rings, so arranged that their surfaces are parallel to the plane in which his equator exists.

"The interval between the lower boundaries of the first

It is true that it discards many things which were regarded as divine truths; but if it is to bring no new light into the world, if the old is to remain, of what avail is it that the angel host communicates with earth?

The pure precepts of the great thinkers of the past will remain forever: they rest on the eternal foundation of man's relationship to man, and cannot perish. But their *interpretations* may be false, we may misunderstand them, or new light may give to them a wholly different meaning. Spiritualism may interfere with many darling beliefs of the churches, but never with their truths. It presents different motives, but the end it wishes man to attain is the same.

spiritual sphere and the second is estimated at thirty miles as a maximum; but this interval is represented to be less as the spheres between which it may exist are more elevated or remote from the terrestrial centre. . . . The first spiritual sphere, or the second in the whole series, is as large as all the other five above it. This is the hell, or Hades, of the spirit world, where all sensual, malevolent, selfish beings reside. The next sphere above this, or the third of the whole series, is the habitation of all well-meaning persons, however bigoted, fanatical, or ignorant. In proportion as spirits improve in purity, benevolence, and wisdom, they ascend."

Prof. Hare divided the spheres into six circles each, the homes of distinct classes; but he admits this division to be somewhat arbitrary. The value of this communication could be better estimated if he had stated how he had received it. There is incompleteness and want of coherence in the statement itself. The inner or second sphere cannot be of larger extent than the external; and, as the second sphere is the

300. Incentive offered by the Church.

The Church offers two reasons for right-doing: fear of punishment, — by far the stronger inducement, — and hope of reward; eternal misery on one hand, eternal happiness on the other. Hell and heaven are foreign elements to be sought or avoided. They are not of the soul.

301. Incentive of Spiritualism.

It is an easy thing to become a Christian, as that name is now employed, — that is, to become a member of a church, to be regular in attendance on Sun-

home of *all* spirits after leaving the mortal body, it cannot be only that of the bad; and it would be just as rational to divide this life, or the first sphere, into six circles, as any of the future states.

It may be truly said that the spirit friends of Prof. Hare stated a great and cardinal truth, — that the spirit-spheres surround the earth; but either from want of knowledge, or from imperfection of their means of communication, they failed to give the details in a perfect manner. However painstaking in his experiments, he seems to have received these communications with almost unquestioning credulity, and did not subject them to the criticism necessary for the elimination of error. Judging from the "internal evidence" of the statement, we infer that he was prone to fashion theories and "submit" them ready formed to the "spirits," rather than to await their spontaneous disclosures. This method is the one most liable to error of any that can be pursued. A positive element is introduced, disturbing in its influence, and shutting out explanation and correction.

days, to be regular in paying quarterage or pew rent, and to be regular in prayers and confessions of short-comings.

302. IT IS NOT AN EASY AFFAIR TO BECOME A SPIRITUALIST.

You have no powerful body to support you when you fail, to conceal your errors, or to praise your virtues; but on your own exertions you must rely, and must achieve your own salvation. Churchianity is a retreat for mental laziness. There the grand problem of salvation is worked out. All that is required for the convert is to *receive the solution.* He must be like an infant or an imbecile, with open mouth ready to swallow the theological pap. The more docile, the more he stultifies his intellect, the better member he becomes.

From this lethargy it is difficult to awake. I always feel uneasy when church-members declare themselves Spiritualists. The bite of the theological mad dog is rankling in their veins: they are ever ready to return. So long have they been led, that, when they find themselves cut loose, they are like children taken into the park, or young colts let out to pasture. The field cannot contain them. They run here, and they run there, and all over the premises, in no time. But they weary of this when they find the old landmarks are washed away, that the old compass is useless, and the log-book obsolete, and their own powers their only reliance,—

they soon weary, and, oh, how they sigh for the flesh-pots of Egypt!

How many have we seen of such poor souls, floating out on the great sea, weary with effort, and ready to catch at a straw for support! How cheery the old days of unquestioning belief appeared to them! How they wished they had *not begun* to think! It is not well to make converts of such unless they have power sufficient to uphold them. You make a poor Spiritualist of a good church-member. You baptize him into a sea of trouble, only to see him in the end grow weary, and return to the fold, when the opiate of formulas drowns his tremulous efforts. The church is necessary for such until it is outgrown. We have often met men who have no business to be outside of its pales. They have not come out by legitimate thought: some friend has broken a paling, and let them out. To such, we say, return,— the sooner, the better. If you cannot walk without using a broken pale for a crutch, out here on the breezy coast of philosophy, you had better return; and, for fear you will come out again, replace the paling carefully after you.

303. Spiritualism the Essence of Philosophy.

Religion is often accused of wanting in philosophy. Spiritualism is the essence of philosophy. It asks nothing without giving a reason, teaches nothing without giving a cause. It causes the individual to become just and pure, because no other being in the universe will receive as great a reward for his right doing as the individual, and because every being in the universe will be better for that right doing. It asks us to improve ourselves by aiding others, in the same effort and time; it teaches that we aid in molding our own immortal natures.

304. THE INDIVIDUAL CANNOT CONTROL HIS OWN ORGANIZATION.

In this imperfect world, he is born, trailing the aggregated sins of his ancestors after him. The sins of the fathers are visited on the children. Nor do we have more control of the conditions which surround us. If the word "religion" means anything, it means doing right. To do right is to obey all the laws of our being. If hungry, it is a religious precept to feed the body; if cold, to protect it; if intellectually starving, to seek for truth. Thus we ascend. Religion, beginning with the head, ascends to the contemplation of eternal laws.

305. THE DOCTRINE OF SALVATION, THROUGH THE BLOOD OF CHRIST, IS A SHAM, AN IMPOSITION, A LIBEL ON REASON AND COMMON SENSE.

We are responsible for the thoughts and actions of all. A crime cannot be committed in the wide world but each individual feels its effects. We are atoms of the social world, and disturbance of one disturbs all. A wrong deed, whether individual or national, re-acts on the whole world. In its larger sphere of nationality we can better observe its effect. We thought, as a nation, we could do wrong with impunity: our statesmen told us we could do so. But the centuries came round; and the higher law, written in the constitution of things, laughed at and scorned by the nation, asserted itself. At once we found ourselves face to face with eternal justice. The cannon booming from Sumter was its voice. The nation found it still had a heart, — *that it could be just!* It met the issue, poured out the blood of a million sons, and billions of treasure, meeting the wrong in a death-grapple, where defeat was annihilation.

So far as it has stood firmly on absolute justice, has it been successful; so far as it has *compromised*, it has met defeat. We fear justice is not yet appeased, or the nation's heart purified. I do not wish to become a prophet, nor to excite fear. I only state what *must* come in the course of events. There are rivers of blood yet to cross, fiery plains yet to pass, before we efface our past wrongs, and plant ourselves on absolute truth and justice, the only basis of a free and noble people.

Talk about the laws of men! They copy those of eternal right; and, if they fail in this, if they are worded by selfishness to meet the requirements of Mammon, alas for the generation they govern! So is it in all history. So in the biography of every man.

306. WE ARE NOT PLACED HERE FOR SELF ALONE.

Beautiful are our relations to others, — relations which are not only for this life, but grow brighter in eternity.

A kind word is never lost. If it bears not fruit in this life, it will in the next. A spirit told me an incident in his own life. When on earth he met a newsboy. He was an impudent, impish rogue, on whose scarred and besmeared face one could not see a line of goodness. Well, the spirit, who was then a mortal, gave him a kind word. A new light brightened that dull countenance; a new purpose seized him. "Come with me," said the man. He placed him at school, where he soon equaled and surpassed his fellows. He entered life with high purpose, and exerted a wide influence.

Said the benignant spirit, "I met that boy in the spirit-world. His gratitude was unbounded. It was the first time we had met since I placed him at school, a boy, with his humanity almost blotted and trampled out. The happiness I received from this little action has brightened the joy of heaven. It is by such deeds we create our heaven."

Oh, let us learn of the angel! The urchins of our streets meet no kindness. They meet scorn, jests, coarse rebuffs, turn where they will. They are in the rough tide, rushing swiftly to the destruction of the little humanity they possess. We stretch not out our hands to help. Instead of helping, *we accelerate the current.*

307. WHAT THE CHURCH HAS DONE.

The Church has for two thousand years been at work. Go down into our back streets and alleys, and answer if this is a Christian land! We have our work-houses, orphan asylums, retreats for the inebriate and insane, our jails and penitentiaries, and our refuges for the Magdalenes: we are benevolent to the individual in a kind of a way, but we make no attempt to control the fountain from which all this disease and death flows. The man of business calls to his workshop his hands, and pays them more or less. What is it to him if they live or starve? Is he not to be in the tread-mill, competitors on every side? and, if he pauses to look after others, will not he go under? If the wheels at the top of society grind so fine, those at the bottom grind to powder. The poor are crushed out, physically and spiritually.

308. WHAT SPIRITUALISM CAN DO.

What we say, we say understandingly. If the grand principles of Spiritualism were put in universal practice to-day, in three generations there would not be necessity for an asylum, a jail, a penitentiary, a lawyer, a judge, a reverend, in the wide land. Time only would be necessary for humanity to outgrow its scars and deformities.

If it is easy to awaken the soul to visions of the beautiful and true, it is equally easy to crush out the little light it may possess.

We scorn the Irishman, who, by oppression and poverty, has become an ignoble serf,— the coal-digger, whose language has been reduced to a few hundred words, and those relating only to his immediate wants. We scorn the outcast, the unfortunate and criminal. Rather should we pity. Let us remember, that, if placed in their situation, with their antecedents, we should do precisely as they do.

Mocking pharisee, who draw your cloak close around you for fear of contact with these, did you have a choice of endowment given you? Were you consulted as to the sphere of life into which you desired to be born? Do you suppose the vagabond, whom you thank God for not being like unto, wished to be born to his estate? Then take no praise for being as you are, nor blame him for not being better than he is.

The missionary may talk religion to starving men; and, when the beggar's children cry for bread, he may give them — tracts. Spiritualism has quite another office. The poor have we with us always; and, because consumption exceeds production, there is misery and crime. It is hideous — this wolf-pang of hungry poverty — to see disease, engendered by want, snatching one's children in its greedy jaws; to see it obliterate the lines of health from their features, and write there the livid lines of death! It is well the law is written in blood,— well that constant pressure obliterates the keener senses of the soul; else these chained savages of society would lay their firm grasp on the bread of the wealthy.

It is not done. But let us not suppose, therefrom, they have no feeling. A human heart in fustian beats as ardently as in broadcloth. The mother in rags has as deep affection for her child as the mother in satin, though sometimes, in its struggle through misery, it appears more like animal instinct than human affection.

I know not that the fault is with the individual: it is with the nation and the times. We rush recklessly forward. The struggle for existence is terrible, and the path of advance is paved with human hearts. The under-structure of society can have, at most, but little pleasure, and the time for the enjoyment of even that is denied to them.

Why wonder at their excesses? The physical frame is prostrated by excessive labor. Stimulants, for a time, restore its tone. It is as natural for the overtasked to seek them, as, when thirsty, to call for water. A passing enjoyment is wrung from the soul-blasting intoxication; but draw the mantle of charity over their failings,— it is all that these poor, crushed souls can obtain.

On the other hand, the man of business, the thinker, and the writer; the men who hold the commerce of the globe, and with ship and sail weave the web of nationalities close and strong; who represent the brain as the others do the hands of society,— by overtasking, fall into the same state. Constant strain produces corresponding depression. The man leaves his desk weary, drooping, enfeebled. Sleep does not refresh him. He cannot enjoy anything. He only feels at home when following the path of business which habit has prescribed.

309. BUT WHAT HAS SPIRITUALISM TO DO WITH THE POOR OR THE RICH?

It has much to do.

Just ahead, there is equality. The green fields of heaven are not owned nor sold by title-deed. There are no mortgages there, — no rents; but as the air is free here, so are all things free there. At once death shakes from poverty its dead weight, and man no longer feels its canker, nor is crushed by what poor mortals call the *justice of the law.* He will not be compelled to see his ragged children grow up in ignorance, and destined to become serfs to Mammon.

How inconsistent we are! We make laws, and rob man of his mother earth, which Nature proclaims belongs to him who will cultivate, and then blame him for poverty and crime. It is well we can go no further. Title-deeds will not hold the sunlight, nor the air, nor the water; else they would be so held, and the unfortunate would then be censured for not breathing and seeing.

310. IN PLAINEST STATEMENT, DO WE NOT ALL DO THE BEST WE KNOW HOW?

Can we not always give reasons for our conduct, satisfactory to ourselves? We censure, because we judge from our own standpoint, wholly ignorant of the thoughts and motives which actuate the censured. We always yield to the strongest influence, right or wrong.

If a tiger spring on a man, and rend him, who blames the tiger? He is only acting out the requirements of a tiger's nature. When a man, born with a tiger's organization, and that inflamed by years of wrong, acts out *his* nature, is he more to blame? Is he more blamable than the man, born with a benevolent organization, who acts benevolently?

Do not understand me as upholding "whatever is, is right." On the contrary, I hold that *"whatever is, is wrong."* We must all join in righting it.

311. "Whatever is, must be."

And there should be no praise, no censure, for its being thus.

This doctrine varnishes no fault. There is only one right way, and that, the obedience to law: and, if you fail, do not support yourself by saying, "I am as I am;" for the first step in progress is the recognition of this very doctrine; and, the next, endeavoring to overcome the impediments of your condition. Your remaining in the wrong plainly says you are ignorant of the right.

The ideal man of Spiritualism is perfect. Would that I could paint to you the beatitudes that cluster around such a one, and breathe into you his lofty aspirations!

That ideal man loves truth for its own sake, because it is truth, — not from any good he expects to derive from it; loves justice because it is justice; loves right because it is right.

There are many who profess to love truth, justice, right; but, on analysis, they love only their special forms, — not the divine, eternal, and universal. We see men, every day, ready to defend what they call by these names; but they so style some speciality, and know little of universal justice, right, and truth.

The love of these, in their universal quality, is the perfection of manhood. This love sustains the martyr, and makes the burning coals a bed of down, compared to their violation. They are the fountains from which flow all the nobleness of a true life, and they never yield bitter waters.

When the love of these exists, the individual never fails in their requirements; for, where the universal exists, the special will well out, as occasion demands, from its exhaustless fountain.

The effect of these three great principles, the representatives of the Spiritual philosophy of ethics on the character of the man, is the development of perfect manhood.

That is the great end and object of living. If we do not advance, we might as well not live. If we are not growing in wisdom, and developing angelic qualities, our life is a waste, and we should make haste to recover the right path.

312. IF THIS BE THE PURPOSE OF LIFE, WE INQUIRE HOW IT MAY BE OBTAINED.

By discarding those things which are only for to-day, and doing those which have an eternal relation.

Every organ has an appropriate function to perform, and the proper action of all is a sacred duty. Take our being as a whole, and the natural, legitimate use of all faculties and powers is equally holy. It is perversion that causes disease and suffering; and the perversion of the morals is as disastrous as that of the passions. To cramp or dwarf one department of our being, and cultivate another to excess, is detrimental, even if the overwrought faculty be the highest moral feeling.

313. WE SAY, DO THAT WHICH HAS AN ETERNAL RELATION.

Happiness, then, is not evanescent, but is an abiding quality. The business of the world is the contrary. Take, for example, the man devoted to the acquisition of wealth. A very narrow portion of his mind is cultivated by his pursuits, and the remainder is dwarfed. Perhaps, morally, he is idiotic. He may be a shrewd dealer in stocks, and thoroughly posted in his business; but, not having cultivated any other department of his being, he is dwarfed. At death, his brokerage is gone; and the man stands on the other side of the grave a miserable, enfeebled soul.

If the angels dealt in stocks, he would feel at home. He finds that he has no treasures laid up in heaven, and that his life has been wasted in an idle chase for brambles, of no consequence to the grand growth of eternal life.

Such a treasure is the proper cultivation of the mind. I say *proper* cultivation, for there is a learning worse than ignorance. The bias given by a creed, or any cramped religious system, is more detrimental to the spirit's growth than absolute deficiency of all learning. Such systems warp and distort the mind. They form a medium through which it views humanity; and that medium, being untruthful, conveys nothing but error.

This culture is founded on the principles of truth, justice, and love. These have their existence in the constitution of man, as well as in external nature, wherein their divine manifestations can be read.

314. The Great Object of Being is a Manly Life.

We are not dwellers on the shores of time, but of eternity. Though we do the best we know how, we have capabilities of doing infinitely better. Life is a school for discipline. We should co-ordinate and harmonize all our faculties, living and acting true to our highest light.

Not in an organization, a party, do we wish to find the excellency of Spiritualism, but in the individual. It makes no difference how strong, how excellent, how pure the party is to which he belongs, if he is wrong. The sacrifice of the world would be of no avail. Sin lies not with the body; all transgression is of the spirit. The higher powers should rise above the lower, and, duly co-ordinated, should control them.

315. WE MAKE OUR OWN HEAVEN AND OUR OWN HELL,

And walk an angel or a devil therein, — not in free realms of spirit-life, but now and here on earth.

Such I consider to be the religious aspect of Spiritualism. It is the combined moral excellence of the world. It is the essence of Christianity; but, while the latter involves itself in creeds and churches, the former acknowledges no other creed than the laws written in the natural world, no other interpreter than reason, no church but mankind.

While the churches descant on the efficacy of prayer, Spiritualism teaches that one good deed is worth all the formal prayers since Adam's time.

He believes in prayer, but in that prayer by which the workman molds iron into an engine, and wood into steamships, — the prayer of the hand as well as of the heart.

While the church prays God to help the needy and suffering, the Spiritualist becomes the messenger, giving that help. Such is he, — large-hearted, open-handed. That is the difference. He has gone past all the churches, and drank at the fountains where the apostles drank. All the trappings are stripped away, and the pure ethics of the world's sages — of Plato, Confucius, Pythagoras, and Christ — are the ethics of Spiritualism.

XIX.

THE OLD AND THE NEW.

CHRIST, very man and very God, has purchased for us an everlasting deliverance. He who died for us is the eternal God. His passion, therefore, is an eternal sacrifice, and has a perpetual efficacy: it satisfies the Divine Justice forever upon behalf of all who rely upon it with a firm, unshaken faith. — ZWINGLE.

Scripture satisfies the soul with holy and wondrous delight: it is a heavenly ambrosia. — MELANCTHON.

We create our own heaven or hell, and walk an angel or a devil therein.

Man is his own saviour.

316. THE RADICAL AND RADICALISM.

THERE is a philosophy of history. Every age furnishes a prophecy of the ages to follow, which, if we fail to read, it is because of our ignorance. The deeds of each century are evolved out of those that preceded it. The past contained the germs of the present, and the present of the future. We call the present the best, rightly perhaps, perhaps wrongly; wrongly to the conservative, in whose mind the golden age glimmers in the remote past, and to whom the future is a dreadful night. The Radical believes the reverse. The sun has yet to rise in full splendor on the glories of that age. One gazes wistfully backwards; the other, forwards.

Society began in savage clans, — began in intense individualism. From thence onward the process has been one of subduing the individual. During the middle ages, Church and State combined to stifle individual thought, and their success was indicated by the ignorance that prevailed, — the brutality and merciless cruelty. There has been a great reaction against these forces; and, moving on in a circle, we have again reached individualism, but in a new form. We began with the individualism of the brute: we end with the individualism of the intellect. Our circle is a spiral.

The conservatives say this is not progress. Progression with them means forever following the same round, just as the squirrel inside its revolving cage thinks turning the cage means getting ahead. So they, blinded by the fog of creeds, think that movement in the same orbit forever is most desirable.

There are those in the world who think otherwise.

You have noticed a large family attaining maturity, and following in the exact footsteps of the father. Perhaps one, however, tires of this method, and seeks out a new path. Fired with youthful zeal, he sets up for himself, and discards the trammels of habit which confine his brothers. He is the radical of the family. Just so do the radicals of society arise. They are prodigal sons, but not fed on husks. They have their sorrows and their joys. They are the pioneers, who clear the pathway across wild continents of ignorance, and from mountain summits obtain the first glimpses of the beautiful regions in store for those who follow. To them comes the inspiration of great thoughts, floating like visions of Eden through the chambers of their minds, lighting the future with resplendent beams, and sending rosy twilight over the gray bleakness of the present.

Radicalism is the *ultima thule* of Protestantism. It is the consequence of the granted right of private opinion. If one man has the right to protest, so has another; and this protestation may go on to the complete separation of all individuals, leaving all believing and acting differently.

This result is quite the opposite of that desired by a respectable class of thinkers who consider harmony the desired end, — that individuals should all think and act alike. On every hand, we hear much said about "harmonious development." They would have us believe that all disagreement should be avoided, and perfection attainable only by means of perfect unity. This view is little better than the conservative idea of sacrificing man to society, making his personality of no account compared to the State. Such will find an example in China of the result of their theory. Disagreement being avoided, the State interfering whenever conflict occurs, harmony results, but it ends in stagnation. The individual is lost in the routine of senseless forms and ceremonies. There is no growth, and Chinese civilization is effete, not in dying with old age, but because it is unable to break through the crust of its concreted ideas. Conflict, radicalism, tempest, is the only cure. So in the world everywhere; thus has it been for all time; and the Protestant of to-day is the conservative of to-morrow.

317. INFIDELITY.

An infidel is a disbeliever in the popular theology of the day. The Christian is infidel to the creed of the Mohammedan, and the latter is an infidel in the estimation of the Christian. The Brahman is an infidel to Christianity, and the Chinese are infidel to Brahmanism. To disbelieve in the current theology is infidelity, and brands "infidel" on the disbeliever. Infidelity, as now used by the church, so far from being a term of reproach, is the most honorable title that can be bestowed; for it means a thinker, one who can and does think for himself, and act on his own responsibility. In all past time, the infidel, he who was branded and scourged by the established theology, has been the reformer of the world. In order to vindicate a new truth, some old and deep-rooted errors must be overthrown; and to those the reformer must become infidel, and show how erroneous they are, as well as prove his own truth.

Jesus Christ was an infidel, as well as his apostles, to the Jewish laws and ceremonies, and dearly paid the penalty usually attached to this crime. Melancthon, Luther, and Calvin were infidels to the theology of their day, as were all the great reformers down to the present. The infidel has good company. Copernicus, Kepler, Galileo, Newton, Laplace, and Herschel are with him in science ; and Confucius, Zoroaster, and Christ are with him in religion. He need not be ashamed of his followers, but rather be thankful that he is allowed to enter a court so august, where all the great minds that earth can boast are arrayed in a galaxy of splendor.

Some minds progress faster than others, and, grasping new ideas, perceive the falseness of the doctrines entertained by their fellows, and attempt to make them believe like themselves. This brings on their devoted heads, from the bigoted opposition, the blighting cry of "Infidel!" The martyr is always an infidel. He cannot be otherwise ; for no one can believe the theology of the day if he reasons on its teachings, and compares them with the revelations of nature. Theologians have always endeavored to shut out the light of nature, and suppress the activity of reason : they have thought that both were blind leaders, and that infallibility could be found only in the Bible and their creeds.

It is well known to every thinking man that we cannot believe without evidence. Believing by faith, having faith to believe, and believing to have faith, are contradictions in terms, and an impossibility. We may be educated into a belief; but, as soon as we reason on it, we cannot believe it, unless it be rational, and appeals to our understanding. We may think we believe, yet we never can believe an unreasonable doctrine.

Slowly the minds of the age are admitting that nature and reason — which is the philosophical interpretation of nature — are the only reliable standards. They must be true. Nature is the same eternal, immutable handiwork of God. When a revelation is given us from God, it will be in accordance with nature, clear and unmistakable, and not ambiguous, and needing succeeding interpretation. Now when a book purports to be from God, infallible in its authority, and binding on us to believe, declaring that we must believe or be damned, it is evident that it is imposible to prevent ourselves from reasoning on it. If we have the right to reason on it, we have the right to reject it if it appears false. God has made nothing in vain. Hence, the possession of reason presupposes the right to reason: this right proves that we also have a right to reject the false, and receive the true, — to subject everything to close and rigid examination, whatever may be its claims.

The infidel is one who asserts this privilege. He knows, that, if the Bible is of God, it cannot be injured by the closest scrutiny; and, if it be untrue, of course he does not wish to believe it, and he feels it to be a duty, if not an honor, to expose its errors. He knows that the truth never suffered by reason or comparison with nature; that only error hides itself away from the light, and loves darkness and mystery!

He takes the book, and compares it with the infallible standard God has given him, — nature. It fails. It presents antagonisms, contradictions, and absurdities. How can he believe it, crush his reason, shut his eyes to the light, and greedily swallow whatever is presented therein? How can he help being an unbeliever? Have faith! He cannot have faith without reasons for faith. He cannot believe without evidence. His eyes are open, and he will not close them. He has not swallowed an opiate, and he is wide-awake. To him, the claims of infallibility for the book destroys it; its antagonism with the facts of nature destroys it; and he cannot help disbelieving it, strive he ever so hard to force himself to its reception. This is the philosophical infidel. It is not from a love of skepticism that he is so, but from the unimpeded action of his reason.

318. Protestantism brings from Catholicism everything but the Pope.

Its basis is the same, — the Bible. Its departure from Catholicism is a departure from reason. Granting its data, the logic of Catholicism is unanswerable: man being incapable of arriving at divine truth, an infinite God delivers to him an infinite revelation. Man, as finite, cannot comprehend this revelation; hence the necessity of inspired teachers or priests to interpret it to him. Protestantism places finite man in direct contact with an infinite God, — a finite comprehension with an infinite revelation. In the latter case, what is the benefit of the exercise of reason, when the object is beyond the grasp of reason? Practically, the two systems are the same; and whatever power the Bible exerts is, by means of the idea of infallibility, attached to its utterances. It is claimed that Protestantism is the system demanded by the present age. We ask, is this a fact? Not only is it what we demand now, but has it elasticity to meet the requirements of the future? Daring questions to ask of a system founded eighteen centuries ago, and claiming for its founder not only the Son of God, but the eternal Father himself. They may be sacrilegious, but they are of vital interest.

319. A Religion of Abnegation.

To analysis what does this religion yield? Emphatically it is of denial and abnegation. It has been well said that "Thou shalt *not*" has a great preponderance over "Thou shalt" in the Decalogue. It is a passive religion. It sets up the preposterous claim, that religion, that morals, can be created outside of man, and forced upon him. Here originate missionary schemes. Contrary to this, the field of the world shows that moral precepts, however calculated to impress themselves, have no power unless received by the intellect. Unless so received, they remain dead beliefs, without any bearing on the lives of their receivers. It is safe to say that such is the state of ninety-nine Christians in a hundred, and that they never gauge their actions by the precepts of their religion. It is received that "It is easier for a camel to pass through the eye of a needle than for a rich man to enter the kingdom of heaven;" that the poor and ill-used of the world are blessed and enviable; that we should love our neighbors and enemies as ourselves; that, if one takes our cloak, we should give him our coat; that we should take no thought for the morrow; that we never should resent injuries, and, if struck on one cheek, we should turn the other also. When Christians say they believe these precepts, we cannot charge them with insincerity. They are not hypocrites and deceivers. They think they do: but if one should practice them; if he began by selling all he had, and giving it to the poor, and some cold day bestowing his last coat on a beggar,—these same Christians would cry, "O fool!" or be swift to thrust him into a mad-house. As for loving their enemies, it is beyond the pale of necessary virtues, unless to burn them for not believing like those in power. The heathen Romans, at the rise of Christianity, exclaimed with surprise, "See these Christians, how they love one another!" They would not say that now.

320. RELIGIONISTS NOT NECESSARILY INSINCERE.

Not insincere: they received certain moral maxims supposed by them to have descended from infallible wisdom, wholly foreign to their intellect, which is pre-occupied by a set of everyday, practical judgments. It is easy to foreknow which must go to the wall. The Christian code becomes from this cause only serviceable to illustrate the beauties of Christianity, not the lives of its professed believers.

321. Is the Present Form of Religion Demanded by the Age?

We question not the origin of Christianity. It is an existing fact. We ask, Is it the religion demanded by the present age? and from it can a religion adequate to the wants of all future time be evolved? In other words, will it continue a foreign element to be foisted upon its recipient, or has it the vitality of growth? Apparently it progresses. Luther and Calvin and Wesley each have done somewhat to improve the old; but, in essence, it is the same. Man grows intellectually, pushing the domain of thought wider and wider; yet he is content with his father's religious formula!

322. Christian and Infidel.

Perhaps we may be severe, if, to the question, "What constitutes a religious man?" we answer, change of heart, baptism, — either by plunging, sprinkling, or pouring, — joining a church, regular attendance at meetings, and regular prayers. If a man do all this, is he not accounted as a Christian, regardless of any moral delinquencies inside of elastic laws? And if he do not do these, but is himself absolutely morally perfect, is he anything else than a loathed infidel? Infidel! Proud name of honor, under which are ranked all the mighty intellects of the ages! He is the thinker, who dares grandly to stand alone in his belief, and to endure the curses of vile-mouthed bigotry and religious hate. This "change of heart" leads to the strangest manifestations of intellectual obliquity. What does it mean? Simply that the individual will forsake his evil ways, and strive to do better. It is the work of a moment. The hardened sinner, with conscience calloused to every emotion of justice and right, can at once become a beautiful Christian! This is Catholicism. The murderer kisses the crucifix, and dies. Paradise awaits him. Had he not kissed the crucifix, hell would have been his everlasting doom.

Does such a religion satisfy? Do we not demand a religion of growth, whereby we may each day feel that we are more manly and nearer to heaven? What is the incentive for well-doing, if coming at the eleventh hour is as well as coming at the first? Rather is it not a premium on guilt thus to be easily pardoned?

323. Can Churchianity Live?

It has been said, that if the church so willed, by adopting Spiritualism as its own, it might bring a new and vivifying element to its aid, and thereby prolong its existence. It could not do this even if it desired so to do. It cannot let go its concreted dogmas for the individualism of the new philosophy. It cannot admit free discussion. Its dogmas must be assented to whether they are understood or not. In this manner, even the truths of the church become superstitions and prejudices. Its dogmas are dead rituals, and, so far from producing activity of thought, they produce moral idiocy, an unresisting passiveness to their voice. Sects in their infancy, when compelled to battle against persecution and antagonistic influences by the free discussion of their beliefs, are forced to gain an honest acquaintance with the beliefs of their opponents, and to have a living interest in their dogmas. When they become established, and a new generation inherit their beliefs, these dogmas form no part in the lives of their believers. There is no life except at distant revivals, when the inanimate corpse is galvanized into contortions resembling the movements of a living being.

Churchianity cannot change without breaking the crusts of its petrified beliefs to atoms, and emerging as something entirely new. It has come to the end of its course. It plants itself directly in the path of human advancement, and, so far from hoping to extend its dominions, it must be content to hold its own.

What are its missionaries doing? Nothing. They honestly complain of want of interest in the Hindoo, the Chinaman, the South-Sea-Islander, the red Indian. They give us no assurance of the Christianization of a single savage. They claim churchizing a few,—that is, persuading them to conform to their ritual, which is being baptized, or sprinkled, and attending church. But, if the missionaries were recalled to-day, in fifty years they would be forgotten, and their labors vanished. Perhaps some cannibal, while feasting on his slain enemy, might relate, as a tradition, that white men once came and taught how they had once crucified God, and thereby saved themselves and as many cannibals as might choose to believe the story. There their labors would end.

324. CHURCHIANITY BED-RIDDEN.

Much has recently been said about a woman who has been bed-ridden for thirty-six years, has had all the contagious diseases of her time, and yet lives, the last of her race, having survived all who cared for her. Yet few have seen the striking resemblance this bed-ridden matron furnishes to the church,—a striking resemblance, only the latter has been bed-ridden for immemorial time, and, still worse, is unconscious of the fact. With a weak spine and a constitutional "general debility," she insists that her wrinkled face blooms with immortal youth, and with a cracked voice she drones songs set to heavenly harmony. She declares she knows more than her generation, and would tie all her grandchildren to her apron-string. Too weak to rise herself, she insists on leading the world. Then she has taken so much medicine in her day that she has become a doctor. For moral ailments there is no end to her herbs and bitters. She is a believer in blood-letting and the cautery. Having had every disease affecting humanity, she understands heroic remedies. From measles to small-pox, from whooping-cough to cholera, she is ready with prescriptions. She has a special class of moral pill-venders, who deal out remedies to sin-sick souls from musty saddle-bags coming all the way down the ages from Moses. Ah me! dear old lady, you have been beautiful in your day; but you are bed-ridden now, and you do not know it. The world has been carrying you on its journey and you did not know it. The people thought you were an ark of the covenant, to be carried on poles, and kept in the van of progress. They have found you to be only human, with nought but conceit left of your charms; with only arrogance and imbecility. Even in your prime you will remember that you thought the Devil rode on a comet, and put your faith in aristocracy, and placed your signet on slavery. The blood of one hundred million martyrs, torn by irons and burnt with flames, is clotted on your mantle. Those palsied hands of yours have kept a tight clutch at the throat of mankind. Now that the sun of truth has arisen, and your aged eyes are blinded, do not insist that you can see better than any one else; but keep to your bed, and the world will bear your moans and mutterings from sheer pity of your weakness.

325. CHRISTIANITY IS DYING.

It has been an experiment serving an important good. It has fulfilled its mission. It has ceased to extend its dominion. As each year passes, it counts proportionally less numbers. Let us not, however, reject it as a whole. Rather carefully garner whatever truth it may contain, to employ in the new edifice which is being built. That edifice is the sum total of humanity,—it is SPIRITUALISM.

326. WHAT IS SPIRITUALISM?

This religion is a philosophy: this philosophy is a religion. It takes man by the hand, and, instead of telling him that he is a sinful worm of the dust, corrupt from the crown of the head to the sole of his foot, it assures him that he is a nobleman of nature, heir to the Godhead, owning all things, for whom all things exist, and is capable of understanding all. He is not for to-day; not acting for time, but for eternity; not a mushroom of a night, but a companion of everlasting worlds. Ay, more: he will bloom in immortal youth when these worlds fade, and the stars of heaven are dissolved. What he writes on his book of life is no writing on sand: it is indelible.

What a position, then, is occupied by man! On one hand are the lower forms of nature,—the brutes of the field; on the other, the archangels of light, towards whom he is hastening, one of whom he will become after death shall have cast from his spirit its earthly garments.

Spiritualism is not a religion descending from a foreign source, to be borne as a cross: it is an outgrowth of human nature, and the complete expression of its highest ideal. Have you a truth?—it seizes it. Has the negro of Africa a truth? Spiritualism asks not its origin, but makes it its own.

You may take the sacred books of all nations, — for all nations have their sacred books, — the Shaster of the Hindoo, the Zendavesta of the fire-worshiping Persian, the Koran of the Mohammedan, the legends of the Talmud, and on them place our own Testaments, the Old and the New: you have brought together in one mass the spiritual history, ideas, emotions, and superstitions of the early ages of man; but you have not Spiritualism, — you have only a part of it. You may take the sciences, — the terrestrial, intimately connected with our telluric domain, teaching the construction and organization of our globe, and the cosmical, treating of the infinite nomenclature of the stars: you have not Spiritualism, — you have but a part of it.

327. SPIRITUALISM COMPREHENDS MAN AND THE UNIVERSE, ALL THEIR VARIED RELATIONS, PHYSICAL, INTELLECTUAL, MORAL, AND SPIRITUAL.

It is the science and philosophy underlying all others. It reaches to the beginning of the earth, when the first living form was created; for even then man the immortal was foreseen, and the forces of nature worked only in *one* direction, — that of his evolution. It reaches into the illimitable future, borne onward by man's immortality.

Would you narrow its domain to the tipping of tables, a few raps, the trance of mediums? You might as well represent the vast Atlantic by a drop of water, the glorious sun by a spark of fire, as to represent Spiritualism by these phenomena. Yet these are not to be spoken of lightly. They are the tests of spirit identity, of which the world has so long stood in need; accidents of the mighty gulf-stream of Spiritualism sweeping past the promontories of the ages, an accumulating flood of ideas and principles.

328. IT IS EMPHATICALLY AN AMERICAN RELIGION.

It was born on American soil, and has all the tendencies of the American mind. The other great religions, the Jewish and Mohammedan, are of Semitic origin; and it has been argued that the Semitic race was ordained for the express purpose of giving true religious systems to the world. Their systems, however grand, partaking of the visions of the Orient, are foreign to us. The new is internal in its growth, practical, and has the coolness and calmness of the West.

The Semitic race, the harsh Jew, the Arab, dictating morals to us! We have taught the world a lesson in government: it is ours to send back to Palestine a new and superior religion. Is it a graft on Christianity, as Christianity was on Judaism? So far as the new always must be on the old, and no more. It is not a "revival" of religious ideas. There has been cant enough, quite, about *morals:* what is wanted is *knowledge.* Give man that, and his morals *will* be right. His demand is not for a revelation embodied in a book, to be expounded by a hierarchy allied with mystery, with partiality for a privileged few; but a system meeting the wants of the people, entering directly into their social, intellectual, moral, and political lives; which is not afraid of the soil of labor; not offended with the jar of commerce, nor abashed at high places.

329. IT IS A PERFECTLY DEMOCRATIC RELIGION,

Presenting a just view of man's duty, destiny, and immortal relations; having its proof drawn from the physical world, and responded to by the intuitions of the soul. Can history yield one page wherein the divinity of man is advocated, and the right of each to perfect that divinity until it becomes a law unto itself? Spiritualists are the only people who have this fire on their altars; who by religion are democratic. Spiritualism is purely so. See how it arose, and how it has advanced. From a simple rap in an old house, in an obscure hamlet, it has steadily marched onward for the last score of years. It never has had a leader; yet its aim and its doctrines are remarkably consistent. The refined and educated medium, enjoying the advantages of the city, and the boy-medium of the backwoods, receive communications enunciating the same great truths, and embodying the same philosophy. All over the land such communications are received, in substance identical. There is harmony amidst diversity; for, however much communications may differ, they do so no more than individual ideas differ, and they substantiate the individuality of the intelligence purporting to communicate. In the fundamental elements of their teachings there is perfect accord. It is a singularity of the Spiritual movement, that it has spread with a rapidity unparalleled in the history of any other innovation, while it has not received the aid of any leader.

330. LEADERLESS.

No one stands at the head of its believers to direct their movements, or to extend, for personal aggrandizement, its philosophy. Its teachings, on the contrary, denounce all leadership, all individual worship, making every believer to rely solely on himself, and seek his salvation through and by his own exertions. There are those who, by a superior mental and spiritual endowment, write and speak more than do others; but their words are severely questioned, and, if they bear not the test of criticism, they are thrown aside. It speaks so strongly of individual responsibility, that the watchword of the true Spiritualist is, "I am a man, and you are another." It has taught equality until leadership is dishonored; and he who would undertake it would immediately be cast down.

It seems to be a great universal movement diffused throughout all ranks and classes of society, and from myriad sources the little streams flow into its vast channel of reform. Other movements have had great and talented men to present and vindicate their claims to the world; they have had leaders who were considered infallible: but Spiritualism sprang into being, and no one can determine when or how or by whom; and, in scarcely a score of years after the first rap was heard, its speakers are declaiming in every city, and its scores of periodicals are scattered broadcast over the land, while its advocates are in number more than those of any sectarian organization in the Union. Is not this an unaccountable fact, unless the myriad spirits of the departed, standing behind the scenes of their invisibility, push on the work?

I say leaderless. The first media are heard of no more. They were wonderful rapping media; and, after serving their time, their oracle departed. A short time since, one of our prominent speakers wailed like Jeremiah over the departure of former workers in the field. He did not understand that men, like seasons, have their time, and afterwards wither away. The spring gives us blossoms; the summer, fruit: each is good for its time.

The individual is his own priest. If he has sins, he must confess them to himself. If Christ did not die for him, God did not make Satan to torment him. What he loses there, he gains here. If he has sinned, he must work out his own salvation. This doctrine is wonderfully egotistical, and brings with it the burdens of isolation. Out of such material are the spiritual ranks filled. It necessitates thought and constant warfare. It is not an easy doctrine. Do you wonder, then, that sometimes recruits go over to the other side? They are tired of the conflict. There is no certainty. The old, loved, and reverenced may any day be overthrown, and wholly unexpected results obtained. They go over where there is certainty and rest. Infallibility of a creed is an easy doctrine. To all questions an answer is ready, — "God willed it." Nothing unexplained; everything set at rest by the mystery of godliness.

Shall we think it desirable that Spiritualists all have one cut of garments? The Catholic said that Catholics should have that a thousand years ago The priests made a suit of baby-clothes, and the laity have worn it ever since. They tied leading-strings to these children, and have never untied them. That we consider folly. The difference between it and fashioning garments for the present, however, is only a difference of time, not of character. Baby-clothed Catholic, or frock-coated Spiritualist, — in principle, the fitting of garments is the same. It is fashioning all men's garments after one pattern, not the pattern, that is disclaimed.

A creed advocating vicarious atonement, or discarding the same, is equally acceptable. It is not what the creed contains, it is the creed itself, which we repudiate. To subscribe to a creed acknowedges the supremacy of its doctrine over the individual. Its boundaries are those set by its makers, and yielding to it is hedging one's self by those boundaries.

331. Its Persistency and Extension.

Christ was born in a manger: how many *centuries* elapsed before a single million believers bowed at his shrine? Mohammed arose out of the royal family of Arabia, and propagated his revelations by the sword; yet how many years before he counted his followers by millions?

The press has used its mighty energies to put down the young giant: the enginery of the church, and all the skillful appliances of public opinion, have been brought to bear, but in vain. Rapidly it springs into strength, and, proving the old fable of Atlas possible, bears the world on its broad shoulders.

The mortal world may be divided, but the nobility of intellect of the spirit-world is one. From it flows the power reposing beneath all manifestations wherever displayed, always the same, varied only by circumstances. The plan is matured in the spirit-world, and from thence measured out to man as he needs. We are engaged in a movement which is ultimately to overturn the fabric of the world's present moral, social, and intellectual philosophies, and its most darling theologies; a movement wide and deep as infinitude. Yet in this desperate conflict we acknowledge no leadership except that of the spheres.

The most humble medium, or obscure circle, is performing a work perhaps greater than that of the most able lecturer on the rostrum. This we assuredly know, — whatever each does, it will harmonize with the work of others. We may walk blindly, but there are eyes which see for us: we cannot go astray. Thus is every individual trained to be a leader of himself,—the ultimate of democracy, a genuine American idea. To this, many millions of Americans assent, and their ranks are rapidly increasing. It encroaches on the desk of the preacher, and enters the halls of legislation.

While we ask, "Can ideas so intensely radical and revolutionary flourish on any other soil?" they pass swiftly the barrier of ocean, and re-appear under the thrones of despots. No police can prevent their utterance in France, they startle the critical sages of Germany, and are received by the autocrat of Russia. The revolution they must work in Europe will be great. They will go forward silently at first, but the red hand of war cannot long be stayed. The *form*, the *idea* around which the masses will rally, the future will determine.

No barrier can obstruct these ideas; for they belong to human nature, and are forced onward by omnipotent spirit-power. They cannot become dead beliefs, for they are of the practical maxims of life. They can be understood by a Carrib or Esquimaux: they supply intellectual food for the profoundest sage. They yield to each just the mental sustenance his capacities require.

332. IT HAS REVEALED NO NEW MORAL TRUTH.

The opponents of Spiritualism loudly exclaim, "Has it presented a single new moral truth? Show it: show what it has accomplished." We do not claim that it has. It would be impossible for it to do so. Christianity, the vaunted engine of civilization, uttered no principle which was not known immemorially before its advent. A new system is not what we demand. We are systematized to death already. We want to be *rid* of what we have. To patch up the ruins of theocratic religion is not the mission of Spiritualism. It comes as the great light of our century, because a sufficient number of advanced minds are educated up to its plane, and are disenthralled from reverence for any system. They receive it because it is not a system; because it is poured out copiously and freely as the sunlight, to be received or rejected, as pleases the hearer.

Would you harness this young giant in theological traces, and compel it to drag the dead systems of the past after it? Then would you defeat its purpose, and set back the hands on the dial of human progress many a weary hour. Spiritualism is the philosopher's highest conception of his relations to the spiritual universe, his fellow-men, and spirits; the living thought of the age, ultimating not in the perfection of religion, but in intellectual superiority, which goes onward and rounds the character in moral completeness.

Man needs not an external revelation, but an internal illumination, whereby he can understand the relations he sustains to himself, his brother-men, and the physical world. Such an illumination is bestowed on, though not perceived by, all. The myriad hosts of the angel world are around us. They mingle in the affairs of men. Their atmosphere is an exhaustless fount from which we draw our thoughts.

Not to the skin-clad prophets and seers of old, fierce wanderers of the desert, are we to look for truth. They may instruct us, but they are not authority. They placed themselves outside of humanity. They were warped and dwarfed by seclusion, and narrow indeed were their views of human needs. Not so to-day. A fountain of exhaustless flow is presented to every one, intoxicating as Castalian waters, as life-giving as the fabled springs of perpetual youth; and every one can become inspired with divine life, and be a lord and prophet unto himself. This is the work of Spiritualism; and the world's cherished creeds are rapidly falling from their bases of sand, undermined by the resistless force of its tide.

333. THE SPIRITUALIST.

SPIRITUALIST! a believer in the Divine incarnated in the human spirit; in the glorious intercommunion of the spheres, from the most insignificant to the great Father of all! Proud name of honor! more glorious than king, emperor, or czar! Why do we hear it hissed and employed as a name of reproach by the churches, which profess to believe in spiritual existence? There can be but two parties,— the Materialists and the Spiritualists. They must be, then, Materialists. They are welcome to the honorable name which, from the purely sensuous plane that they occupy, they so well deserve. We receive the name of Spiritualist with joy. We do not wish to tone it down with an adjective. We are not Progressive nor Liberal nor Christian Spiritualists, but SPIRITUALISTS, — by that word signifying that we are liberal, progressive, and Christian. Let us take this firm and decided stand, never ignoring our name, nor striving to pass for anything but what we are. We should be proud of our name, so broad and catholic, and write our professions in dignified lives. When we compel respect by making the churches fear us, we shall gain it, but not before.

334. PLEASURES OF A BELIEF IN SPIRITUALISM.

With what pleasure we contemplate the world of spirits that surrounds us! There are congregated the wise men, the sages, the prophets, and the philosophers of the ages gone. They have all passed up the glittering pathway to the immortal land. We are travelers up the same way, and they are our instructors and guides. True, the veil of invisibility divides the world of spirits from the world of men; but otherwise there is little distinction. Do you think Clay and Webster feel less interest in the republic than when they made the nation tremble with their eloquence? They are more cosmopolitan, — feel more universal love for the race, not less for their own nation.

Intricate and beautiful are our relations to the angels of the spirit-world. They are our friends, our relatives, the good and great gone before us; superior in knowledge and experience, with love and friendship increased in the measure of their greater capacity.

Ah! you who profess to believe that the spirit at death is removed to a far-off country, — that it has no communion with earth, — you should behold the groups of those spirits as they bend over their earthly friends, and the intense interest they manifest in their welfare.

We have all a greater interest in the hereafter than in the present: our deepest hopes lie there, and we listen with rapture to the voices from the great beyond.

My gray-haired friend, years ago you were called to lay in the cold and narrow grave the loved companion who made life a constant June day of joy. You wept then; and now, as I lift the misty curtain of the past, you weep. The heart grows sad as I tread the halls of sacred memories. The years have come with iron feet; but they never can obliterate the memory of the departed, which beneath the searching frosts, like the mountain evergreen, grows fresher. Ah! you consigned the body back to the mother-earth: the spirit, fledged in immortal life, rested over you unseen, perhaps unfelt. Has that spirit departed? Are you left lonely, forsaken, a weary pilgrim without hope? Let me raise the veil, and show you how intimately the world of spirits blends with the world of men. Could I open your spiritual perception, could I quicken your sight, I could show you that loved one, the same as when you first knew her in youth and beauty, a guardian angel by your side. You are susceptible to her holy influence, and have recognized many times in the past a gentle voice saving you from paths of disappointment.

Mother, you have wept for a darling child, a young bud you had watched with tenderest care, and saw him, with the joy a mother only can feel, bursting into bloom. Just when you thought your fruition complete, when life became most involved in the loved one, a chilling breath snatched it from you.

A little grassy hillock in the churchyard, a little white slab with a name! Is that all?

Nay, the body resting there is not your CHILD, but his worn garment. Your CHILD basks in the sunshine of heaven. It was a cruel stroke which tore him from your bosom, and your very heart-strings broke with the blow. You are sad now, as you look though the long vista of events, and a tear wells from your mother-heart. Is your child lost? Does he sleep with the body? Has he gone far away, where not until death can you behold him? Nay, he is here, in radiant beauty, with an affection for you heightened by the harmony of his angel-life.

Many of you — alas! how many! — sent your loved ones forth to red-handed battle. One died in the fierce struggle of Antietam, pierced by sharp bayonets; another was torn to fragments by a Parrott shell, and scattered like chaff to the winds; another went down in a fierce cavalry charge, his dear form battered by the iron heels of a thousand horses as they swept like a whirlwind over the plain; another lay wounded amid the dead, and his precious life went out beneath the crushing wheels of ponderous artillery; another died a thousand deaths in the prison of horrors, the name of which is too loathsome to utter.

Mother, the vacant chair at your hearth is a source of unending affliction. Weeping wife, when your infant asks for its father, you will say, "He went forth to the strife, and was drawn into the fierce whirlpool of death: all that he has left us is his proud name and immeasurable sorrow."

Patriotism supports you not. Your country's gain is your countless loss. Brothers, fathers, sons, and friends, who went forth with high hopes and lofty ambition, are now beyond the veil of darkness, and on earth write their names no more. The poor privilege of gazing on their inanimate clay was denied you; and you think of them as bleaching in a Southern jungle, or with rude hands concealed in a common grave, where the wreck of valor was indiscriminately plunged.

Is this the reward for your sacrifice, bitter anguish, and tears? Ask the question of Spiritualism, and its answer is a balm more precious than Gilead's. Like the sound of the waterfall to the parched traveler in the desert come the silvery voices of departed friends, softening and subduing the asperities of life, cheering us onward to better aims and loftier endeavors. They call, sweetly and musically call, "O man, brother, sister! come up hither: partake of these fountains, and thirst no more."

You have heard of the happy dying. How beautifully shone the light of heaven over their reposing features! and even after the dissolution a smile like the radiance of sunset played upon their calm faces. Ah! death is the key whereby the spiritual perceptions are unlocked; and, long before its final stroke, it opens man's vision to the future, and he sees the bright springs and clear waters and green fields and radiant spirits immortal.

From this standpoint we can take a broad survey of our relations to the future. We are not creatures of a moment: our existence is not like that of a cloud sweeping the sky, to be dissolved into nothing; but ours is a companionship of worlds and stars,—ay, more enduring than are they. Friends, relatives, neighbors, have preceded you, whom you will greet in the hereafter. Sages, philosophers, the great and good of the ages past, await you there, where you shall mature in the light of angelic wisdom.

We have many lessons to learn from this contemplation. By it we comprehend our duty to lower, and our relation to higher, orders of intelligences. The brutes of the field (our ignoble brethren), all the forms of life beneath us, require our kindness, love, and sympathy: the angels of light, our elder brothers, call forth our emulation, reverence, love, and wisdom.

335. THE COMING CONTEST.

Spiritualists cannot be held by organizations, except such as draw them together by the ties of universal brotherhood. Its purpose is to disintegrate and to individualize. Organization has been attempted, but with disastrous results. It is willed by the vast motive power of this measure that hero-worship shall form no part of its gospel. Truth alone shall be praised. You might as well take the fragmentary granite boulders of the field, and endeavor to mold them into one, as to unite so many Spiritualists, and form them into an organization, acknowledging a creed or a leader. All the creeds in the world cannot hold them. There are no holy books for them, no holy days. If you appeal to their superstition, you appeal in vain.

Spiritualism, embodying the glorious ideal of the freedom of body and mind, absorbs all that elevates and ennobles our conceptions of this life and the life hereafter, of nature, and of human relations. It is a gigantic system of eclecticism. It seizes the good everywhere. Like the bee, drinking nectar from the poisonous nightshade as well as from the fragrant rose, it absorbs the *truths* of Catholicism, of Mohammedanism, of Buddhism, of Philosophy. It is not a religion; it is not a philosophy: it is a perfect union of the two with science.

Witness its results in the world. All reforms are marshaled under its banner. The temperance movement, woman's rights, land reform, magnetism, phrenology, all the new and unprotected issues which look to the amelioration of human burdens, whether physical or mental, have become parts of its gigantic scheme. Their only advocates are the spiritual press. A conservative Spiritualist is a rare object, and either becomes a reformer or goes over to the party to which he of right belongs.

You have heard of Spiritualists becoming Catholics. It is a very wonderful change, but not so wonderful when understood. As Spiritualists, they learn that there are but two issues, — going ahead, and going back. They are not capable of going ahead, and hence at once take the fearful leap into the lap of the mother church. Be not alarmed if men forsake the light, and return to the old. Leaders may desert the standard of the new to rest at ease in the lap of the mother church, or to enjoy the offices she gives. These are accidents to be expected: they have no universal significancy, except as they show the necessity of standing with the one or the other cause. Those who are fully vitalized by Spiritualism never can desert: with them, there is no falling from grace.

In Spiritualism, Protestantism has worked itself clear of Romanism; cast off creed, church, and priest, and allowed freedom to all.

Catholicism is a child of the old world; Spiritualism, of the new. The former has grown old, is in decay: the latter is in its infancy. The result is easily seen: it is not in a distant future. The intelligence, learning, and hope of the age are on the one side: on the other are bigotry, superstition, and darkness. On the one hand is conservatism, or Catholicism, resting on the infallibility of a book expounded by infallible teachers, surrounded by gorgeous trappings calculated to excite the attention of rude natures, to stifle inquiry, denying the right of reason, ignoring the individual, and absorbing all into its masses: on the other hand, Spiritualism, setting the individual free, trampling on the traditions and mythologies of the past, declares MAN to be the most sacred object in the universe.

The two systems are diametrically opposed. One looks to the past; the other, to the future. Which shall triumph?

Humanity never goes backward: it moves ever towards the right; for there is a Divine Power which wrenches human actions after an omnipotent plan. The leaf torn from the branch by the autumn winds, the bird caroling its song of gladness, the sand-grain rolled by the tide, the drop of dew on the flower, — all things, from the least active of tiny life to the gigantic efforts of the elements, — work after a prescribed plan, from which there cannot be the least departure. So with man. He works, seemingly fortuitously; but there is no chance. He puts forth his bravest efforts in the tide, striking out for this or that object; but the strong current bears him onward to a goal well known and undeviatingly approached, however unknown to him. The Divine Energy has marked out a plan, an archetype to be attained in future ages; and the powers of darkness, though they ally themselves to hold the wheel of progress, will find that they do so only to be crushed into oblivion. They will retard it only for a time. The bringing-together of such opposing forces will, of course, produce conflict. They already begin to mingle in our national affairs, in the affairs of all great nations.

Spiritualism in France speaks through its past heroes, and she feels the effects of superior wisdom. It is the dawn of a new day, when departed intelligences will mingle in the affairs of men. Again, it speaks to the Czar of Russia, through a spiritual medium; and the people of the vast steppes, stretching from the Baltic to the Pacific Ocean, from the Altai to the Arctic Sea, feel its breath: the chains of the serf fall from his festered limbs; and millions arise, free men, ready for a glorious career of progress. In England, the higher classes are impressible to spirit thought, and its civilization begins to glow with new vigor. The garroted masses awake at the new voice. Priest and king feel that what they considered solid earth — earth formed of prostrate human beings, cemented together by concrete blood and tears — has no consistency, but heaves like the billows of the stormy sea. The breath of the Divinity is abroad. They hear its call, and arise.

Thus marshaled, the two forces are to wage a war of extermination. Not here alone, but over the whole world; and the end, after misery and suffering, will be the destruction of creeds, superstition, and dogmas, the severing of all shackles, whether of body or spirit, and the production of a universal brotherhood of *free* men.

336. THE TOTALITY OF SPIRITUALISM

May be expressed in a few words. Its aim is the aim of nature, — the production of a perfect man, and the elimination of a perfect spirit. That has been the ideal of Creative Energy through all the vicissitudes of the past from the chaotic beginning. The stars sang together, "Let us make a perfect man." The terrible saurians of the primeval slime, the gigantic brutes of prehistoric ages, chanted the same.

In the perfect man, there can be no self-abasement; there can be no appeal to any one else; there can be no dwarfing of any faculty of the mind. Go by, blear-eyed Theology, that calls the body sinful and corrupt; that would blot out the noblest emotions of the soul. Your ideal is the Stylite on the top of his high pillar, flagellating, lacerating, and starving the flesh, that his miserable soul may gain heaven.

Evolved from and by the elemental forces of nature, being their concentration, or rather centrestantiation, man is an integral part of the whole universe. In him everything is represented. He is capable of comprehending all, because a part of all. In his mind is laid the orbits of starry worlds:

solar systems and galactic universes dance through the congeries of his brain. He makes grooves in which he compels the elements to run, by embodying his ideas in matter. All he does is the concretion of pre-existing thought. The engine, — beautiful, perfect, a miracle of workmanship,—the telegraph, and the steamship, are ideas clothed with matter, embodied thoughts.

For a moment lay aside all prejudices; let your religious education be as though it had never been; and calmly contemplate this being, with such antecedents, such universal relations, such boundless capacity, and such a destiny. Will you not SCORN any system that offers violence and insult to the integrity of his character? ay, trample underfoot the supposition that he is destined for anything but the unlimited progress of angel-life?

Such are the broad deductions of Spiritualism.

Man is not to be miserable on earth to enjoy heaven in the hereafter. We stand in the courts of heaven as much this hour, we see as clearly the presence of God now, as we shall a thousand ages hence. We are our own saviours, achieving our salvation. This is the religion of the future, the highest type of civilization. Other systems will linger with the races of men whose highest ideal they represent; but from the courts of the world's intellectual nobility they will vanish, and be spoken of as myths which once aided infantile progress, leading-strings necessary to walk by until the use of our limbs had been attained.

LIST OF AUTHORITIES.

Abercrombie.
Alger, "The Future Life."
Barrow, "Bible in Spain."
Bellows, "Re-statement of Christian Doctrines."
Berbiquin.
Blockhouse, "Australia."
Brittan, "Man and his Relations."
Bruce.
Buchanan, "Anthropology and Journal of Man."
Brierre.
Büchner, "Stoft und Staft."
Bucknill and Tuche, "Insanity."
Capron, "Modern Spiritualism: its Facts and Fanaticism."
Cahagnet, "Celestial Telegraph."
Charlevoix.
Child, L. M., "Progress of Religious Ideas."
Cicero.
Collins, "New South Wales."
Cook, "First Voyage."
Confucius.
"Correlation of Forces."
Colquhoun.
Columbus, Letters of,
Crow, "Night Side of Nature."
"Curiosities of Medical Science."
Davis, A. J.
Davidson, Lieut. Col., "Illustrations of Magnetism."
Deleuze, "Animal Magnetism."

List of Authorities.

Denton, "Soul of Things."
Draper, Prof.
Dubois, "Mœurs, Peoples de l'Inde."
Esdaille, James, M.D., "Mesmerism in India."
Fishbough, "Macrocosm and Microcosm," and Contribution to "Univercœlum."
Furgerson, J. B.
Gregory, "Lectures on Animal Magnetism."
Gregory of Nazianzen.
Hardinge, Emma, "History of American Spiritualism."
Hare, Prof., "Spiritualism Scientifically Demonstrated."
Herschel, "Astronomy."
Howitt, "History of the Supernatural."
Lane, "Modern Egypt."
La Place, "Théorie au des Probabilities."
Leger, "Animal Magnetism."
Livy.
Liebig, "Animal Chemistry."
Locke.
Keisser, Prof.
Macacio, "Reports et Discussions," 1833.
Mayne, "British Columbia."
Macnish, "Philosophy of Sleep."
Moore, "Soul and Body."
Munzinger, "Ostafükanische Studien."
Müller, "Physics."
Newman, "Fascination."
Owen, "Footfalls on the Boundaries of Another World."
Parsons, "Creeds."
Parker, Theodore.
Peucer.
Polac, "New Zealand."
Pliny.
Ravenstein, "Manhat."
Rebold, Father.
"Resurrection of Spring."
Reichenbach, "Dynamics of Magnetism."

Rivero and Tschudi.
Sahagun, "Hist. de N. Espagne," quoted by **Prescott.**
Schoolcraft, "Indian Traits."
Spencer, "Psychology."
Socrates.
"Spiritual Magazine," vol. ii.
St. John.
Swedenborg, "Arcana Cœlestia."
Talmadge, "Healing of the Nations."
Tertullian.
Townshend, "Facts, etc., of Mesmerism."
Tyndal, "Heat as a Mode of Motion."
"Univercœlum."
Vogt, Carl, "Anthropology."
Ward, F. de W., "India and the Hind**oos."**
Williams, "Figii."
Youmans, "Chemistry."
Zoroaster.
Zschokke.

INDEX.

Adamic creation a myth, 364.
Adam Clark, belief of in regard to Spiritualism, 289.
Affinity, 97–105.
Animal life, 112.
Animals can influence man magnetically, 138.
Apollonius of Tyana, 175.
"Arcana," the, quoted in support of Materialism, 132.
Atheism, 35.
Atom, what is an, 93, 118–120. Divisibility of, 121. Form of, 124. The chemical, 122. A centre of force, 124.
Attributes, definition of, 119.

Belief educational, 61.
Berkeley's idea of the atom, 60.
Body, how far does it affect the spirit? 266. Resurrection of, a myth, 273.
Brain, organ of the mind, 164. Impressibility of, 134.
Bruce, anecdote by, 171.

Cahagnet, experiments of, 66.
Charity, 404.
Change of properties by chemical union, 128.
Circles, how they should be formed, 312. Dark, value of, 72.

Clairvoyance, 68–230. Value of as evidence of man's immortality, 250. Applied to the realm of spirit, 230.
Coming contest, 442.
Compensation, 114.
Communications from spirits, why contradictory, 310. All from one source, 16. Influence of persons present on, 305. Influence of the circle, 310.
Conscience, its authority, 173. Test of conduct, 173.
Conduction, 101.
Conducting power of metals, 126.
Confucius quoted, era of, 35.
Correlation of forces in the realm of life, 110.
Crystallic flame, or od force, 147.
Crystals, influence of on sensitives, 144.

Dead, mourn not for the, 286.
Death, 14. Process of, 265–284. Maturity desirable before, 284. No occasion for rejoicing, 285. Reception of the spirit after, 286. Greek conception of, 271. Terrors of, 272. Of man and animals apparently the same, 36. Spiritual perception of, 301. All faculties retained after, 166.

Dreams, 316. Of animals, 318. Prophetic, 332. Psychometric, 161. Why allegorical, 350. Spiritual communion in, 320.
Double presence, 237.
Duality, 206.

Earth, effect of its being suddenly brought to rest, 108.
Eden, garden of, 353.
Elysium, 354.
Elements, undiscovered, 129. Progress of the, 258.
Electricity, 101. Positive and negative state of, a baseless hypothesis, 101. Quantity of, 106. Velocity of, 50.
Election to heaven, how known by the church-member, 367.
Esdaille's experiments in India, 214.
Evil spirits, are they the cause of spiritual phenomena? 48. Communications referred to, 195.

Force, 74–107. In animals, 101. Explanation of, 95. Vital, 112.
Formation of mineral veins, 103.
Fox family, 64.
Facts from Prof. Hare's experience, 70. From Mrs. Gourlay's experience, 71. From R. D. Owen's experience, 76.
Fortune-telling, 187.

Ghost-seeing, 156–158.
Goethe, quoted, 198.
Grey, quoted on magnetism, 222.
Gregory of Nyssa, quoted, 58.

Hades, 354.
Hallucination, 43. Instances of, 43. Poet Cowper, 43. What is? 46. Are spiritual phenomena referable to, 47.

Hare's apparatus for testing communications, 74.
Heat, 106. Heat and cold, 99.
Healing by laying on of hands referable to organic laws, 196.
Heaven, popular ideas of, 362. Where located by the ancients, 351–355. In the sun, 356. The actual of desire, 357.
Hell, terrors of, 370. Located in comets, 356.
Hermits of the Ganges, 292.

Ideal and real, 19, 20.
Ideas, their force, 21. They cannot be kept, 22.
Identification of spirits, 81.
Ignorance the cause of crime, 24.
Impenetrability, an error, 123.
Impressibility, 181. Of the brain, 134–184. How induced, 298. Conditions requisite for, 303. By narcotizing drugs, 298. Influence of mental excitement on, 299. Exaltation produced by sickness, 300. Induced by fasting, 301. Manifested in insanity, 303. In animals, 134. Impressibility and sympathy, 138. Natural or organic, preferable to induced, 303. Mrs. Denton's testimony, 160. Distinction between spiritual and mesmeric, 53.
Impressions never effaced from the mind, 240.
Immortality, necessity of, 198. And science, 36. Arguments in favor of, 39. Why to be sought outside of physical matter, 264. Impossible with physical elements, 37. Conditions of, 37. Why asked for, 357. Failures of all religious systems to prove, 200.
Inertia, 119.

Index.   453

Infant depravity, 364.
Influence of the external world on the spirit, 141. Of animals over animals, 179. Duration of, 159. Of man over man, 182. Of controlling spirits, 277.
Infidelity, the infidel, 415.
Instinct and intellect, 165.

Knowledge, how obtained, 30.

Law, as supreme in the spiritual as in the physical world, 260, 376.
Leadership, its causes, 26.
Life, what is? 269. Its purpose, 408. Animal and vegetable, distinction, 111, 112.
Light, its analogies, 97–104. Relations of to matter, 261.
Likes and dislikes, explained, 188.
Living beings, a balance of forces, 36.
Locality, influence of on the mind, 156.
Laura Bridgeman, 251.

Man, a dual being, 14, 206. Perfection of, 131. The ideal, 173. Intellectual nature of, 169. His desires insatiate, 170. His spiritual aspirations, 171.
Matter, indestructible, 94. Impenetrability of, a false theory, 123. Elements of, 116, 117. What is? 118. Impossibility of moving without force applied, 41. Moves without visible contact, 73.
Materialism, 58.
Magnetism, 105. Effect of on the operator, 214. Charging objects, 159, 217. Intensifies the spiritual perception, 222. Not imagination, 222. As a curative agent, 191, 192. Why the word is retained, 174. Among the ancients, 175.

Esdaille's experiments in India, 214. Application of to Spiritualism, 194. The cause of spiritual phenomena, 51. Magnetism and electricity, 146.
Magnetic state, classification, 211. description of by Iamblichus, 213. By Tertullian, 213. One of insensibility, 214. Magnetic influence of animals over man, man over animals, and over man, 177, 178. Magnetic healing among savages, 194.
Magnets, influence of, 141. Electro-magnetism, influence of, 143.
Mediumship, 16. Among savages, 289. Of the Australians, 289. Of the Maori, 290. Of the Africans and New Zealanders, 290. A physical state negative to, 306. Possible to all, 304. Developed by sleep, 349.
Medium, how to become a, 304. Responsibility of the, 313. Position of the, 293. Not excused for waywardness because sensitive, 294. Why disreputable media are employed, 293. Influence of on communications, 295. Necessity of culture for, 314.
Memory quickened by death, 243.
Mental phenomena, 52.
Mind, does it perish? 38. Correlation of, 115.
Miracles, in the spirit-world, 377, 386.
Motion, 96. Equivalent of, and resolvability, 97. Economy of in living beings, 101, 110. Of cosmical bodies, 104.
Mysteries, the Druidic, 273–275. Of the Incas, 274.

Nervous sensibility, 181.

Nervous sensibility, facts in proof, 189.
Nerves, use of, 112.
Necessity, 399.
Necessity of culture for mediums, 314.
"New Jerusalem," the, 358.

Od force, the cause of spiritual phenomena, 52.
Organization, 17.
Oxygen, creator and destroyer, 114.

Paganism and Christianity, 274.
Passions, use of, 167. In animals, 168. Perversion of and cause, 169.
Phenomena, mental, 52.
Polarization, 102.
Polarity of the body, 108.
Positive, the, 59.
Prayer, use of, 193.
Prescience, 225.
Present tendency of thought, 93.
Presentiments, 322, 330. Of death, 344.
Prevision, 194.
Pre-existence, 203.
Principle, definition of, 119.
Principles on which all agree, 13.
Progress of the elements, 258, 259.
Prophecy, explanation of, 244. Through trance, 246. Of Bonaparte, 246. Explained, 247.
Prophetic dreams, 332.
Properties, definition of, 119.
Psychometry, 184. Evidence in support of, 77. Applied, 185.
Pythoness, the, and oracles, 292.

Radicalism, 412.
Resurrection, 273. Of Christ, 277. Teachings of the Bible, 278. Objections of science, 279.

Refinement of matter, 380, 381.
Reformers, levelers and builders, 28.
Reichenbach, experiments of, 141.
Right, whatever is, 407.

Salvation, how attained, 14, 402. Dependent on intellectual growth, 172.
Saul, consults the woman of Endor, 176.
Science, ancient, 92. Science and immortality, 36.
Scientists, failure of to explain Spiritualism, 40.
Second sight, 245.
Seeress of Prevorst, 231.
Senses, are they reliable, 42, 60. Deception of, 43.
Sensations while drowning, 241. Imperishable, 242. Abnormal in sleep and disease, 153.
Sensitives, influence of the earth, planets, sun, etc., on, 153, 154.
Sensibility of the nerves, 131.
Sleep, 315. May be development of mediumship, 349. Relation of night and day to, 155. Sleep-walking, 319.
Somnambulism, 319.
Sound, compared with electricity, 103, 104.
Space, is there such an entity? 125.
Spheres of influence, blending of individual, 163.
Spirit, definition of, 61, 201, 266. Origin of, 15, 203. Eternal progress of, 200. Organization of, 255. Destiny of, 15. Loses nothing at death, 166, 209. Condition of after death, 250. Does it leave the body in trance? 336. Comprehension of, 91. Identification of, 57. Independent of the body, 251.

Spirit-healing, charlatanism connected with, 190.
Spirit-body, words of Paul, 207. Words of St. Augustine, 207.
Spirit-elements realities, 259.
Spirit-presence, Victor Hugo quoted, 292.
Spirit-world, the, 15. Where located, 378.
Spirit-zones, 382, 392.
Spirit-communications, how obtained by the eastern hermits, 292. By the Indians, 292. Relation of to the spirit-world, 388.
Spirits, influence of, 17. Employment of in heaven, 361. Of animals, 260.
Spiritualism, definition of, 13, 426. Incentives furnished by, 17. Objects of, 17. Can have no creed, 17. Qui bono? 83. Personal experience in, 83. Science opposed to, 40. Why not given to the world before? 61. Ideal man of, 407. Not new, 63. First modern manifestations of, 64. Advent of in France, 66. Is it electricity? 50? Is it magnetism? 51. Is it the work of evil spirits? 48. Parker's opinion of, 58. A democratic religion, 429. Religious elements of, 394. Leaderless, 430. Incentives of, 396. Its persistency and extension, 433. The essence of philosophy, 303. Has revealed no new moral truth, 434. Pleasures of a belief in, 437. Totality of, 446.
Spiritual phenomena, legerdemain, 41.
Spiritual universe, how formed, 377. Where located, 378.
Spiritual beings, of what composed, 202.
Spiritual body, origin of, 266.
Spiritual attraction and repulsion, 260.
Spiritual ether, 184.
Spiritualists, who are, 13.
Sun, force from, 263. The fountain of life, 109.
Superstition, 291.
Swedenborg, instance of his impressibility, 176.

Trance, how produced by savages, 194.
Test of truthfulness, 197.
Testimony, negative, 60.
Thought, independent of the senses, 255.
Transformation of force, 100. Cycle of, 110.

Ultimate of nature's plan, 282.

Vital force, 112.

World of the dead, 354.

Zschokke, experience of, 189.

www.ingramcontent.com/pod-product-compliance
Lightning Source LLC
Chambersburg PA
CBHW022133300426
44115CB00006B/165